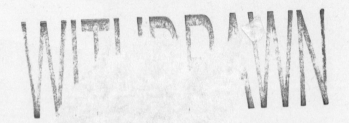

Contemporar **.al/sis**

Contemporary Sociology and Policy Analysis:

The New Sociology of Public Policy

Dr Roger Sibeon
University of Liverpool

TUDOR

© R. Sibeon

This version first published in Great Britain by Tudor Business
Publishing Limited.

A CIP catalogue record for this book is available from the British Library

ISBN 1 872807 86 0

The right of the authors of this work has been asserted by them in accordance with the
Copyright, Designs and Patents Act 1988.

Typeset by Deltatype, Ltd, Birkenhead, Merseyside
Printed and bound by Biddles Limited,
Guildford, Surrey

CONTENTS

Foucault and the question of whether power can be stored
The relational nature of interests and power

Actors: some issues for consideration

The state is not an actor
Policy networks and agency
Organizational actors
International actors: the European Union
Agency and social actors

Forms of thought

The conditions of action

Contingency

Unintended consequences

Time-space

Network analysis

Material diffusion

Role/positional, dispositional, and situational-interactional dimensions of social action

The state/civil society, postindustrialism, and citizenship

The state/civil society distinction
Postindustrialism
Citizenship

The institutional framework through which public policy is mediated

The principle of parliamentary democracy
Central government
Central/local relations
Local government
The ''new public management''
The European Union

The state and public policy

Conventional theories of the state
A post-Foucauldian sociology of governance

PREFACE

In an attempt to cut across an institutionalized academic division of labour, this book will demonstrate that developments in contemporary sociology and social theory have significance for political science and, more particularly, for policy analysis. There are a few books on public policy (including quality texts by Ham and Hill 1993; Hill 1993a, 1993b; M J Smith 1993; Harrop 1992; Lane 1993, and Parsons 1995) that attempt to "bring in" sociology and social theory, but these are written by political scientists and policy studies writers rather than by sociologists; while important in their own right, their sociological content tends to be sparse and unrelated to current transitions in the discipline. Among the better texts on public sector organization and policy are Metcalf and Richards (1990), Lawton and Rose (1991), Farnham and Horton (1993), Isaac-Henry et al (1993), Flynn (1993), Hughes (1994), Ranson and Stewart (1994), McKevitt and Lawton (1994), Mullard (1995), and Kirkpatrick and Lucio (1995); none of these, however, acknowledge present-day sociology, still less assess its relevance to the study of public policy. Conversely, and despite some insightful accounts of the relation of sociology to policy (Bulmer 1982; Bulmer et al 1986; Bryant 1976, 1991, 1995; Weiss 1986, 1993), sociologists have in general contributed very little to this field. Theoretical sociologists and social theorists, including those who are ostensibly interested in the relation of sociological theory to policy-related matters, tend to be uninformed when it comes to the field of policy studies.

This is not to say that texts of the kind just referred to have little value. (To the contrary, those listed above are excellent in their own terms). It is to say, rather, that the *sociology of public policy* is one of the least developed fields within the discipline; it is, however, a field of enquiry that is potentially capable of transforming policy analysis. There are good reasons for suggesting that the new conceptual frameworks in sociology, when they permeate the public policy literature, will re-shape the assumptions that currently influence policy analysis; nor, on a dialectical note, should we underestimate the beneficial effects on sociology and social theory of closer sociological engagement with public policy concepts in an expanding body of writing that is unfamiliar to many sociologists.

It would be inappropriate to suppose that readers interested in the *new* sociology of public policy should not address the central theoretical (and methodological) concerns of present day sociology. Thus, although concerned with public policy, and in particular the policy process, a distinctive feature of this text is the importance attached to the exploration of connections between sociology, contemporary social theory, and public policy analysis. The book will appeal to lecturers, postgraduates and advanced undergraduates in sociology, applied social science, public policy and policy analysis, government and politics, and social policy. Readers primarily concerned with sociological theory, and who may wish to explore the relation of theoretical ideas to governance and to public policy issues, will also find much in the book that is of interest and value to them.

INTRODUCTION

When it was published in 1972, Hill's *The Sociology of Public Administration* was something of a rarity. Today the gap between sociology and the study of public policy is as wide as it was when Hill wrote his book. For example, Parson's (1995: xvi) text on public policy acknowledges that sociology is relevant to policy analysis, yet current theoretical and methodological concerns in sociology are almost entirely absent from his book. Policy analysis has been much closer to political science than to sociology, with the result that policy analysis as an academic field is largely uninformed by the major theoretical, methodological, and empirical transitions that are currently taking place in sociology. Some policy texts, it is true, make use of conceptualizations and methods of analysis that have been developed in sociology; but the material that is employed tends to be oversimplified and out of date, with little or no analysis of current theoretical and methodological developments. This state of affairs is widespread and is true of some of the best-known texts on the policy process, a point noted by Bolderson (1994: 272). But there is another side to this. It is important to acknowledge that important conceptual and empirical developments in the disciplines of political science and public policy are unfamiliar to many if not most sociologists. This has long been the case, to the cost not only of political science and policy analysis, but also of sociology. It can be argued, for example, that had sociology as a discipline been more exposed to developments in political science, the fanciful and essentialist ideas that influenced some fields of sociology in the 1970s and afterwards, might have been avoided. Sociology, public policy as an academic discipline, and political science, have much to learn from each other; hence there is, I suggest, a lot to be said in favour of an *interdisciplinary* orientation.

As a contribution to the longer-term collaborative work that will be necessary in order to develop a more integrated and up-to-date interdisciplinary approach to the study of public policy, this book's main purpose is to demonstrate the relevance of contemporary sociology to policy analysis. This, as already noted, involves breaking new ground and is an attempt to bring current sociology into a field of enquiry that is usually thought of as the province of political scientists and policy researchers. Hence my objective in this book is to develop a contemporary sociology of public policy and thereby demonstrate what sociology can offer to the longer-term development of an interdisciplinary field that, in common with Ham and Hill (1993:

4), I will refer to as *policy analysis*. This is something to which I shall return later.

I have indicated that this is essentially a sociological book about public policy. When, however, I refer in the book's title to *the* sociology of public policy, what do I mean? Like other social sciences, sociology has always been multi-paradigmatic (Heller 1986: 150). Perhaps, therefore, there can be more than one sociology of public policy? There are no good reasons for trying to impose a single paradigm upon the discipline. This is not to say that synthesis which draws critically on a number of paradigms is undesirable (Bauman 1992: x). There is room in sociology for special theories and paradigms *and* for synthetic and integrative frameworks (Bryant and Jary 1991b: 30), my own inclination being towards an integrated and synthetic approach. I recognize, however, that in principle there can be as many *sociologies* of public policy as there are sociological paradigms (structural-functionalist, rational choice, neo-Marxist, feminist, structuralist, poststructuralist, etc). Hence my reference to *the* sociology of public policy is purely a terminological convenience, and I do not seek to deny the legitimacy of attempts to construct alternative sociologies of public policy. That having been said, it should be observed that the approach outlined in this book is to some extent eclectic, and is explicitly synthetic. I believe that this wide-ranging approach, and the fact that in places I deal with underlying metatheoretical as well as theoretical considerations, will help to equip the reader to form his or her own judgement about the theoretical and methodological framework offered here, while at the same time providing material that is relevant to the evaluation of any possible alternative sociologies of public policy.

It will not have escaped the reader's attention that so far I have referred to public policy, rather than to public administration. Earlier, I mentioned Hills's (1972) *The Sociology of Public Administration*. Depending on the context of its usage, it is conventional to suppose that the term *public administration* can mean (a) public organizations (for example, central government departments) and inter-organizational networks that comprise the administrative machinery of the state; or (b) institutionalized policy-related practices that are carried out in the public sector; or (c) an academic discipline, that is, an academic discipline normally associated with political science and which studies both of the above (the organizational and practice dimensions of public administration) in their social-political and economic contexts. In the following chapters it will be necessary to refer to all three variants; on each occasion it will be clear from the context which variant is under discussion. In common, however, with current practice in the political science and policy literature I will for the most part refer to *public policy*, which for reasons associated with the 1980s movement towards a "new public management" (Hoggett 1991) has, at least in the European countries, largely replaced use of the term "public administration" (Chandler 1991; Gilliatt 1991).

In the following chapters it will be necessary to confront theoretical concerns that unavoidably underpin social scientific analyses, whether these be analyses of public policy or of anything else. In the remainder of the present chapter, however, I want only to introduce three general themes that relate to the sociology of public policy. These are the ontological status of social science generalizations; the difference between sensitizing theory and substantive theory; and the distinction between analysis *of* policy and analysis *for* policy. Let us briefly examine each of these in turn.

Social Science Generalizations

In the next chapter, it will be observed that in the social sciences there has been a general shift away from "grand theory". Grand theories, such as Parsonian structural-functionalism and Marxism, attempt to explain the historical and present-day totality of social behaviour and social structure. Another way of putting this is to say that grand theories overgeneralize: they produce large, sweeping generalizations that bear little relation to concrete empirical happenings in particular times and particular places.

There is, however, a danger of overreaction against grand generalizations. Nomothetic (or generalizing) forms of knowledge refer to *categories* of persons, places, events, etc; idiographic (or particularizing) knowledge refers to a *particular* person, place, or event. The social sciences deal mainly in nomothetic knowledge; this is acceptable, indeed necessary (the reasons for saying this will become apparent in the following chapters). The approach adopted in this book is that social science generalizations are entirely appropriate, provided they are of more limited scope than the generalizations associated with grand theory. As Mouzelis (1995: 34) observes, grand or universal generalizations in the social sciences "tend to be either inconclusive (holding only in certain conditions not specified by the theory) or trivial". Substantive generalizations should aim to strike a balance between the idiographic and the nomothetic; statements that refer only to a particular person, place or event cannot constitute the whole of sociological knowledge, but nor should we engage in analysis that is so overgeneralized that it becomes "vacuous" (ibid.). This last statement does not mean, incidentally, that general sociological propositions must refer only to particular societies or to specific nation-states: as Morgan and Stanley (1993: 2) observe, cross-cultural differences should not be seen as "an inhibitor of theoretical generalization, but rather, as influencing the kind and scope of generalizations the discipline is concerned with".

A policy-related example of inappropriate generalization is to be found in post-Fordist theory of the welfare state (Burrows and Loader 1994). A post-Fordist perspective identifies "new" features of the welfare state such as de-skilling, employment via short-term contracts, organizational decentralization, increased service flexibility, and increased responsiveness to consumer preferences. It is often claimed that a fully-fledged post-Fordist welfare state has come into existence. Such a claim, despite the fact that the above features of "post-Fordism" do to some extent exist in some welfare sectors, is far too sweeping. A generalization of this kind is, in effect, a universalistic statement about the impact of post-Fordist social change on the welfare state; the problem with such statements is that they have a crude broad-brush approach that ignores complexity and variability among different sectors of the welfare state (Williams 1994: 56–57). Post-Fordism and other "grand" theories of social change deal in crude generalizations that fail to come to terms with a "messy" empirical reality in which the nature and impact of social change is often variable and uneven.

The point I am making here is that cautious generalizations of limited scope are desirable. Not that general (nomothetic) statements can be avoided. In the social sciences, it is impossible to avoid generalizations of one kind or another. As Best and Kellner (1991: 72) note, a problem with Foucault (1972, 1980a, 1980b, 1982) and other post-structuralist (and post-modern) theorists is that while at a formal level they attack the idea of generalizations, they are inevitably unable to avoid general statements and nomothetic understandings: for example, Foucault (1980a: 142) describes relations of power in terms of "general conditions of domination". Generalizations of one kind or another are unavoidable and therefore the real question for social science, and for the sociology of public policy, is not *whether* but *which* generalizations to employ.

Sensitizing Theory and Substantive Theory

Most of the theoretical material contained in the following chapters is in the form of sensitizing theory, rather than substantive theory. Sensitizing theory can and should stimulate the development of substantive theories, but the two types are distinct. Sensitizing conceptual frameworks are relevant to the development of specific substantive theories and relevant to empirical work (here the meaning of "sensitization" is broadly similar to its meaning in Blumer (1954: 8), in Berger and Luckmann (1972: 26–27 and 207–11), and in Giddens (1989b: 294–301)). Substantive theories aim to provide us with new empirical information, whereas sensitizing theoretical frameworks are intended to furnish general orientations or perspectives; they are intended to equip us with ways of thinking about the world. Sensitizing theories are theoretical frameworks or perspectives (ways of thinking) that are intended to be a precursor to the development of specific substantive theories and an aid to the design of empirical studies. Put another way, substantive theories and empirical studies endeavour to explain social happenings, whereas sensitizing theoretical frameworks, such as Giddens's (1984, 1993) structuration theory, give us "a broad idea of what we might be looking for and some ways of thinking about it" (Craib 1992: 5). The job of sensitizing theory, in other words, is to provide conceptual tools that prepare the ground for the construction of substantive theories and for conducting empirical investigations. To the extent that this book contributes to the theoretical development of the sociology of public policy, it is a contribution towards the development of *sensitizing* theoretical ideas that are relevant to the subsequent formulation of specific substantive theories and to the design of empirical studies of public policy and the policy process.

Notwithstanding the earlier remarks to do with social science and nomothetic knowledge, it should be noted that some sensitizing theories legitimately formulate "large" generalizations pertaining to common social processes that may be found in a wide variety of social settings. For example, the main postulates in Giddens's (1989b: 295) structuration theory "are intended to apply over the whole range of human social activity, in any and every context of action". This, however, is a far cry from the universal (grand) generalizations associated with reductionist substantive theories such as Marxism and radical feminism, theories which are rightly criticized by post-modernists; see, for example, the criticisms by Nicholson and Seidman (1995: 7). Marxism ultimately reduces social life to an expression of class interests or "the interests of capitalism", while radical feminism simplistically reduces the complexity of social relations to the notion of "patriarchy". This amounts, in both cases, to a theoretical and methodological closure of the range of possible empirical interpretations and explanations that might be drawn upon to account for social phenomena. In contrast, Giddens's theory of structuration attempts to provide a sensitizing theoretical orientation to the study of general social processes pertaining to agency/structure (the relation of social action to social structure, see chapter 1). But this involves no reductionist theoretical closure. Rather, it leaves the door open for the subsequent development of a wide range of possible substantive theories and for relatively "open-ended" empirical investigation and empirical interpretation that does not commit Giddens to explanations that rely on generalizations of the kind associated with reductionist substantive theories (on this, see Cohen 1993:279–80, 285, 289, 297). In Cohen's terminology, the kind of generalizations that are contained in Giddens's theory of structuration are "ontologically flexible". I happen to believe that Giddens's theory of structuration has much to offer; the more general point that I want to emphasize here, however, is that the theory of structuration is a good example of a *sensitizing* theory that constructs generalizations that are based on a legitimate theoretical protocol.

Analysis "Of" Policy/Analysis "For" Policy

The sociology of public policy is a sociological sub-field in its own right; but potentially it is also a major disciplinary contributor to the larger, interdisciplinary field of study known as *policy analysis*. In the terms used here and by Ham and Hill (1993: 4–21), policy analysis is an interdisciplinary social scientific field of enquiry that is concerned with analysis *of* policy (including its institutional context) as well as analysis *for* policy. I shall be concentrating mostly on the former; the book's purpose is to outline a contemporary sociology *of* public policy, and in this way to contribute to the longer-term development of policy analysis as an interdisciplinary field of study. In a moment, however, I shall make the point that this approach to the sociology of public policy has applied spin offs in so far as some of the social science developments outlined in the following chapters are likely in the future to significantly influence research and analysis carried out "for" public policy.

The distinction between analysis of/for policy serves to indicate that the sociology *of* public policy is an exercise in intellectual understanding, its purpose being to sociologically investigate public policy as an organized social activity, rather than to provide sociological knowledge of a kind intended for practical application. In other words, the prime objective in the sociology of public policy is to add to the sum of knowledge *about* policy. This objective rests upon intellectual values which regard knowledge as worth having for its own sake. In contrast, a sociology *in* or *for* public policy may be defined as the provision of conceptual insights and empirical data of a kind that are intended for practical application by policy-makers and practitioners. This distinction between analysis "of" and analysis "for" policy is analytically important, for it relates to questions of purpose. However, in reality the distinction sometimes becomes blurred. In the social sciences, as in the physical sciences, "pure" research far removed from practical concerns may later turn out to have unanticipated practical applications. Also, some substantive empirical topics are intrinsically difficult to assign to one or the other of the two categories just referred to. An example is sociological analysis of organizational structures: this topic is integral to a sociology *of* public policy, but analysis in this area is also capable of generating a range of insights and data that have practical value for policy-makers and practitioners.

The Structure of the Book

The first two chapters are focused mainly on theory; in these fairly lengthy chapters the intention is to survey contemporary social theory, in particular sociological theory, and to also identify some methodological implications of theory. The first chapter explores core concerns in sociological theory, and in social science theory in general. The chapter contains material on the postmodern challenge to social science, and on the recent history of and background to current theoretical debates, particularly debates surrounding *agency/structure* and *micro-macro*; these theoretical debates, as will become clearer later in the book, are methodologically and empirically relevant to the task of engaging in social scientific analysis of public policy. The second chapter identifies concepts and themes associated with current social science transitions towards anti-reductionist and non-reified methods of analysis. In the second chapter, as in the first, reference to policy-related issues will illuminate the necessarily abstract discussion of the theoretical and methodological assumptions that inevitably underpin policy analysis. I have a very good reason for saying that theory "inevitably" influences policy analysis. Theories and concepts, whether informal and homespun or formal and academic, or some combination of the informal and formal, are *unavoidable*. They are intrinsic to human thought in general, and to formal social scientific analysis. Therefore, rather than allow theories and concepts to exert a hidden, unexamined influence on methodology and on the analysis of empirical events, it is far better to make theories fully explicit and thereby expose them to critical scrutiny and evaluation.

Chapter three, which is rather less concerned with theory than the earlier chapters, focuses on the institutional context of public policy. As well as outlining the framework of government and recent public sector developments, the chapter introduces empirically-relevant conceptual schemes that refer to analysis of the state, governance, and policy networks. In order to take a more detailed sociological look at the policy process, the fourth chapter re-examines earlier material to do with agency/structure, social chance, and micro-macro. These are, as I shall demonstrate, perennial concerns that underlie not only sociological studies of public policy but virtually all forms of social scientific enquiry. Chapter five pulls together the various theoretical and methodological materials that constitute the "new" sociology of public policy. In this chapter it is also observed that *post-national* dimensions of policy will require closer attention in the future, together with continued attention to the distinction between analysis *of* and *for* policy.

A Terminological Note

A comment on terminology is appropriate, bearing in mind that readers' disciplinary backgrounds are likely to span sociology, political science, and public policy. In the following chapters, whenever I use the term "agency" I will usually be referring to a volitional capacity of actors (as in the agency/structure debate, which is introduced in the following chapter). To avoid the possibility of confusing this sociological reference to agency with political science uses that tend to employ the term (as in the expression "public agencies") to describe state organizations, I shall for the most part refer to central government departments as state organizations or as state departments, rather than refer to them as public agencies or state agencies. An exception will be when I allude to state organizations as agencies in the sense that they are *actors* or agents; unlike social classes, social movements, etc, actors (whether individual human actors or organizational actors) may be defined as entities that are capable of formulating purposes, of making decisions, and of engaging in action (see the anti-reductionist conception of agency discussed in the first and second chapters). Also, it should be noted that my generic use of the term *social* (as in the expression "social life") follows sociological convention; more often than not, I shall use the term to encompass all of the various dimensions of social existence – including cultural, political, and economic dimensions.

In a book of this kind the use of sociological language is, of course, entirely appropriate. However, as far as possible I have tried to avoid highly specialized jargon. This does not mean that the book shies away from complex, controversial, or unresolved issues in social and political science and in the sociology of public policy. To the contrary, I have sought to expose and explain such issues in the hope that the interested reader will feel sufficiently stimulated and sufficiently equipped to explore them further.

CHAPTER ONE

CORE CONCERNS IN SOCIOLOGICAL THEORY

The main purpose of this chapter is to introduce topics that lie at the heart of sociological theory and method. These relate, in one way or another, to agency/structure and micro-macro. Following a short introduction, the chapter opens with a critical examination of the post-modern rejection of social science. This is followed by a review of structural-functionalism (a macro-to-micro approach); a discussion of rational choice theory (a micro-to-macro orientation); and a review and summary of methodological individualism and methodological collectivism. The final section of the chapter examines a number of anti-reductionist concepts and postulates to do with agency, locale, materials, social networks, and social systems.

Some Basic Theoretical Issues

For reasons that will become clearer later, it can be argued that agency/structure and micro-macro are conceptual constructs that underpin not only sociology but the whole of social science knowledge (Crespi 1992; Layder 1993, 1994; Mouzelis 1989, 1991, 1993a, 1995; Ritzer 1990, 1992; Watson 1990; McLennan 1995; Bryant 1995). *Agency/structure* refers to agency in terms of the purposiveness and causal powers of agents (or actors); and to structure in terms of constraints upon actors, constraints that stem from social structure. An illuminating alternative conception of structure is developed by Giddens (1976, 1981, 1982, 1984, 1987, 1993). He regards structure as "rules" and "resources" which may constrain *or* enable actors, depending on the circumstances. *Micro-macro* refers to differences in the units of and scale of analyses concerned with the investigation of varying extensions of time-space. For micro-researchers the spatial unit of analysis normally is small groups of people who interact with each other in micro-settings (in the street, home, workplace, etc), and the research focus is the "negotiation" of meanings, intentions, and activities that arise *during* the course of face-to-face interaction in the setting. In a temporal sense, the unit of analysis tends to be a relatively short period of time. Micro-sociologists' data refer, in the main, to events and stretches of interaction that take place over a period of days, weeks, or months. Macro-researchers, in contrast, tend to be more interested in the study of spatially extensive phenomena such as social institutions or whole societies, viewed across stretches of time (years, decades, or even centuries) that are usually much longer than those involved in micro-studies.

Before embarking on a sociological exploration of agency/structure and micro-macro it is first of all necessary to acknowledge the relatively recent emergence of a challenging body of thought – post-modern theory – that denies the very notion of social science and rejects disciplinary knowledge of the kind associated with sociology, political science, economics, psychology, philosophy, etc. In the period since the mid-1980s the so-called "post-modern turn" has affected all of the social sciences (Lyon 1994: 18) and nowadays it is impossible to ignore the post-modern rejection of social science knowledge. The challenge posed by the post-modern is thus an appropriate starting point for this chapter on sociological forms of theoretical knowledge.

The post-modern challenge

It is often said that theorists associated with post-modernism, such as Baudrillard (1983, 1994) and Lyotard (1986), write in an arcane and almost impenetrable style. I shall not employ post-modern jargon. But nor, unlike some, shall I dismiss post-modernism as a shallow cultural movement bound up with chicness, Madison Avenue, and media hype (Hills 1993: 380). Once we penetrate the needlessly obscure jargon used by post-modern theorists, we are still left with intrinsically complex and far-reaching issues that cannot legitimately be ignored (Hollinger 1994: xi). Engaging here in critique of post-modern thought will also conveniently allow me to introduce a number of general sociological themes that will re-appear later in the chapter as well as in the later chapters.

The post-modern can be thought of in two main ways. Firstly, as a historical periodization. Let us call this a *type of society* approach: here the post-modern claim is that we exist in a post-modern type of society that has certain identifiable characteristics (these include social diversity, cultural pluralism, post-industrialism, and consumerism). Secondly, the post-modern can be thought of as a *type of theory*. Post-modern theory argues for "small narratives" (sometimes called "local" narratives) that do not involve social science generalizations. Post-modernists also claim social science knowledge is flawed for the reason that it fails to recognize that the social world that we perceive is nothing more than a product of discourse, including social science discourse. Let us briefly examine both of these strands of post-modernism, beginning with the post-modern as a theoretical perspective.

The post-modern as a type of theory

Post-modernists reject what Lyotard calls "grand narratives". Marxism, structuralism, structural-functionalism, radical feminism, etc, are rejected as overambitious "grand theories" that set out to explain "everything": far better to have small-scale, particularistic "narratives" (Dickens 1990: 105). Holist and general approaches are rejected not only in favour of "small" narratives and "local" knowledge; they are also rejected in favour of a *relativism* which presupposes that theories "produce" the social reality to which they refer, rather than reflect in mirror-image fashion an ontologically prior or pre-existing reality (Seidman 1994). On this view, the world is *theoretically* constructed; there is no ontologically prior, pre-theoretical, or materially "real" social world. There are, so to speak, as many social worlds as there are languages and theories.

All knowledge, including academic knowledge, is regarded by post-modernists as an "embedded" product of the context of its production (Bauman 1987: 4). That is to say, post-modernists suppose that a person's knowledge and ways of thinking are largely determined by that person's structural location in the social totality (as a man, let us say, or as a woman or a black or white person), and by social, historical circumstances that are particular to a specific time and place. Knowledge is also regarded as a fragmented pastiche that has no coherence. Vincent (1992: 188), a political scientist, notes that post-modern thinkers "oppose all closure, totalizing discourse and erasure of difference. They do not believe in truth, rationality, knowledge, subject-centred inquiry or the search for a coherent epistemology . . . Contradiction, difference and incoherence are welcomed".

The aspect of post-modernism that I wish to emphasize here is the post-modern rejection of "foundational" knowledge. Language constitutes or "constructs" the social world (Tiryakian 1992: 72). For the post-modernist, *the world is a product of language and discourse; there is nothing more to reality than discourse.* Actually, this post-modern postulate is not new. Versions of it have been widely discussed by sociologists and philosophers such as Berger and Luckmann (1972), Holzner (1968: 1), Sapir (1966: 68–9), Whorf (1956: 6), and Schutz (1962: 348), and the postulate is also a feature of post-structuralism and ethnomethodology. The adequacy or otherwise of this post-modern conception of language and reality construction is something to which I shall return shortly.

The post-modern as periodization (the "type of society" approach)

It was observed earlier that the idea of the post-modern refers not only to a type of theory, but also to a *type of society* (Kumar 1995). It is claimed that modern society is characterized by an emphasis on producers and production, whereas post-modern society is characterized by an emphasis on consumers and consumption (Bauman 1989: 46). It is worth noting that these aspects of post-modernists' image of society are, as Gurnah and Scott (1992: 146) have noted, not particularly new: they can be found in the neo-Marxist writings of Castells in the 1970s and in the work of theorists of "post-industrial society", such as Alain Touraine (1974) and Daniel Bell (1973). For example, Bertens (1995: 123) observes that Lyotard's (1986) post-modern notion that *information* in the computerized society is replacing the centrality of the manufacture of goods, is a theme that was developed some years earlier by theorists of postindustrialism.

Diversity, heterogeneity, and pluralism are said to be the crucial defining features of the post-modern. Instead of the simpler class-based divisions of modern society, diversities in post-modern society are linked to multiple and cross-cutting values and affiliations to do with gender, race and ethnicity, religion, sexuality, generation, regionalism, and localism. Alongside this social fragmentation and the breakdown of the "grand narrative" is an extreme cultural pluralism (Heller and Feher 1988: 5), so that post-modern societies are said to be "a babble of ... mutually uncomprehending discourses, lacking a coherent ideology or central authority" (Gurnah and Scott 1992: 148).

Post-modernism: a critique

While theorists such as Gellner (1993) see almost nothing of value in post-modern thought, I take the view that aspects of post-modern theory are relevant to the development of sociological theory (Lemert 1993) and to methodological concerns relating to the design of empirical studies (Fox 1991). Post-structuralist and post-modern views of contingency (Lyon 1994: 4; Bauman 1992), locale, and power can be said – subject to the conceptual and methodological modifications described in later chapters – to have a theoretically sensitizing part to play in sociology. Post-modern notions of contingency, locale and spatial variation, though not in the particular form conceived by post-modernists, are relevant not only to sociology but also to political science (Wilsford 1994) and to policy analysis (Fuller and Myers 1941; Cooke 1989; Harloe, Pickvance and Urry 1990; Gyford 1991). Post-modern theory also has a certain amount of merit in so far as it rejects "modern" theories that are reductionist and essentialist. In general, however, post-modern theory contains so many deficiencies that it cannot be regarded as a viable critique of social science knowledge nor as a suitable basis for developing a sociology of public policy. Let us briefly examine these deficiencies.

Language and the social construction of reality

Post-modern theory refers to the question of the relation of discourses – whether cultural, political, legal, professional or academic discourses – to their social contexts (or to "society"). Post-modernists along with post-structuralists and ethnomethodologists believe that discourses constitute or "construct" the social context (Parker 1992: 3–5, Rustin 1993: 191). The social world is not preconstituted. There is no real, pre-existing social reality "out there": there are only languages and discourses (the latter are sets of linked meanings and practices) which construct the "reality" that is experienced by the language-user. For reasons that will be developed later in the chapter, and also in chapter two, I incline, at least in regard to this matter, towards the position of Berger and Luckmann (1972), Harrison White (1992: 305) and Law (1986c: 3–4, 1991a: 18), each of whom regard the relation of discourses to social contexts (or to "society") as loosely dialectical. That is to say, actors' discourses – their forms of thought and social practices – both *shape and are shaped by* the social world(s) of which they are a part: in this sense, *actors are both products and creators of society*. To say this is to reject the idea of a one-way causal determination: neither discourse or context are determinant, rather each shapes the other. It should also be noted that the idea that there is a dialectical ("two-way") relation between actors' discourses and the social context, is associated with a non-reified and non-reductionist conception of what an actor (or agent) is. This is something that I shall take up later in the chapter.

A complicating factor, however, is post-modernists' contradictory tendency to argue on the one hand that discourses *produce* (or "determine") social contexts, and to argue on the other that discourses are largely *determined by* the context! Here we have a theoretical contradiction made up of two opposed forms of determinism. The first insists that it is discourses that produce contexts, the second that it is contexts that produce discourses. In regard to the second of these two positions, there is a distinct post-modern tendency (as in Seidman 1994: 325) to imply that actors' discourses are structurally predetermined in the sense that actors' forms of thought are said to be largely shaped by their memberships of various social categories such as "men", "women", or "class" as well as by specific ("local") social-historical circumstances. This deterministic epistemological stance seems to be suggesting that it is "society" that shapes actors' forms of thought, and not the other way round: indeed, it is a stance that curiously echoes the determinism in some "modern" reductionist macro-structural theories (such as Marxism, and structural-functionalism) of the kind that post-modernists reject. What we are left with, then, is an incoherent post-modern insistence that discourses are a product of their social context while in the same breath post-modernists claim that social contexts are the product of the discourses that constitute them. As I have already intimated, my own inclination is to endorse the view taken by those theorists who argue that neither discourse or context is determinant, but that each shapes the other to a degree that is a matter for empirical investigation in each instance; this is my preferred approach to, for example, the investigation of the relation of political and policy discourses to their social contexts.

The question of "foundations"

Post-modernists reject "foundational" knowledge. Put another way, they reject theories which eschew relativist epistemology. As I have just noted, post-modernists claim that knowledge and theories rest on nothing more than a standpoint that has been determined by the structural location of the theorist in terms of his or her membership of social categories like race or gender, or in terms of the allegedly cognitively determining effects of "local" circumstances. This is a deterministic and reductionist conception of agency. It is, too, a conception that sits uneasily alongside an opposed, idealist epistemology that is also a part of the post-modern genre. I pointed to this epistemological and ontological confusion in the preceding section. For the moment, though, I simply want to make the point that post-modern rejection of foundations and of "foundational" knowledge is linked to the post-modern rejection of "grand theory" and of holistic generalizations (though it is not only post-modernists who reject "grand theory': see the discussion of generalized knowledge in the introductory chapter). The epistemological rejection of holistic generalization, however, is highly problematical; indeed, it is self-negating. This is because the post-modern statement that there can be no general theory, *is itself a general theory*! As Gurnah and Scott (1992: 148) observe, post-modern theorizing rests on "a grand narrative . . . It thus reproduces precisely those totalizing characteristics of which at the level of intellectual critique it is most critical".

Lack of a systems perspective

Later in the chapter it will be observed that although post-structuralist and post-modern views of power and social action, including Foucault's (1972, 1980a, 1980b, 1982), have a certain amount of merit, they suffer from a failure to appreciate the significance of the *systemic* aspects of social life (Best and Kellner 1991: 72). Social systems are patterned relations between positions/roles and social institutions. Social systems, though often thought of as macro phenomena (for example, the political system) may also be micro systems involving face-to-face interaction in local settings. As well as the micro and macro levels, systems are also to be found at the mezo (organizational and inter-organizational) level of social process. Later in the chapter I will show that so long as reified and reductionist conceptions of systems are avoided, the concept *social system* is an important analytical tool in sociology and in political science; it is also significant in policy studies in such fields as, for example, policy-network analysis (see chapter four). Post-modern theory, however, lacks a systems perspective and this severely limits the usefulness of a post-modern approach.

Social determinism

I have already touched on problems of determinism. Social determinism, which refers to agency/structure, is an issue that will re-appear throughout the book. Although macro-structural theory and post-modern theory are in many ways opposed, what they share in common is a determinist conception of social action (B.S. Turner 1990: 248) and also a failure to perceive the analytical significance of a non-deterministic conception of the micro-social ("interactional") order (Best and Kellner 1991: 66). In this sense, though not in this sense alone (see the anti-reductionist definition of the concept *actor* later in the chapter), it can be argued that post-modern theory displays an inadequate grasp of agency/structure.

Problems associated with the post-modern as historical periodization

The "type of society" version of post-modernism tends to assume that modern and post-modern societies are two readily identifiable and distinct structural types that are almost entirely unalike. In fact, the dividing line between modern/post-modern societies is probably far more hazy than most post-modernists recognize (Smart 1991: 20). On this issue, Rose (1988: 362) is critical of post-modernism: "in social theory the notions of the 'modern' and the 'postmodern' are, in the first place, fundamentally the same, and, in the second place, are not 'modern' or 'new' – for want of a neutral term". In brief, the point to be made here is that post-modernists generally fail to recognize that there are empirical discontinuities *and* continuities as between the so-called "traditional", "modern", and "post-modern" types of society.

The post-modern as a "type of society" and as a "type of theory": a problem of epistemological incommensurability

The strong, distinctive form of post-modern "anti-foundationalism" is itself a meta-narrative that is foundational in a way that fails to rigorously analyze the implications of epistemological incommensurability between the post-modern as periodization (the "type of society" approach) and the post-modern as a type of theory. In its *type of society* mode, post-modernism specifies that a post-modern society is "real", a preconstituted, actually-existing social form that exhibits certain structural features (diversity, pluralism, consumerism, etc). But postmodernism in its *type of theory* mode goes off in the opposite direction and insists that no societies are "real"; rather, they are effects of discourse. There is an evident contradiction here. On the one hand, post-modernism confidently insists that there is a (post-modern) social world "out there", an "objective" ("real") type of society that is preconstituted and which exhibits definite structural features; on the other, post-modernism insists that the social world, far from being "real", is no more than a product of language and discourse. This classic case of trying to have it both ways led Parker (1992: 10) to observe: "One cannot combine an idealist epistemology and a realist ontology and expect to produce coherent theory". Actually, this is not necessarily a problem for post-modernists who, as noted earlier, welcome incoherence. The inchoate, however, is not a suitable way forward for the social sciences and nor, therefore, for the sociology of public policy.

The post-modern: an overview

Sociology can derive some useful insights from post-modern theory: these are to do with contingency, the idea of temporal and spatial variation and discontinuity, and (despite some post-modern theoretical confusion on this score) the idea of anti-reductionist and non-essentialist theory and methodology. However, post-modernism's relativism and hypercontextualism (Alexander 1992) and the various problems discussed above, suggest that a post-modern approach to the study of public policy has little to commend it. In view of the difficulties referred to earlier it is not surprising that, as May (1993: 558) put it, "the modernity/post-modernity debate . . . has currently ground to a halt".

Nor is it surprising, in view of the perceived inadequacy of the post-modern assault upon disciplinary knowledge, that there have been calls for a "return" to sociological theory and method. This is reflected in, for example, Mouzelis's (1991) *Back to Sociological Theory*, his *Sociological Theory: What Went Wrong?* (1995), and is also featured in McLennan's (1995) "After post-modernism: back to sociological theory?". Mouzelis's work (1989, 1991, 1993a, 1993b, 1995, 1996) is of particular importance and I shall refer to it from time to time in this and the later chapters. The current post-postmodern movement towards a "return to sociology" is not, however, a call for sociological "business as usual". To the contrary, post-modern and other critics have highlighted a number of problems in sociological theory and methodology; these problems are addressed in *anti-reductionist sociology* which is a new form of analysis that, as I intend to demonstrate, has massive implications for the development of a contemporary sociology of public policy.

The major theoretical approaches

Earlier, I mentioned the *agency/structure* debate and the *micro-macro* distinction. I suggested these are core theoretical concerns that underlie the whole of social science theory, methodology, and empirical enquiry. Bearing these central theoretical concerns in mind, and related ones that I shall introduce shortly, a comprehensive theoretical map of sociology would need to include the following types of theory:

• theory focused primarily on *agency* and constructivism, such as phenomenology, ethnomethodology, symbolic interactionism and structuration theory;
• theories focused mainly on the idea of *social system*, such as structural-functionalism and neo-functionalism;
• theories focused on *rationality* and on actors as rational, utility-maximizing beings. Historically, such theories have included utilitarianism and, more recently, rational choice/public choice theory and exchange theory;
• theories concerned with *social structure*; these include critical theory, structuralist Marxism, and post-structuralism.

This typology, which is derived from Waters (1994: 7), is a convenient guide to the major sociological theories and paradigms. Since this book is not exclusively concerned with theory, it is not intended to cover in detail all of the theories referred to in the above classificatory framework. In order, however, to identify central sociological themes that are bound up with agency/structure and micro-macro, I shall in the next two sections of the chapter look at *structural-functionalism* (this is a macro-to-micro theoretical perspective that gives more emphasis to the macro and to "structure" and large-scale social systems, than to agency); and *rational choice theory*, a micro-to-macro perspective that focuses upon individuals and upon (a particular conception of) agency in a way that, however, is unable to account for the "emergent" properties of macro (and mezo) social systems.

Macro-to-micro: structural-functionalism

The early development of functionalism is largely associated with the writings of Auguste Comte (1798–1857), Herbert Spencer (1820–1903) and Emile Durkheim (1858–1917), together with the work of Radcliffe-Brown (1881–1955) and Bronislaw Malinowski (1884–1942). The highpoint of structural-functionalism was American sociology from the late 1930s to the early 1960s, under the leadership of prominent functionalist theorists such as Talcott Parsons, Robert Merton, and Kingsley Davis. By the early 1960s functionalism had become the dominant paradigm in American sociology, and it also had a fairly secure foothold in European sociology. This position of dominance was not sustained. In the period from the early 1960s to the mid-1980s, academic interest in structural-functionalism declined sharply. The mid-1980s, however, saw the beginnings of a revival of interest, based largely on neo-functionalism as represented in, for example, the work of Alexander (1985), Munch (1987) and Luhmann (1982, 1988). For the most part this has involved, as Munch (1987: 116) and Robertson and Turner (1991: 1) observed, an attempt to revise and develop aspects of Parsonian sociology. Even Habermas, whose neo-Marxism and critical social theory might have seemed to place him in the opposite theoretical (and political) camp to Parsons, turned in his later work (1986, 1987) to the task of incorporating elements of Parsonian sociology into his theoretical framework.

The theoretical basis of structural-functionalism

Structural-functionalism is a holist perspective that focuses upon society as a whole, conceived as a system of interconnected "parts". The parts are the state, the economic system, the family as a social institution, mass media, social class, education, religion, general cultural meanings and values, etc. The early functionalists, as well as modern functionalists such as Parsons (1947, 1951, 1954), had a particular concern with the problem of social order (the problem of how it is that a society "holds together" as a whole). As part of this concern the early functionalists and a number of more recent functionalists employed an *organic analogy*. This analytical device compares social systems with biological systems. A biological system, such as a human being viewed as a biological entity, is a whole that is made up of interrelated components ("parts") such as the heart, the liver, and the lungs. Each of these parts performs a vital function for the other parts, and for the larger biological system as a whole (for the human being, in this illustration). Likewise the social system ("society") is a whole that consists of various interrelated parts (the state and public administration, education, the family as a social institution, industry, the legal sub-system, cultural beliefs, etc). These parts perform important functions for each other and for the social system as a whole. Functionalists, then, emphasize *interdependencies* and it is assumed that the meaning, purpose, or function of a "part" can only be understood *in terms of its relation to other parts and to the whole*. To attempt to study an element of society in isolation from (its relation to) other elements, would be to lose sight of the basic premise of structural-functionalism (Abrahamson 1978).

In structural-functional analysis, emphasis is given to roles and social positions (positions such as father, bus-driver, politician, administrator, etc). *Roles*, which prescribe the norms and behaviours associated with particular *positions* (or "statuses") are important features of social systems, for it is roles that, so to speak, "link" individuals to social systems (Parsons 1954: 230). *Social institutions* are clusters of meanings, values, rules, and recurrent practices associated with segments of the social world that have come to be regarded as important. Examples of social institutions are marriage and the family, private property, science, religion, the market, the polity and so on. In structural-functionalism, these are regarded as key structural parts of social systems. Roles and social institutions perform functions for the larger social system ("society") of which they are a part, and roles as well as social institutions are said to operate in a way that satisfies system "needs', such as the need for system integration and cohesion (Parsons 1947).

I referred above to the organic analogy; this has been criticized on at least three grounds. Firstly, the structure of social systems ("societies") changes over time, whereas the structure of biological systems does not (other than over exceptionally long periods of time). Secondly, it has been argued that while the health or normal functioning of a biological system can be objectively assessed without recourse to value-judgements, this cannot be done in the case of society as a social system. For example, some regard the liberalization of divorce law and of sexual mores as progressive ("functional") manifestations of a more rational and tolerant social order; others regard such liberalization as unhealthy symptoms of social malfunction and moral decline. Thirdly, the idea of system "needs" in biology is fairly clear, as in the statement that animals require a heart in order to survive. In animals, the heart serves a vital function, *and the function performed by the heart is said to explain its existence.* In social systems, however, there may be *functional alternatives* (Merton 1968): for example, the social system's "need" for a healthy population might be satisfied by a service based largely on public medicine as in the United Kingdom, or by private medical insurance as in the United States. By and large, in biological systems functional alternatives do not exist (an exception might be a mechanical device to replace, say, the heart); in social systems, however, functional alternatives are far from rare and very often system "needs" may be met in a number of different ways so that it is not always possible to claim that a social or cultural item is indispensable or that the functions it performs cannot be performed by some other, alternative social or cultural item.

It is appropriate at this point in our discussion of structural-functionalism to introduce an analytical distinction between a *social integration* approach (the study of agency/actors and of social relations – whether cooperative or conflictual – between actors), and a *system integration* approach (this refers to the study of relations between roles/positions and social institutions). I shall clarify the nature of this distinction at various points throughout the rest of the chapter. In terms of the matters under discussion here, we can say that society has at least two "faces", each of which requires investigation. In Mouzelis's (1995: 127) terminology: "a social whole can refer both to a system of interrelated *actors* (to a figurational whole) and a system of interrelated *rules, roles or social positions* (institutional whole)" (emphases added). In the social sciences, it is necessary to investigate *both* of these dimensions, and to also study linkages between them. Although Parsons recognized the distinction between social integration and system integration, his primary concern in *The Social System* (1951) was system integration. Social integration (a focus on actors and actor-actor relations) and system integration (a focus on rules, roles/positions and institutions) are, as I have just noted, different modes of analysis and both are important; but Parsons neglected the former and gave too much emphasis to the latter.

A related issue to which I shall return later is the problem of *teleology* that is associated with some forms of functionalist explanation. It is important to recognize a distinction between *causal explanation* and *functionalist explanation*. Durkheim distinguished between the *causes* of something (the factors which bring a social or cultural item – such as religion or a cultural belief system – into existence in the first place) and the *functions* of something (the consequences of that item for the social system, once the item has come into existence). Illegitimate teleological explanation conflates causal and functionalist explanation and attempts to explain the *cause* of a social or cultural item in terms of the item's "functions", that is, in terms of the item's consequences or *effects* (one of the best discussions of this is still Cohen 1968: 47–8). As well as structural-functionalists, Marxists and feminists tend to engage in illegitimate teleological forms of explanation. For example, teleological and reductionist analysis might start with, say, an observed public policy or social practice then try to "work backwards" to infer that the policy or practice is the "realization" or "expression" of someone's or something's "interests", such as the interests of taxonomic collectivities (the interests of "capitalists", of "men", of "white people", etc). As we shall see later, a problem with teleological analyses is that unless intentional planning was involved we cannot discover *causes* by examining *effects* (Betts 1986: 51); and planning can only be done by *actors* who, moreover, cannot be said to have "objective" or structurally-given "interests". It happens that many features of society are unplanned, *unintended* consequences of the exercise of agency; but to suggest that the unintended consequences of action embody "objective" interests (discussed in the next chapter) is to employ a muddled methodology based on inadequate theoretical reasoning. In one way or another, structural-functionalism together with radical structural analyses such as Marxism and radical feminism, have been bedeviled by the problem of teleological explanation. In sum, it is not legitimate to try to explain the causes of something in terms of its effects.

Social system as a concept in structural-functionalism

Parsons regards systems (the economic system, political system, legal system, etc) as self-maintaining and boundary-maintaining entities that are made up of interdependent parts which form a usually orderly and stable whole. It is also assumed by Parsons that any instances of system change will tend to be orderly rather than "revolutionary". Parsons's theoretical scheme refers to systems and sub-systems of varying scale, ranging in size from the personality system and dyads (two-person systems) to organizations and larger social systems such as whole societies.

A controversial aspect of functionalist thought is the previously mentioned notion of social system "needs" (or *functional prerequisites* in the language of structural-functionalism). The idea of system needs may be applied at the micro (small-group) level, the mezo level (for example organizational needs), and at the macro (societal) level. Functionalist macro-theorists such as Aberle (1967) observe that for its survival a society has to satisfy certain functional needs. These include such basic needs as a population living in a distinct geographical area; some degree of consensus and shared values; means of socializing the society's members including children; methods of internal social control; means of protection from external attack, and so on. A highly formalized statement of social system needs is provided in Parsons's (1967) work; later I will come back to this, although at a general level of analysis without going into the details of Parsons's work on system prerequisites.

Critique of structural-functionalism

Knoke and Kuklinski (1991: 174) refer to "the *emergent* properties of social systems that cannot be measured by simply aggregating the attributes of individual members" (emphasis added). It is to Parsons's credit that he drew attention to the emergent properties of social systems. In the Durkheimian tradition, Parsons insisted that different types of social phenomena exist at different levels of social reality. For example, he argued that the personality system, the social system, and the cultural system each have different properties that are peculiar to the system in question. Hence it is not legitimate to try to explain phenomena which occur at one level (for example the social) in terms of phenomena that occur at another level (for example the psychological). *It can be argued that there are connections between micro, mezo, and macro, but these are nevertheless separate levels each with distinct properties of their own; rather than remove or collapse the distinction between them, we should build bridges between these levels of social process* (Layder 1994). This question of emergent properties to do with the relation between different levels of social reality is an aspect of the micro-macro distinction (Mouzelis 1995: 180, n.11), and it is a theme that will be discussed later in the chapter in connection with methodological individualism and rational choice theory.

As well as recognizing the emergent properties of social systems (the idea that the whole is "more than" the sum of the parts), Parsons also deserves credit for tackling the question of system "needs" (these are sometimes referred to as a social system's "conditions of existence"). In focusing on system needs it is important, as Mouzelis (1991, 1995) observes, to draw upon the previously noted distinction between *social integration* (agency, and figurational wholes/relations among actors) and *system integration* (institutional wholes/relations between institutions or between roles/positions). If the social integration approach is lost sight of in analyses that refer to a social system's conditions of existence ("needs"), then the theoretical and methodological problems of *reification* and reductionism arise; in reificationist theories, structural *"parts"* (rules, positions/roles, and social institutions) *are wrongly treated as though they were actors with decision-making powers*. In order to avoid teleology (explaining a cause of something in terms of its effects) and reification (attributing agency to entities that are not actors), it is necessary to employ the following methodological principle. When a social system is inspected in *institutional* terms (a system integration mode of analysis) it is legitimate to enquire into the system's conditions of existence, providing that *figurational* analysis (a social integration approach) is also brought into the investigation so as to examine the part played by *actors* and actor-actor relations in the reproduction or change of the system. This relates closely to the problem of teleology. Functionalist enquiry concerned with the question of whether certain practices contribute to the reproduction, change, or destruction of a social system, is an entirely legitimate form of enquiry so long as the *consequences* of any existing social item or practice (whether these contribute to the reproduction, change, or demise of the system in question) are not regarded as a *"cause"* of that item, that is, are not regarded as an explanation of how the item came into being in the first place. As noted earlier, causal explanation, which is important in its own right, is distinct from functionalist explanation.

An important aspect of the matters under discussion here, is the distinction between *necessary* conditions and *sufficient* conditions. Let me provide a policy-related illustration of this distinction. It might be argued that certain general economic and political conditions may be "necessary" conditions for, let us say, the emergence of publicly funded welfare states: but those general conditions are not "sufficient" to provide a *causal analysis* of the coming into being of any *particular* welfare state. For this we also have to look at specific "local" and national factors, the intentions and activities of particular national actors, the intended and unintended outcomes of specific actions, and so on. For example, an illegitimate teleological functionalist explanation of the emergence of a welfare state in a particular society (for example, Britain) might take the form that advanced industrial societies in general exhibit certain structural features or have certain functional "needs" (for example, a healthy and literate labour force) and that it was those general systemic needs that made the particular (British) welfare state necessary, and that this therefore explains how and why the British welfare state came into being. The problem here is that this so-called "explanation" cannot account for the fact that the *types* of welfare states that exist in advanced industrial societies such as Britain, Sweden, Australia, the United States, Japan, etc, are very different (Esping-Anderson 1990; Mishra 1990; Ginsberg 1992; Gould 1993). Nor, by way of further illustration of this point concerning "necessary" and "sufficient" conditions, can teleological functionalist theory account for cross-national variations in political systems (Lane and Ersson 1994a, 1994b) or in public policy regimes (Heidenheimer et al 1990), nor for variations in the causes and forms of political revolutions (Defronzo 1991; Dunn 1989). Thus, although functionalist analysis of the *consequences* of an already-existing social item is perfectly legitimate, it is always necessary to distinguish *functional* analysis from *causal* analysis (the latter consisting of analysis of the factors that brought the item into being in the first place). In the light of this, it is possible to agree with Mouzelis's (1995: 132–3) contention that Merton's (1968) long-standing distinction between teleological (that is, illegitimate) and non-teleological (that is, legitimate) functional analysis is a perfectly proper analytical distinction that, despite the controversy that continues to surround functionalist analysis, should be retained and incorporated into social scientific methods of investigation. Thus we should reject blanket condemnations of functionalist analysis; to throw out the whole of functionalist analysis would be a classic case of throwing out the baby with the bathwater. Underlying these observations, it should be remembered, is Parsons's neglect of a *social integration* approach. As observed earlier, Parsons deserves credit for his work on system integration (the study of system "parts" – positions/roles and social institutions – and relations between the parts), but he neglected a social integration form of analysis. This to some extent accounts for his being unable to provide an adequate account of the parts played by agency and by social relations and specific ("local") social conditions in the construction and reproduction or change of social systems.

In addition to, or in some cases as an extension of, the general theoretical and methodological issues to which I have just referred, there are a number of specific criticisms of structural-functionalism that require our attention. In turning to these, the distinction made below concerning substantive criticisms and methodological and logical criticisms is a convenient classification that I derive from Ritzer (1992: 258–62).

Substantive criticisms

The neglect of social change. Structural-functionalism has for many years been criticized (Cohen 1968; Mills 1970) for its alleged failure to provide a convincing account of processes involved in social change. Functionalists tend to employ a synchronic rather than diachronic approach; in Comte's terminology, their focus is generally upon "social statis" rather than "social dynamics". It should be noted, however, that there are a number of functionalist accounts of social change, such as Smelser's (1962) study of social change in the Lancashire cotton industry during the Industrial Revolution; and in his later work, Parsons (1966, 1971) himself turned to the investigation of social change. Critics such as Cohen (1968) argue that functionalism, because of its particular kind of focus on society as a system of interlocking parts, is inherently unable to account for social change; others, such as Turner and Maryanski (1979) argue that functionalist theory is in principle able to deal with social change but that most of the major functionalist writers have, for whatever reasons, chosen not to focus upon this topic. My own view of this matter is that in so far as structural-functionalism has an inadequate conception of agency/structure and micro-macro, it is not, despite the analytical usefulness of a number of functionalist conceptualizations, a theoretical perspective that in its traditional or neo-functionalist forms can adequately explain either social change or social continuity.

Failure to account for social conflict. A long-standing criticism that relates to the previous one, is the complaint that functionalism focuses almost exclusively on value consensus and social stability. (The recent history of this criticism is well documented: see Cohen 1968; Dahrendorf 1959; Rex 1961; Horowitz 1967; and Mills 1970). Gouldner (1971: 220–21) portrays functionalism as a conservative ideology, and many years ago Lockwood (1956) commented on Parsons's neglect of possible conflicts of values and of material interests as between different social groups structured along the lines of social class, gender, race, ethnicity, and religion. Merton's (1968) notion of "dysfunction" attempted to rescue functionalism from these criticisms, but at the end of the day it can be argued that the failure to deal adequately with social conflict is part of the functionalist's larger failure to adequately address the complexities of social life (Giddens 1993: 26).

Social determinism and agency. Bourricaud (1981: 108) is of the view that Parsons allows considerable scope for agency; but probably a majority of sociologists incline towards the opinion of Gouldner (1971: 218), Wrong (1967) and others who suggest that structural-functional theory employs a deterministic conception of the actor. Garfinkel (1967) and Blumer (1969) argued that in Parsons's scheme the actor is seen as a passive being who typically internalizes and conforms to pre-existing, socially patterned rules and role-scripts. Parsons's highly abstract classification of the elements of action led Turner (1988) to argue that Parsons is describing how, in his view, people "ought" to behave rather than engaging in analysis of how people actually behave. These criticisms, it should be noted, reflect Parsons's overemphasis on system integration and his neglect of social integration. Another way of putting this is to say that Parsons concentrates on social action in its *positional/role* dimensions; this is important but, as I shall observe in chapter two, so too are the *dispositional* and *situational-interactive* dimensions of social action (Mouzelis 1991: 168, 1995: 136, 174).

Methodological and logical criticisms

Grand theory. It has long been argued (Mills 1970; Abrahamson 1978) that structural-functionalism, as in Davies and Moore's (1945) functionalist theory of stratification, is an unproductive exercise in "grand theory". This requires no lengthy discussion here, since the topic of grand theory was examined in the introductory chapter and was also mentioned earlier in the present chapter in connection with post-modernism. Merton's (1968) functionalism was critical of Parsons's "grand theory" functionalism, and Merton argued for a more modest ("middle-range") level of generalizations. In later years, the nature of the debate shifted. As we saw earlier, by the 1980s debate over grand theory had become part of the modernist/post-modernist controversy. In terms of the distinction made in the introductory chapter concerning *sensitizing* theory and *substantive* theory, most sociologists would agree that some generalization is possible and legitimate in both types of theory. This is not, despite what post-modernists may claim, a question of an either/or choice. We no not have to choose between reductionist and modernist grand theory on the one hand, and post-modern relativism/hypercontextualism on the other (Alexander 1992: 323). To reject Parsonian grand theory (or Marxist or feminist or structuralist grand theory) is one thing. To revert to the opposite extreme of post-modernism and to suppose that all knowledge is particular, "local", or idiographic, is quite another. For the moment it is sufficient to reiterate the points made in the introductory chapter and to observe that the overwhelming majority of theorists and empirical researchers are agreed that cautious, limited general-izations are legitimate and that, in any case, generalizations of one kind or another are unavoidable in academic and lay discourses alike.

Teleology. The problem of teleology associated with some forms of functionalist explanation was discussed earlier. We saw that teleology, the attempt to explain the *causes* of social phenomena in terms of their *effects*, confuses the distinction between causal explanation and functionalist explanation. Illegitimate teleological explanation involves reification in so far as entities that are not actors are assumed to have purposive powers. It is supposed in teleological explanation that society has needs, and that therefore "society" brings into existence social items to fulfil those needs. The problem here is that societies are not actors; to argue otherwise is to engage in reification. I have already observed that it is legitimate to suppose that social systems of whatever type or size (whole societies, policy-networks, organizations, small groups, etc) have certain general and basic conditions-of-existence, but that these, however, must be regarded as "necessary" rather than "sufficient" conditions when it comes to the task of providing an adequate explanation of any *particular* social system or any particular social item. This relates to the importance of holding in view both a *system integration* and a *social integration* perspective. As observed earlier, the former refers to the "parts" (rules, positions/roles and social institutions) that comprise systems/institutional wholes, and to relations between the parts; the latter refers to actors (agency) and to actor-actor relations. In the anti-reductionist conception of social action that is introduced later in this chapter and discussed further in chapter two, illegitimate teleological explanation is avoided altogether.

Structural-functionalism: a concluding comment

I have suggested that structural-functionalism offers potentially useful theoretical and methodological insights. Structural-functionalism helps to establish the understanding that "system" is an analytical idea that should not be ignored. Structural-functionalism also raises, though does not satisfacto-rily resolve, the problem of how to combine systems integration and social integration perspectives. And Mertonian structural-functionalism helps to establish the notion that, providing teleology is avoided and providing that both system integration and social integration methods of analysis are employed, it is legitimate to investigate social systems' conditions of existence ("system needs") and to investigate the effects/consequences of the existence of social and cultural items. I have also shown, however, that structural-functionalism is in various ways a flawed perspective. In sum: it can be argued that structural-functionalism in general is not an adequate sociological paradigm, but that a number of ideas drawn from structural-functionalism may usefully be incorporated, in a modified form, into the sociology of public policy.

Micro-to-macro: rational choice theory

The philosophy of utilitarianism was developed in the eighteenth and nineteenth centuries by British social philosophers such as John Locke, Adam Smith, Jeremy Bentham, and John S. Mill. Utilitarianism has in various ways influenced modern social theory, particularly rational choice theory. Following Olson's (1965) analysis of agency and collective action, rational choice theory (RCT) attracted interest in sociology and economics, and also – mainly in the form of public choice theory – in political science.

In essence, RCT rests on two postulates. The first is that individuals act rationally to maximize their personal gains; the second is methodological individualism (Hechter 1988: 264), a micro-to-macro postulate which specifies that "individuals make society". The term *rationality* as used in RCT indicates that individuals select the *means* that best serve their personal advantage. The image of rational, self-interested actors who are intent on maximizing their *personal* rewards does not, however, preclude recognition of the existence of generalized goals that are common to many individuals. Thus, Hechter (1988: 269) suggests that we can safely assume that "everyone prefers more wealth, power and honour to less, because attaining these goals makes it easier for individuals to retain other (perhaps more idiosyncratic) goals".

Exchange theory is an important variant of RCT. Homans (1958, 1961, 1974), who attempted a sociological re-formulation of Skinner's psychological behaviourial theories, is widely regarded as the founder of sociological exchange theory. Unlike ethnomethodologists, symbolic interactionists, and phenomenological sociologists, Homans had little interest in actors' subjectivity or inner mental states. Rather than delve into individuals' consciousness we can simply assume, argued Homans, that people usually will attempt to satisfy their wants and that they will rationally select the means that seem likely to satisfy those wants. Social life is largely a process of responses to stimuli so that, for example, people tend to repeat behaviour for which they were rewarded in the past and avoid those behaviours that had attracted unpleasant sanctions in the past. In exchange theory, individuals exchange with each other various goods and services (such as money, food, shelter, support, love, social approval) and this involves rewards and costs. For instance, in exchange for a reward (for example a pay rise) a factory worker may have to "pay" or incur a cost (such as undertaking a less congenial kind of work). People decide whether to enter an exchange relationship – or whether to remain in or withdraw from an existing exchange relationship – according to their assessment of the balance of costs and rewards available to them in the relationship, and according to their assessment of whether any *alternative* rewards or any other equally rewarding or less costly relationships are available to them (Blau 1964: 99).

Blau's (1964: 117–18) version of exchange theory, though in some ways similar to Homans's, paid more attention to exchange and power, including imbalance and asymmetry in exchange relationships. Also, whereas Homans was mainly concerned with individuals, Blau was very much interested in the relation between the micro-social level and the cultural and macro-social levels (Uehara 1990: 525). Blau believed engaging in social exchange builds up trust and also strengthens people's commitment to common values, thereby contributing to social integration. More so than Homans, Blau (1964: 260) argued that as well as person-person exchanges (direct exchange) it is also necessary to recognize the significance of person-collectivity exchanges (indirect exchange), as when the collectivity gives its social approval (a "reward") to individuals who carry out socially approved role performances (ibid. 257–59).

Rational choice theory (RCT) and exchange theory are *micro-to-macro* orientations that are highly critical of macro-to-micro approaches such as structural-functionalism and structural Marxism. Whereas macro-structural theories tend to emphasize society as a whole and then "work downwards" toward the individual as a culturally shaped and socialized being, rational choice theory goes in the reverse direction. In RCT, macro-*cultural* explanations of individuals' behaviour in terms of individuals' internalization of cultural values, are rejected (Hechter 1988: 266). Instead, rational choice theorists argue that exchange is rooted in self-interest which is based on a combination of economic and psychological needs. However, RCT and exchange theory do not entirely dismiss normative ("cultural") explanations of behaviour; rather, an attempt is made to combine the notions of self-interest maximization, power, and *equity*. Equity, of course, is a value and this brings normative factors into RCT/exchange theory. Homans (1974), for example, referred to "distributive justice"; by this he meant that most individuals restrict or modify their self-interested behaviour in so far as they believe they *and others* should have what is due to them by right, or because they have earned it. Another example of the introduction of normative factors into the utilitarian/rational choice paradigm, is Blau's (1964: 92) assertion that there exists a generalized norm of reciprocity which underpins social exchange: "the need to reciprocate for benefits received in order to continue receiving them serves as a 'starting mechanism' of social interaction". As these examples from Homans and Blau show, RCT attempts for explanatory purposes to combine two different lines of thought. These are (a) the notion of rational choice/self-interest maximization that stems from personal economic and psychological needs, and (b) the idea that normative factors are additional sources of influence upon behaviour.

There are other strands of RCT that it is not possible to discuss without a lengthy theoretical detour. These include Emerson's (1981) work on exchange networks; Roemer's (1981, 1982a, 1982b) game-theoretic Marxism; Elster's (1989) attempted reconciliation of Marxism with methodological individualism and rational choice; and Coleman's (1990) attempt to relate RCT to the micro-macro linkage, as well as his interesting proposition (ibid. 542) that organizations as well as individuals display agency. However, one particular form of RCT that should be mentioned here is public choice theory.

Public choice theory is associated with political science and public policy. Lane (1993: 150) observes that the Virginia School of public choice as represented by, for example, Buchanon (1975, 1977), Gwartney and Wagner (1988) and Tullock (1965, 1975), is associated with an anti-state right-wing philosophy that in some respects is critical of politicians and of public officials. However, Lane argues (1993: 156, 160, 161, 164) that the public choice approach can also be employed as a relatively objective social-science perspective that is not inherently normative, and therefore not inherently neo-liberal or right-wing. Lane's case is that public choice theory rests on two postulates (ibid. 155). Firstly, public sector actors – like any other actors – typically engage in self-interest maximization (ibid. 5–6). They seek to expand their budgets and bureaucracies; retain working practices that benefit themselves rather than their clients or customers; enhance their status and salaries; and preserve their security of employment (Mueller 1989). Secondly, social wholes (such as society) are the products of individuals: this is the doctrine of methodological individualism ("individuals make society") to which I have already referred. Lane (1993: 161) argues that these two theoretical postulates are not intrinsically neo-liberal or right-wing; it is only when other assumptions are added to them that we arrive at the neo-liberal philosophy of the Virginia School of public choice theory. Lane's contention is not entirely without foundation, although it has to be said that public choice theorists' view of the public sector does tend to coincide closely with the political philosophy of neo-liberalism.

Critique of rational choice theory

Unlike structural-functionalism, structuralism, structural Marxism, and radical feminism, rational choice theory (RCT) is in some respects a useful reminder that individual agency linked to "rational choice" is a significant factor in social life. There are any number of situations where utility-maximizing decisions by individuals have significant intended or unintended social effects. Consider, for instance, the following unintended effect: if a very large number of people decide on health grounds that it is in their best interests to eat white meat rather than red meat, an aggregated and unintended consequence of these individual self-interested decisions might be to make chicken farmers rich and beef farmers poor. Another example is Boudon's (1982) study of individual decisions made by French students faced with deciding whether to apply for a place at a University or at a Technical Institute. RCT also highlights other interesting aspects of "the problem" of collective action (Olson 1965), such as "the prisoners' dilemma" and the "free rider" problem (these are discussed in Heap and Varonfakis 1995). Certainly it can be argued that aspects of the idea of social exchange can be put to good analytical use, as will be demonstrated in the discussion of policy networks in chapter four. It should also be acknowledged that, as documented by Mayer (1994), RCT has contributed to recent developments in Analytical Marxism. In general, however, the rational choice approach is open to a number of serious criticisms, and it is to these that I now turn. In discussing them, I intend to simultaneously draw out a number of *general* sociological themes that, as will be shown in the later chapters, are theoretically and methodologically relevant to the task of constructing a contemporary sociology of public policy.

The problem of "rationality". It is likely that individuals frequently engage in self-interest maximization, but RCT has a tendency to push this to extremes and convey an image of actors as, so to speak, decision-making "scientists". The image in RCT is quite often one of actors who systematically identify and sift through the range of options available to them in the various situations in which they are involved; who rationally explore different methods for implementing their plans/strategies; and who monitor and methodically evaluate progress toward the achievement of their goals. Against this image, the notions of "bounded rationality" and "satisficing" (Simon 1957; March and Simon 1958) are probably far more realistic. Actors, whether lay people or politicians, officials, or professionals, often have to "make do" with less than perfect information. In addition, it has been evident ever since the time of Weber's sociology of action that such things as emotion, habit, and value commitment, or some combination of these, are invariably to be found among the constitutive elements of social action. Collins (1992: 90), who argues that Giddens (1984, 1993) gives too much emphasis to the "knowledgeability" of actors, observes that most of the available sociological evidence (provided by phenomenologists, ethnographers, and conversation analysis researchers) suggests that individuals deal mostly in cognitive typifications and routinized taken-for-granted forms of reasoning (Collins 1992: 80–81). Actors' decision-making very often relies on habitualized ways of thinking that mentally "simplify" the social environment and to some degree "screen out" diversity and complexity (89). An in some ways similar argument concerning actors' habitualized use of institutionalized meanings is set out in Berger and Luckmann's (1972) *The Social Construction of Reality*. There are, then, grounds for questioning the validity of at least some aspects of RCT's model of the actor as a decision-making being.

Overconcentration on individual actors. Aside from rare exceptions such as Coleman's (1990: 531, 542) version of RCT in which he explicitly acknowledges the existence of organizational (or "corporate") actors as increasingly important components of the social fabric of modern society, the rational choice approach tends to concentrate almost entirely on individual human actors. The significance of this overemphasis on individuals will become clearer later in the chapter when I shall define and discuss the concept *actor*.

Ontological emergence and the relative autonomy of micro, mezo and macro levels of social process. An analogy will serve to illuminate the important concept of *emergence*, a concept which was introduced in the earlier section on structural-functionalism. The human organism (the person) is "more than" the sum of the parts (molecular cells) that constitute the whole. The whole (the person) has *emergent* structural properties (for example, consciousness and causal powers) that *arise by virtue of the structure of the whole*. These are properties that cannot be found in any of the individual parts (molecular cells) that constitute the whole. In this sense, the whole is "more than" the sum of the parts.

Likewise in the social world it is possible to find "new" or *emergent* structural properties. These emergent properties can be found at micro, mezo, and macro levels of social process. At the micro level, a small group is "more than" the sum of the individual members' personalities, forms of thought, dispositions, intentions and goals. For example, a formal committee in the public sector is likely to have institutionalized mechanisms of legitimation, resource-attraction, decision-making, etc, and more generally causal powers, of a kind that cannot be reduced to the level of its individual members. *Informal* groups also have emergent properties in the form of, for example, patterns of interaction that emerge simply by virtue of the group's existence. And at the mezo level, organizations have emergent structural properties that cannot be reduced to the level of individuals. The same is true at the macro level. An example of the latter is provided by Mouzelis (1995: 32) who observes that in order to understand a revolution we must take account not only of the decisions and actions of *individuals*, but also of "emergent" macro phenomena to do with, for example, the relative power positions of the armed forces and political elites; the condition of the economy and general level of economic wellbeing in the country in question; international relations as between that country and others; and the possible involvement of international actors such as the United Nations. None of these phenomena are reducible to the decisions and actions of individuals.

Emergent structural properties – whether at micro, mezo, or macro levels – are not adequately addressed in the micro-to-macro theoretical framework that is associated with RCT. We saw earlier that it is important to avoid the reification and reductionism of *methodological collectivism* (for example, structural-functionalism and structural Marxism); methodological collectivism is a macro-to-micro perspective that portrays individuals as beings whose forms of thought and practices are largely macro-determined. Equally, however, it is important to avoid the opposing reductionism of *methodological individualism* which, as in RCT, is a micro-to-macro perspective that portrays society as the aggregated outcome of the decisions and actions of countless human individuals; this is a micro-reductionist perspective that cannot account for emergent structural properties that are "more than" the aggregated outcome of individuals' intentions, decisions, and actions. As we have seen, there are emergent properties – at mezo and macro levels, for example – which require analysis and investigation *at the level of social process at which they occur*; the methodological implication of this is that emergent properties require analysis of a kind that does not confine itself to the study of individuals or of person-person social exchanges.

RCT's hidden reductionism: macro-structural determination. Despite the rational-choice school's commitment to methodological individualism, there is actually a sense in which some versions of RCT tacitly subscribe to methodological collectivism and to the notion of a macro-structural determination of actors' forms of thought. It was observed earlier that in RCT some preferences are not seen as individually specific or idiosyncratic but, rather, as group-patterned (Mason 1988: 17). Hindess's (1988: 22–24) critique of Marxist versions of the rational choice approach, such as Elster's (1989), shows that such approaches, though formulated on an avowed commitment to methodological individualism, nestle on a tacit theoretical assumption that actors' forms of thought are structurally predetermined in so far as it is presumed that what counts as "rational" action is a function of the actor's membership of a social collectivity such as social class.

Failure to adequately account for normative factors. Although RCT and exchange theory are highly critical of cultural and macro-structural explanations of behaviour, we saw earlier that rational choice theorists do attempt to incorporate normative (cultural) factors into their model of the rational utility-maximizing actor. The examples that I referred to were Homans's concept of "distributive justice" and Blau's "norm of reciprocity". But given that RCT argues that rational utility-maximizing behaviour based on economic and psychological need is pervasive, it is unclear – in the absence of any suitable explanation – how and why normative factors should influence behaviour. Herein lies one of RCT's weaknesses. Instrumentalism undoubtedly is one aspect of social action, but in the final analysis RCT fails to provide a convincing account of the part played by normative factors. In other words, the rational choice approach cannot adequately account for the *ends* of social action. Actors may, it is true, act rationally in the sense that they select means that will help them achieve their ends, but RCT is in general so hostile to cultural explanations of behaviour that insufficient attention is paid by RCT theorists to the part played by culture in actors' formulations of their goals and in social action generally.

A narrow conception of actors' forms of thought. The criticism of RCT that I wish to make note of here, overlaps with some of the earlier ones. It is by no means clear how in any particular instance an observer or empirical researcher should decide what is to count as rational action. Rather than become involved in making judgements about whether actors' behaviour is "rational" or "non-rational', it can be argued that we should instead employ anti-reductionist methods of analysis for the purpose of investigating what actors *actually* do, how they view situations, and how in practice they relate ideas and values to particular situations and to possible courses of action. Moreover, actors' ways of thinking are related to social situations and contexts, and thus to the availability of discourses. Hindess (1988) observes that actors employ a wide variety of deliberative tools (oral traditions, written materials, commonsense, mythology, science, religion, the reading of tea-leaves, cost-benefit analysis, etc) and these discourses and deliberative tools may be differentially available not only to different actors but also to the same actors in different time-space locations. Hindess (1988: 68), who is one of the leading writers on anti-reductionist methods of analysis, notes that a problem with the rational choice approach is that it obscures important questions about the processes of evaluation, calculation and reflection that figure in actors' decisions and actions. To simply assume a holistic rationality without enquiring into, for example, actors' methods for assessing and reflecting on situations, and actors' techniques for turning decisions into actions, is to ignore large and important areas of social scientific research.

Neglect of the interactional order. It was noted earlier that RCT's commitment to methodological individualism is associated with a failure to account for the emergent structural properties of macro-social systems. In other words, RCT is a micro-reductive perspective that fails to provide an adequate account of the macro-social order. Given RCT's rejection of macro-social analysis and its rather "extreme" micro-orientation (Ritzer 1992: 630), it might at first sight seem strange to accuse RCT of also neglecting the significance of the micro-social ("interactional") order. It is important to recognize, however, that RCT's micro-orientation is *individualist*, not situational or interactional. Micro-situational approaches such as symbolic interactionism (Charon 1995) are well attuned – in a way that RCT is not – to the *emergent* nature of micro-social happenings. What RCT does not properly acknowledge is that actors' forms of thought, criteria for assessing situations and for formulating and acting upon decisions, are to some extent formulated, altered, "negotiated", etc, *during* the course of face-to-face interaction in micro settings. These are the settings of everyday life in families, pubs, schools, the workplace (offices, the factory shopfloor, committees, informal meetings) and so on. Rational choice theorists are in some sense correct to say that actors' forms of thought are not macro-structurally determined: but RCT tends to ignore the significance of the notion that actors' meanings, intentionalities, and decisions are almost always to some extent *situationally emergent*. Meanings and intentionalities, at least in part, are a product of the ebb and flow of social interaction in micro situations. Micro-sociology in the form of the symbolic interactionist perspective recognizes this and addresses its implications, whereas RCT does not. Micro-sociology is *inter*actional (Mead 1967: 78) and *inter*subjectivist: it is not concerned with individuals as single actors but with interactions and "negotiations" among actors in micro (face-to-face) situations and *regards* *social action as arising from the interlocking of intentionalities rather than from their singular existence* (Knorr-Cetina 1981: 8–9 and 16–17). Undoubtedly, the "self" is important: methodologically speaking, this entails a focus on life-career and the unique psycho-biography of self (Layder 1993: 72). In micro-sociology, it is worth noting, "the self" is a more complex concept than in RCT. However the wider point that I am making here is that – without in any way denying the importance of "self" – social behaviour nearly always has an *interactional, micro-situational and emergent component that can not be adequately grasped in terms of the individualism promulgated by RCT*. It is true that efforts have been made to broaden RCT so as to include micro-situational factors and also to refine RCT's conception of the micro-macro linkage (for example, see Friedman and Hechter 1988, 1990); but most of the problems that I have referred to above remain unresolved in the rational choice approach. This is hardly surprising, for the approach is reductionist.

Reductionisms: methodological collectivism and methodological individualism

Rational choice theory, as I have just noted, is a form of reductionism. Earlier, I identified methodological individualism and methodological collectivism as two major forms of reductionist theory. *A reductionist analysis is an analysis that illegitimately attempts to explain social life in terms of a single, unifying principle of explanation*, such as "the interests of capitalism" (as in Marxism) or "the interests of patriarchy" (as in radical feminism). *Methodological individualism* boils down to a reductionist claim that it is possible to explain the nature of society in terms of a single explanatory formula which specifies that "individuals make society". This reductionist postulate is, as we have seen, employed by rational-choice theorists. Methodological individualism is reductionist, then, in so far as it is based on a single general principle of explanation which decrees that social life is reducible to the constitutive actions of individual actors (Hindess 1988: 36). *Methodological collectivism*, in contrast, is a macro-to-micro form of reductionism that "decentres" the actor. Methodological collectivism, as in structural Marxism and in teleological and reified versions of structural-functionalism, is a reductionist attempt to explain agency and social action as an effect of and in terms of internal structural exigencies, principles, or "needs" of social systems. The reification involved in methodological collectivism alludes to so-called "deep" or "hidden" macro structures (such as "patriarchy" or a deep linguistic structure) which are said to function as the generators or "prime movers" of social action. Such theories are very often of the type that explicitly claim or tacitly imply that social aggregates such as "the middle class", "men", or "white people" are actors. The problem here is that an *actor* is, minimally, an entity that has the means of formulating and acting upon decisions, and therefore a social collectivity such as "men" cannot be regarded as an actor (or agent). From time to time in the later chapters I will come back to these matters, and re-inspect methodological individualism and methodological collectivism from policy-related angles.

A "New" Anti-Reductionist and Non-Reified Sociology

In the preceding section it was established that major forms of reductionism are methodological individualism (as in rational choice theory) and methodological collectivism associated with, for example, Marxism and radical feminism. *Reductionist* theories, it was noted, wrongly attempt to reduce the complexity of social life to a single unifying principle of explanation, such as "the actions of individuals", or "structural necessities" bound up with "the needs of the system" or with the so-called "interests of capitalism" or the "interests of patriarchy". In the recent history of sociology and social theory there have been a large number of left-orientated macro reductionist theories in such fields as organizational studies (Marglin 1980), the sociology of education (Sharp 1980), the sociology of welfare (Cockburn 1977) and social work (Dominelli and McLeod 1989), the sociology of professions (Poulantzas 1975, Braverman 1974, Ehrenreich and Ehrenreich 1979), and the sociology of medicine (see the discussion in Bury 1986).

Although the term *essentialism* is closely related to reductionism it tends to be more specifically linked to the reductionist notion that taxonomic collectivities – such as "women" – are a relatively homogeneous category comprised of individuals (individual women, in this instance) who have more or less common (and "objective") interests that are structurally given to them by virtue of their structural location in the social totality, that is, by virtue of their membership of a taxonomic collectivity called "women" (see the discussion of power and interests in the following chapter). It is in relation to feminism that contemporary critique of essentialism is most noticeable. Essentialist feminist theory mistakenly supposes that "women" *as represented in the theory* is a social category that is empirically "real" – a category that is "given" by nature or by society rather than a socially constructed definition or a feminist theoretical construct (Elliott and Mandell 1995: 17). Essentialism, then, presupposes on *a priori* grounds a unity or homogeneity of social phenomena. The phenomena in question might be, for example, the state, the law, or culture, or taxonomic collectivities such as "women", "men", "white people", "the middle class", etc.

Critique of the inadequacies associated with certain kinds of social and political theory need not, however, end on a negative note. In the remainder of this chapter I shall begin the task of identifying a range of concepts that, when they are combined to form a new and synthetic conceptual framework, lead to a form of sociological analysis that transcends the previously described problems of reductionism and essentialism, teleology, and reification.

Actor

A crucial component of anti-reductionist methodology is Hindess's (1986a: 115) formulation of social action: he defines an *actor* as "a locus of decision and action where the action is in some sense a consequence of the actor's decisions". Actors in terms of this definition may be individual human actors, or they may be social ("organizational") actors (ibid.) of the kind that are referred to by Harre (1981: 141) as "supra-individuals". This distinction, which draws upon the previously mentioned idea of *emergence*, is important in so far as corporate or organizational actors are capable of engaging in actions that are not reducible to the actions of human individuals (Hindess 1986a: 124, 1990: 25–29; Clegg 1989: 187–188; Holzner 1978). In the following chapters I shall use the term *individual actor* to refer to individual human actors; the term *social actor* will be employed to refer mainly to organizations, but also to families, committees and some other small-scale micro-groups (Harre 1981: 144, 150–152). Thus, social actors are, for example, committees (such as a local tenants' association, or the cabinet) or "organizations" of various kinds such as central government departments, private firms, local government departments, professional associations, trade unions, organized pressure groups, and so on. It is important to note that only actors have causal powers. Merely taxonomic collectivities like "society", "classes", "men", "black people", "white people", etc, are not actors. They are collectivities that cannot do anything or be held responsible for anything; this is because they are social aggregates that "have no identifiable means of taking decisions, let alone of acting on them" (Hindess 1988: 105). And certainly it can be argued – in regard to what has until recently been one of the major theoretical and empirical foci of sociology – that social classes are not actors (Hindess 1988: 104–5; Harre 1981: 157; Goldthorpe and Marshall 1992: 385). Those theorists who insist that classes are actors or that classes may be actors under particular circumstances (for example, Touraine 1981: 32; Mouzelis 1991: 126, 129, 130; Layder 1994: 4) are engaging in reification. Nor are social movements actors, despite widespread claims to the contrary by, for example, Touraine (1981: 31–32, 77–78), Giddens (1984: 203–4), Scott (1990: 6), Mouzelis (1993a: 677), Eyerman and Jamison (1991: 80), Demertzis (1993) and Munck (1995: 677–8). To repeat: *for an entity to be an actor (or agent) that entity must have means of formulating and of acting upon decisions.*

This anti-reductionist and non-reified conception of agency has profound implications for the sociology of public policy. For example, only actors as defined earlier can be said to have causal responsibility for existing social conditions (including forms of inequality) and only actors are capable of formulating and implementing social and political actions and public policies that reproduce or alter those conditions. Viewed in these terms, the notion that, let us say, "white people" are an entity (an actor) that has causal responsibility for or can take action to remedy racial (or any other) inequalities, can be seen to be an absurd notion that, it should be noted, has implications for the sociology *of* public policy as well as the development of sociological knowledge *for* public policy. Nor can "men", who are not an entity that can be said to be an actor, be held responsible for gender inequalities, and nor are "men" an entity that can undertake actions designed to reproduce or alter inequalities. We should reject, on the grounds that they are reductionist, both methodological individualism and methodological collectivism. With regard to the latter, to impute causal responsibility for social conditions to social aggregates ("society", "the middle class", "men", "white people", etc) that do not have the means of formulating or of acting upon decisions, is to refer to "fictitious actors" (Hindess 1986a: 116). This has the two unfortunate consequences of obscuring the social processes resulting in those conditions, and of obscuring analysis of what can be done to change them (ibid. 116–17).

Locales, materials, and social networks

In later chapters I shall return to the importance of the temporal dimension of social life, a dimension that forms part of the concept *time-space*. For the moment, however, let us examine those *spatial* aspects of time-space that refer to non-reductionist conceptions of locale, materials, and social networks.

Locale

Ideas concerning the significance of locale have been neglected in the past, but currently they are becoming more widely recognized in sociology and in social science in general. Harrison-White (1992: 130) observes: "Social science has shied away from locality . . . To meld social with geographic concepts is very hard . . . Localities are intersections between physical space and social networks". Giddens's (1984: 376) emphasis on locales and their interconnections is an important part of the theory of structuration, in terms of which social action is viewed as "the structuring of social relations across time and space". Much of the credit for bringing the idea of locale and time-space into sociology and social theory, must go to Giddens (1984, 1993). Some years ago, he had argued (1979: 201): "At first sight nothing seems more banal and uninstructive than to assert that social activity occurs in time and space. But neither time nor space has been incorporated into the centre of social theory."

Locale can usefully be used as a bridging concept that spans micro, mezo and macro dimensions of social life. Sites, or settings as some sociologists prefer to call them, are particular time-space locations of face-to-face interaction. This means that, for example, the medical training school which currently exists at the University of Liverpool is, for analytical purposes, a *site* or *setting*: but "medical training" is not. In her study of the practices of shoppers, Lave (1986) defines supermarkets (plural) as an *arena*, that is, a general type or category of institutional settings. In Lave's terminology, a setting (a supermarket) is a singular, actually experienced place, as distinct from an arena (supermarkets) which is an institutional category ("a type of place"). Shoppers can walk into a setting (a supermarket) and directly experience it: they cannot do this in respect of the arena, because the arena consists of many places (supermarkets) scattered through time and space. *Sites and arenas are linked in various ways, and this has methodological implications.* To study only an arena as an institutional category (for example "medical training") without also investigating the internal properties of local sites, runs the danger of failing to check empirically for the existence of possible situational specificity *within* a particular site(s) (for example, a particular medical school). Because no structural predetermination is involved, some local events may be relatively site-specific, or be part of empirically significant patterns of variation across sites within the particular institutional sphere ("arena") in question. Conversely, an exclusive preoccupation with micro-situational analysis is too narrow an approach, by virtue of the failure to analyse *time-space* linkages *across* sites and the relationship(s) of sites to arenas and to wider (macro) social, economic and political conditions.

Implicit in my anti-reductionist conception of locale, a conception which avoids macro-structural theories of structural predetermination, is the notion that public policies (in terms of their contents and how these are interpreted, their methods of practical application, etc) might vary from one place to another. This is bound up with the general idea – to which I shall return shortly – that society is neither a unified nor structurally predetermined totality. Policy examples of spatial variation are plentiful. There has been, for example, an increasingly empirically-based awareness of not only national variations (Bryant and Mokrzycki 1994) but also regional and local variations in responses to trans-national political, economic, and social change. Two interesting research-based accounts of regional and city-based differences in policy strategies in response to de-industrialization, are the analyses provided in Cooke (1989) and in Harloe, Pickvance and Urry (1990). This is not to say that spatial variation (or spatial "discontinuity") is necessarily ubiquitous; spatial as well as temporal *continuities* also exist, though this does not mean that continuities are structurally predetermined. An example of public policy continuity is the reproduction of a relatively unchanging policy agenda within a policy community over a lengthy period of time, as in the case of British post-war agricultural policy (Smith 1990). It is important to emphasize that if reductionist analyses associated with methodological collectivist approaches such as Marxism, structuralism or feminism are to be avoided, any such continuities should be analyzed as *contingently reproduced* phenomena. That is to say, it is important to recognize that they could have "happened otherwise"; *continuities are not "necessary effects" of the social totality*. In other words, if some particular policy materials are reproduced across large stretches of time-space in more or less the same form, we have to look for the specific actor involvements and conditions of action that resulted in the policy reproduction. When reductionist theories of structural predetermination are abandoned, we have to search for specific and non-reductionist explanations of the social reproduction or change of the policy materials in question.

Materials

In anti-reductionist sociology, the term *materials* is a convenient theoretical shorthand. Following Callon and Latour (1981: 284) and Latour (1986), I employ the term in a very general way to include a wide variety of discourses (such as religious, technical, professional, or political discourses or any combination of these), laws, rules, resources, written contracts, and policies, together with value-articulations, social practices, and typifications of the kind associated with the ordinary routines of everyday life. The point I wish to make here is that it is useful to give analytical credence to a deceptively mundane anti-reductionist postulate. This is that materials *flow spatially and temporally across locales.* And in anti-reductionist sociology, the form and effects of any particular materials, including the extent of their time-space *mobility* and *durability* (Law 1986a), are seen as relational and contingent outcomes of social processes: they are not seen as given by nature or by the social totality.

There is a sense in which materials (for example, policy materials) flow into and out of contemporaneously existing locales (Duster 1981, Lidz 1981), and in addition to spatiality the movement of materials also has a temporal dimension. This theoretical approach has methodological implications. That is, the approach sensitizes the empirical policy researcher to the importance of investigating – in open-ended (ontologically flexible) and non-reductive fashion – the movement of policy materials as they travel from one time-space location to another. In terms of the theoretical/methodological framework developed in this and the later chapters, an important research task is investigation of the extent to which some policy materials are *transmitted* in relatively unchanged form from one time and place to another, and the extent to which some policy materials may be *transformed* as the material travels across time-space (Latour 1986). When, where, by what means and with what effects policy material is transmitted, or else transformed, are, providing they are examined in non-reductive terms, crucial empirical questions in the sociology of public policy. My reason for saying this is that, to repeat the point made earlier, *no structural predetermination of the material is involved.* Once reductionist theories of structural predetermination are jettisoned we can no longer simplistically "read off" policy material as a manifestation or expression of a "deep" or "primary" structural generator of material; no such generator or "prime mover" exists.

I am aware that it is likely that not every reader of this book will be familiar with some of the sociological themes to which I have just referred, including the idea of material diffusion. Indeed, the notion that the social world is in part made up of materials and that materials "travel", might at first sight seem odd, or else "obvious". Nevertheless, there are significant analytical advantages in thinking about social life in these terms. Cohen, a theorist who is sympathetic to Giddens's (1984) work, refers to "circuits of reproduction" and he to some extent recognizes that in regard to material diffusion processes across time-space and across social networks there is an explanatory deficit in Giddens's theory of structuration (see Cohen 1989: 87, 105–6, 124, 127, 199). Also relevant here is the theoretical work of Fararo (1992: 275):

> the diffusion process ... is one answer to Giddens's (1984) "re-constructed problem of social order". The time-space separation of concrete actors (with memory traces of distributed procedural knowledge constitutive of the generators of institutions) is bridged in terms of the spread of typifications and of associated ... rules.
>
> In this way, Giddens's reconstructed social order problem of how entities get connected is solved in principle. Namely, the objects of diffusion, among them potential candidates for institutional embodiments throughout the ... system, are spread beyond localized networks through ... ties that bridge them.

The postulate that I am seeking to establish here in regard to materials and material diffusion processes (Lidz 1981; Latour 1986, 1991; Callon 1991; Braithwaite 1994; Fararo 1992) can be conveniently illustrated with reference to housing policy. Let us assume a sociological interest in the investigation of housing policy in Britain (Cole and Goodchild 1995: 49). In this policy field it can be argued that the relevant policy materials (Hill 1993a: chapter 10; Saunders 1990; Fimister and Hill 1993; Garside 1993) can for analytical purposes be regarded as consisting of housing law; housing policy; norms and conventions associated with housing organization, management, training, and professionalism; conflicting moral-political conceptions of the nature and purposes of housing policy; and everyday housing policy "practice" in local settings. In this as in any other policy arena, it is appropriate to regard policy as a *process*. The policy process exists spatially and temporally within and across a range of relevant "micro" sites of face-to-face interaction, together with larger locales such as organizations that collectively constitute a relational policy network (Marsh and Rhodes 1992a). The micro settings and organizational locales that constitute the policy network are, in this illustration, central and local government departments; local housing offices; the housing advice sections of neighbourhood law and advice centres; professional housing management training courses in academic institutions; the central and local offices of building societies, housing associations, and housing pressure groups. This illustration, and the earlier observations concerning rejection of the idea of structural predetermination, are intended to demonstrate that an anti-reductionist sociology of public policy is concerned with the following: the detailed study of *how* time-space linkages between relevant locales are maintained or changed; analysis of micro (interactional) processes pertaining to the handling and application of policy material *within* locales; and investigation of the actors, media and mechanisms involved in material diffusion *across* policy locales that, in the very nature of things, are scattered across time and social space.

Social networks

A social network is an assemblage of actors, positions/roles, locales and materials that exhibit a degree of patterned interconnectedness and continuity across time and social space, and where the network is sufficiently self-contained to be distinguishable from other networks and from the larger social environment in which it is located. In a number of respects, policy networks (see chapter four) may be regarded as a type of social network; an example of a policy network is the housing policy network to which I have just referred. Some aspects of Callon's (1991) sociological conception of materials and social networks are relevant to the concept of time-space that I associate with anti-reductionist sociology. Although I reject (for reasons that I have already discussed) Callon's claim that materials such as money and written materials can in some circumstances be *actors* (ibid. 140–41), and I am critical of his neglect of system integration and its linkage to social integration in the terms that I discussed earlier in the chapter, I nevertheless take the view that some parts of his work can usefully be incorporated into sociological methods of analysis.

Callon's (1991) notion of "intermediaries" (ibid. 134–40) is in some ways similar to my conception of materials; indeed he sometimes prefers to use the term "materials" (143). An intermediary is "anything passing between actors which defines the relationship between them" (134). He suggests (140): "Action works via the circulation of intermediaries. These tirelessly carry messages which describe . . . the networks in which they are inscribed". The various kinds of materials found in a social network will usually have different levels of *durability* or "resistance", and here Callon suggests "there is a gradient of material resistance stretching from inscriptions embedded in idle canteen talk, through laws and legal codes" (150). Another factor is that some social networks are more *tightly integrated* and more institutionalized than others. Differing material durabilities are linked to characteristics of their relational networks, so that, other things being equal, institutionalized materials circulating within tightly-coupled networks are more difficult to disturb or change than materials in looser material-network configurations that have low levels of "irreversibilization" (149). Callon's sociological distinction between tightly-coupled networks and less tightly-coupled networks, has a parallel of sorts in the political science literature. For example, Marsh and Rhodes's (1992b: 251) typology of policy networks draws a distinction between policy communities and issue networks. Post-war British agricultural policy is widely cited in the political science literature as a good example of a policy community. In a *policy community* such as British agriculture there are relatively few actors (the Ministry of Agriculture, the National Farmers Union, and at European Union level the Council of Agricultural Ministers and Directorate General VI of the EU Commission), and these have a relatively stable and continuing relationship with each other. Other characteristics of policy communities are that there tends to be a high frequency of interaction among the actors; membership of the network does not fluctuate; there is a fairly high degree of consensus within the network in regard to values and policy-objectives; and each of the major actors involved has some power in so far as they have resources (technical or professional knowledge, financial resources, legal power, political influence, etc) that they can "exchange" with the other actors in the network. In contrast, an *issue network* is a far looser, less integrated type of policy network. Examples are American agricultural policy and British industrial policy. Issue networks tend to have a relatively large number of state actors and numerous non-state participants (individuals, organizations, and pressure-groups) and a shifting rather than stable membership; the frequency and quality of contact among actors in the network fluctuates; there may be a certain amount of agreement over values and policy, but there is usually also conflict over numerous issues; and there tends to be a number of network participants who have very few resources to exchange with others and who are therefore likely to have only limited power within the network. It should be noted that I am referring here to a continuum, rather than a sharp dichotomy. Policy networks are located somewhere along a continuum with policy communities at one end, and issue networks at the other. It should also be noted that these categories are not static or structurally predetermined: in principle, an issue network may become a "closed" and tightly integrated policy community, and for a variety of reasons a policy community might become a loosely coupled issue-network. Once again, we observe that social phenomena, in this case social networks, are not structurally predetermined.

Social Systems

A social system is in many respects similar to a social network. This statement requires some qualification. For example, while society is sometimes referred to as a (large) social system, it is rare to hear of society referred to as a social network. In some sense, society may be thought of as an amalgam of social networks (Fararo 1992; Law 1994). More often, however, society is referred to as a (macro) social system. Systems, then, are to be found at the macro level. They can also be found at the micro level, and at the mezo level in organizations and in inter-organizational relations. At the mezo level, a policy community has certain system-like characteristics; this is demonstrated in Freeman's (1965) notion of "policy subsystems", Thurber's (1991: 325) concept of "policy systems", and Mayntz's (1993) analysis in which she describes policy communities as social systems (19–20).

Luhmann (1982: 70), a neo-functionalist, suggests that a social system exists "whenever the actions of several persons are meaningful, interrelated and are thus . . . marked off from an environment". In Giddens's (1984: 377) sociology, the concept *system* refers to: "The patterning of social relations across time-space, understood as reproduced practices. Social systems should be regarded as widely variable in terms of the degree of 'systemness' they display and rarely have the sort of internal unity that may be found in physical and biological systems." For Giddens (1993: 128), social systems are "groups, collectivities, etc". Of course, Giddens's conception of systems does not involve him in methodological individualism. He is well aware that the idea of *emergence*, discussed earlier, applies to social systems. In this connection it is worth noting Knoke and Kuklinski's (1991: 174–75) observations on emergent properties in industrial and medical social systems:

Relational measures capture emergent properties of social systems that cannot be measured by simply aggregating the attributes of individual members. Furthermore, such emergent properties may significantly affect both system performance and the behaviour of network members. For example, the structure of informal friendships and antagonisms in formal work groups can affect both group and individual productivity rates in ways not predictable from such personal attributes as age, experience, intelligence, and the like. As another example, the structure of communication among medical practitioners can shape the rate of diffusion of medical innovations in a local community and can determine which physicians are likely to be early or late adopters.

Notice that to recognize the emergent properties of social systems is not the same thing as pushing the argument to the point of *reification*. Reification, as I have already noted, is an illegitimate method of analysis that attributes agency to entities that are not agents (or actors, in the terms used earlier). For example, Luhmann argues that systems are self-referencing (1988): he claims (1982: 265) systems are self-referential in that they are able to reflect and have consciousness of themselves as systems, and are also able to take decisions. In other words, he is claiming that social systems are actors. Luhmann fails to adequately address the agency/structure debate. It is true that social systems have emergent structural properties that arise for reasons that cannot be "reduced" to the agency exercised by actors (whether individual or social actors), but it is quite another thing to claim that social networks/social systems are themselves actors with capacities for reflection and with causal, decision-making powers. Here Luhmann is engaging in reification and in a mystification of agency. As I have already noted, a more adequate approach to agency/structure is, following Mouzelis (1995: 127), to make a distinction between a social whole (whether a small group, an organization, a policy network, or a society) viewed (a) as a system of interrelated actors (a figurational system); and viewed (b) as a system of interrelated rules, roles or social positions (an institutional system). In the study of any particular social system it is also important, as Mouzelis (ibid. 155) notes, to explore *linkages* between the figurational and institutional dimensions of the system. The significance of this last observation will become increasingly apparent in the following chapters as we continue to examine and illustrate in policy terms some key postulates associated with agency/structure and micro-macro.

Recursion

The concept *recursion* is frequently employed in connection with social systems and social networks. Recursion refers to self-generating processes (Law 1994: 14–16). A "strong" and ultimately reified and reductionist version of recursion is to be found in Luhmann's (1982, 1989) theory of "autopoietic" systems. These are tightly-coupled systems that have considerable autonomy from their environment and that are seen as self-reproducing in a way that, as I have already noted, involves a reductionist conception of agency which treats the system itself as if it were an actor with causal, decision-making powers. In an anti-reductionist and non-reified methodology, an entity that is to be regarded as an actor must, as observed earlier, have the means of formulating and of acting upon decisions.

However, it is entirely possible to acknowledge the importance of recursive (self-reproducing) tendencies in social systems and in social networks without having to also endorse reductionist and reified conceptions of recursion, such as Luhmann's. Amin and Thrift (1995: 53) argue that an aspect of the "socioeconomic" approach to the study of governance, is the growing interest in policy networks and recursive processes: they refer to "the tendency to emphasise path-dependent evolutionary change ... the degree to which networks constructed in particular contexts for particular purposes are sedimented over time". M J Smith (1993: 225) observes that within a policy network, especially if it is a tightly-coupled policy community, "standard operating procedures" (institutionalized procedures and rules) tend to shape events and limit the number of options open to policy actors, and in most circumstances the existence of standard operating procedures in a policy network tends in the direction of recursion and network self-reproduction. As Cerny (1990: 27) put it: "Once established ... structural patterns tend to be reproduced, whether because of biases built into the structures themselves, or the expectations held by agents, or the linkages built into structural fields". Once in existence, structured patterns in policy networks – and particularly in policy communities – tend to be reproduced through institutionalized "rules" and regularized interaction among the policy actors who are involved in the network. A closely related argument is developed by Kickert (1993: 192) who defines governance as the management of inter-organizational networks, which he examines in terms of recursive tendencies and relatively high levels of network autonomy from "external" controls. A similar theme is taken up by Mayntz (1993). However, in discussing recursion Mayntz does not examine the concept *agency* and she exposes herself to the charge that she comes close to a reified conception of social systems. She claims that social systems and social networks "under certain conditions are able to define their own boundaries, and to actively protect themselves from external intervention" (17), and that systems have an "ability to organize . . . capacity to act" (18). Mayntz's remarks are open to challenge, for reasons that I have already discussed: to say that an entity (for example, a social system) may have recursive (self-reproducing) tendencies, is *not* to say that the entity in question is necessarily an actor in the anti-reductionist terms referred to earlier.

Also worthy of attention is Wilsford's (1994: 269) path-dependency model of recursion: "In a path-dependency model, existing policy (that is, the institutions and the rules of the game in place in a particular policy domain at a particular moment) acts as a focusing device for policy . . . to channel future policy movement along a certain path". Wilsford, writing from a political science perspective, also brings out the point that a path-dependency model (the idea that events, circumstances, and decisions predispose future events) is not the same thing as historical determinism (253). Though he rightly rebuts the idea of historical and structural predetermination, he provides little conceptual underpinning for this rebuttal. However, it seems clear from his paper that he rejects theories of structural predetermination without wanting to replace them with the equally problematic assumption that the world is entirely "chaotic"; instead, though he does not state the matter in quite these terms, he recognizes that time-space stability and policy continuities do occur, but that these are *contingently reproduced* continuities and not "necessary effects" of the social totality.

Society is not a unified totality

Implicit in some of the earlier observations concerning the contingent nature of social life and rejection of the idea of structural predetermination, is an understanding that society is not a unified totality. Mann (1986: 1, 4) argues as follows:

> Societies are not unitary. They are not social systems (closed or open); they are not totalities . . . I operate at a more concrete, socio-spatial and organizational level of analysis. Societies are constituted of multiple overlapping and intersecting socio-spatial networks of power. Societies are much messier than our theories of them.

Thus, for example, Mann suggests that the social, political, and economic advances that took place in Europe during and after the Middle Ages, and which served for a time to establish European dominance over much of the rest of the world, were advances that were "not the result of the dynamism or the contradictions of a preceding social system" (ibid. 506); rather, they were a "gigantic series of coincidences" (505). That is to say, patterns of social development are relatively contingent and unpredictable; they are not the expression of some structural principle or structural exigency. A broadly similar conception is evident in Miller's (1993: 695) distinction between *factorial* and *essentialist* theories of the interconnectedness of the parts of a social whole such as a nation-state or society.

> In a factorial theory, the tendency for a society to fit together as a system is just the product of the action and reaction on one another of all its different components. None is privileged with a special explanatory power. As in certain kinds of puzzle, everything can be a key to everything else. But in an essentialist theory the tendency towards system involves some sort of dynamic at the heart of things, pushing, pulling, shaping them to fit in with one another by fitting in with the pattern which it contains.

Notice that Miller uses the term "essentialism" in a way that is synonymous with reductionism, whereas I prefer to keep the two terms separate. However this does not affect the significance of the point that he is making. The argument developed by Mann, Miller and various other theorists and empirical researchers, is that the world of public policy – like the social world in general – is relatively indeterminate. Thus, we should give up the search for analytical "prime movers" in the social sciences (Lyman and Scott 1970: 16). That is to say, we should, as I have argued in various places in this chapter, abandon reductionist theories which attempt to reduce the complexity of social life to a *single* substantive explanatory principle such as "the interests of capitalism", "patriarchy", "post-colonialism", "post-industrialism", "post-Fordism", "the information society", "globalization", and so forth.

Reductionist theories that portray society as a relatively unified social totality have tended to be *macro* theories based on methodological collectivism: this involves, as we saw earlier, a macro-to-micro ("downwards") reduction of the kind that is to be found in structural functionalism and Marxism. However, let us not forget that – for the reasons introduced earlier in the chapter – we should also avoid the reductionism of methodological individualism that is associated with a micro-to-macro ("upwards") reduction as happens in, for example, rational choice theory. As Mouzelis (1991: 138, emphases added) puts it:

> *Downward reductionism* rests on the a priori assumption that the lower levels of analysis point to phenomena which have no dynamic of their own, and can therefore be entirely explained in terms of regularities grasped at higher levels. *Upward reductionism* rests on the equally false

assumption that developments on a higher or more encompassing plane can be entirely derived from those on a lower one.

The arguments developed by Mann, Miller and Mouzelis suggest, firstly, that society is not a unified totality; and secondly, that in studying society, governance, and the policy process it is necessary to formulate a non-reductionist methodology that does not try to reduce social life to a single, general principle of substantive explanation.

CHAPTER TWO

ANTI-REDUCTIONIST SOCIOLOGY AS A BASIS FOR POLICY ANALYSIS

In the introductory chapter it was observed that, although special theories and paradigms have a legitimate place within the sociological community, there is also a place for integrative theoretical frameworks (Bryant and Jary 1991a: 30) that employ concepts and ideas drawn from a number of different paradigms (Bauman 1992: x; Crespi 1992). Anti-reductionist sociology, in the terms defined in the introductory chapter, is a sensitizing framework rather than a substantive theory. The framework is to some extent eclectic and pragmatic, and it emerges through a process of "intertradition boundary work" (Alexander and Colomy 1992: 41). Above all, anti-reductionist sociology is a *synthesis*. Its large-scale pluralistic and methodological reach owes something to its drawing on several theoretical schools. These include micro-sociology, in particular symbolic interactionism; Elias's figurational/process sociology; Berger's constructivist sociology; Foucault's sociology of power and post-Foucauldian conceptions of governance; the sociology of translation developed by Callon, Latour, and Law; Hindess's anti-reductionist perspective which refers to actors, forms of thought, interests, social relations, and the conditions of action; Giddens's theory of structuration; some concepts that until recently have been aligned with (but which are not exclusive to) post-modern theorizing; and recent work – pertaining to agency/structure and micro-macro – that forms part of the post-post modern "return to sociological theory" associated with, in particular, Mouzelis's attempted reconstruction of sociological theory and methodology. To this wide-ranging and synthetic *sociological* framework are added, for the purposes of this book, a range of conceptual materials drawn from political science and also from public policy as an academic discipline. Thus, one of the most obvious features of the theoretical framework for the "new" sociology of public policy is that it involves large scale integration and synthesis.

However, is large scale synthesis a legitimate analytical procedure? There are, it was noted in the previous chapter, post-modern and other objections against synthesis and against "grand theory" (Gurnah and Scott 1992: 161).

Of relevance here is the distinction between *sensitizing* theoretical frameworks and *substantive* theories. In the introductory chapter and also in chapter one, it was observed that anti-reductionist sociology's constructs are intended – like Giddens's theory of structuration – to have analytical application in the study of social action and social processes in all manner of social contexts. They are legitimate sensitizing constructs that, far from being reductive or essentialist, are explicitly non-reductive and *ontologically flexible* (Cohen 1993); they are, in other words, resources for the development of a wide range of substantive theories and empirical explanations. In principle, it is only the development of *reductionist* substantive theories that is excluded from – or to put it another way, cannot be derived from – anti-reductionist sociology's relatively empirically open-ended (ontologically flexible) sensitizing framework. The framework, in a nutshell, is a sensitizing device that is designed to stimulate the development of non-reductive substantive theories and empirical studies. It should be emphasized that anti-reductionist sociology is a large-scale synthetic theoretical framework that has none of the narrow explanatory dogma associated with the reductive and archetypal "modern" substantive theories that post-modernists justifiably reject as "grand narratives". This is a crucial point. To challenge post-modern "anti-foundationalist" orthodoxy is *not* to defend the single-order foundationalist theories (such as Marxism) that post-modern writers rightly reject. Moreover, it was also observed in the first chapter that the post-modern prohibition of nomothetic knowledge, of synthesis, and of cumulative social science, is a self-denying edict (Krokidas 1993: 534; Larrain 1994): the post-modern statement that there can be no general theories is itself a general theory. Notice also that although post-modernists are "for" theoretical fragmentation, the idea of theoretical consolidation via synthesis is, paradoxically enough, compatible with the post-modern notion that the boundaries between theories should be subverted or dissolved (Kellner 1990: 277). Of course, not all objections against synthesis are post-modern: others also exist (Jackson and Carter 1991). These very often take the form of a claim that it is logically impossible to integrate concepts drawn from antithetical theories and paradigms. Such objections only hold good in one sense. That is, what they ignore is that it is sometimes possible to "re-work" concepts drawn from mutually opposed theories (Wallace 1992: 62–63). In response, therefore, to traditional objections of the kind outlined by Hamilton (1974: 150) in his rejection of the idea of synthesis, it will be evident from this and the following chapters that synthesis and theoretical integration is legitimate provided the integration, if it combines otherwise unaligned or mutually exclusive concepts, does not contradict itself through failure to re-work the cluster of imported conceptualizations so as to make them mutually compatible.

With the above remarks in mind, I propose in this chapter to describe a number of the concepts and postulates that collectively comprise the synthetic theoretical framework that, borrowing Hindess's (1986a: 114) term,

I refer to as "anti-reductionist" sociology. Some of these, a number of which were introduced earlier, are of such significance that it will quite often be necessary to return to them in the following chapters. The particular concepts and postulates that I want to highlight in the present chapter are the following: power and interests; actors; forms of thought; the conditions of action; contingency; unintended consequences; time-space; social networks; material diffusion; an important typology that refers to the role/positional, dispositional, and situational dimensions of social life; and three themes that often figure in the literature on politics and policy (these are the state/civil society distinction; postindustrialism; and citizenship).

Power

So far, I have said relatively little about the sociology of power. In classical theory, power is associated with resistance. Weber (1921,1978: 53) argued that power is "the probability that one actor within a social relationship will be in a position to carry out his will despite resistance"; power is "the chance for a man or a number of men to realise their own will in a social action even against the resistance of others who are participating in the action" (ibid. 926). The association of power with resistance, and by implication with conflict, raises the question of whether it is possible to recognize the existence of power in the *absence* of observable conflict. Power and conflict and the observable exercise of power in concrete situations are, following Weber, often seen as interrelated in the sense that some theorists argue that power is only real if exercised; an implication is that sociological analysis of power should be confined to investigation of concrete decisions (Dahl 1958). In contrast, other theorists warn against confining analysis to only those occasions when power and conflict are expressed and observable: powerful groups may be able to exercise power to construct a false and manipulated consensus, and it has been claimed that "the crucial point is that the most effective and insidious use of power is to prevent . . . conflict arising in the first place" (Lukes 1974: 23). Lukes, in his account of what he calls the first dimension of power, acknowledges that Dahl's type of power exists and that the study of concrete policy decisions is therefore important. In this way we can discover who dominated the policy agenda and who, therefore, held the greater amount of power in the policy-making process. There is, though, a second dimension of power. Lukes observes that powerful actors can sometimes employ coercion or subterfuge to keep potentially conflictual issues *off* the decision-making agenda. This implies that the researcher who finds no evidence of struggle over concrete policy decisions would be wrong to simply assume that no power is being exercised.

Providing a non-reductionist approach is employed, there is no reason to disagree with the view that power can exist in both of these dimensions. Lukes also argues, however, that there is a third dimension of power. This arises when dominant elites are able to shape actors' preferences in such a way that, even though there may be no experience of or expression of conflicting interests on *or* off the decision-making agenda, there may nevertheless exist a hidden form of power. Actors, who are brainwashed by the power elite, exist in a condition of "false consciousness" so that they fail to understand what their "true" or "real" interests are. They therefore often do not, according to Lukes, perceive that their "real" interests are under threat and they accordingly "fail" to engage in conflict in the political decision-making arena. Thus, and as Hindess (1982: 508) observed, a conception of so-called "objective" or "real" interests underlies Lukes's view of power.

The problem of "real" ("objective") interests

Anti-reductionist sociology rejects the notion that actors have "real" or "objective" interests that are a necessary consequence of the actors' structural locations in society. Reductionist and reified theories of interests presume that actors have *structurally "given" ("real") interests that inhere in actors simply by virtue of their membership of a taxonomic collectivity such as "the working class", or "men", or "women".* Abell (1977: 20) comments: "The Marxian/Lukesian view is . . . [inadequate] . . . and the possible authoritarian implications in over-riding preferences of those suffering from 'false-consciousness' have disturbed many a liberal mind." Problems associated with the idea of "real" interests are long-standing (Barker and Roberts 1993) and it was many years ago that Child (1941: 218) asked: "How is one to know *which* thoughts, feelings, etc, are, in point of fact, the ones rationally suited to a given class's position?" The answer, stated in non-reductionist terms, is that no particular thoughts and feelings are "necessary" to or "rationally suited" to a "class's" structural position: nor, come to that, to "men's" position or "women's" position (Clegg 1989: 113). As Hindess (1986b: 128) puts it: "The notion of interests that are real or objective (unlike other interests that actors may believe themselves to have) have no explanatory significance with regard to the actions of those whose interests they are thought to be". Of course, actors regularly *formulate* (a sense of having) particular interests, and sometimes act or attempt to act on the basis of their formulated interests, but this is entirely different from the reductionist presupposition that some particular interests are the structurally predetermined (structurally "given") properties of actors.

Translation Sociology

Translation sociology is a somewhat unconventional school of sociology that has some bearing on the topics of power and interests, and therefore this is as good a place as any to introduce the "translation" style of analysis.

Translation sociology, which is mainly associated with the writings of Callon (1986, 1991), Callon et al (1983), Callon and Latour (1981), Callon and Law (1982), Callon et el (1986), Latour (1986, 1987, 1991) and Law (1986a, 1986c, 1986d, 1991a, 1991b, 1994), is influenced by post-structuralism, including Foucault's conception of power and social action. Other influences on translation sociology are actor network theory and, to a lesser extent, symbolic interactionism.

Translation sociology is a mode of analysis that emphasizes strategic agency and processes by which actors "enrol" or "translate" other actors. Methodological collectivism and theories of structural predeterminism are rejected, as also is methodological individualism. Marxism, structural-functionalism, and rational choice theory are dismissed in favour of an alternative approach in which power, interests, intentions, social conditions and relationships are seen as strategically and relationally constituted. For example, getting other actors (individual as well as social actors) to want what a strategic actor wants them to want, is a process of *enrolment* through which other actors' "positions, desires, what they will want . . . is channelled" (Callon and Latour 1981: 289). Enrolment is a process that figures strongly in Callon's (1986, 1991) translation sociology, and, as we shall see in the next chapter, in Foucauldian sociology of governance (Miller and Rose 1988, 1993; Rose and Miller 1992). A policy-related instance of the process of enrolment (or "translation") is when a strategic actor gets a range of other actors to commit financial and other resources to a particular programme: once this happens, the resultant network of actors have been "translated" in that they themselves come to have a vested interest in the continuation (and perhaps the expansion) of the programme to which they have committed themselves. It is in this and other ways that new networks of power, interests, and social relations are constituted and "consigned" (institutionalized), sometimes by chance or through unexpected shifts and unplanned alignments in social relations and in the relevant conditions of action, and sometimes intentionally and strategically (Callon 1991, Latour 1991, Rose and Miller 1992). There are different shades of emphasis within the school of translation sociology, some of which are particularly insightful. One is Callon's emphasis on sociotechnical networks. It can be argued that not enough attention has been given by sociology, political science, and public policy to Callon's (1991) valuable though underdeveloped insights pertaining to the analytical role of network analysis, exemplified in his array of network concepts (actor-network, intermediaries/materials, convergence, irreversibilization, alignment, coordination, network boundaries, and punctualization).

The deficiencies of translation sociology are fourfold. Firstly, the approach lacks an explicitly anti-reductionist and non-reified conception of the concept "actor" (or "agent"): all manner of entities (for example, networks of social relations) and materials (for example, money) are said, wrongly in my view, to exhibit agency. It would be better to regard such entities and materials as part of the *conditions of action*. (This is discussed later in the chapter). Secondly, and in contrast to, say, the work of Mouzelis (1991, 1995), the approach does not pay sufficient attention to systemic/structural features of large scale social systems. Thirdly, translation sociology's commitment to Foucault's view of power is so unswerving that translation theorists and researchers ignore that there is, as I shall shortly demonstrate, a sense in which power, though relational and contingent in some part, is also something that can be "stored" in positions/roles and in social systems and social networks. Lastly, although Callon (1991) and his colleagues claim that translation sociology can account both for stability and continuity as well as change and discontinuity, the approach is in fact rather weak when it comes to accounting for extensive time-space continuities in respect of materials and social systems. Despite these problems, there is, as noted in this and some of the other chapters, no good reason for ignoring translation sociology in the way that many sociologists and almost all political scientists and policy analysts have done. Providing they are modified and aligned with the anti-reductionist framework outlined in this chapter, the insights of translation sociology can be put to good use in social and political analysis. As I have already indicated, aspects of translation sociology relate to conceptions of power and in what follows it will be necessary from time to time to refer to the work of translation theorists and researchers.

Power as an outcome

Analyzed in non-reductionist terms, and in terms of translation sociology and Foucauldian social and political theory, power is not a structurally predetermined or structurally pre-given capacity of actors: it is not a fixed-capacity that inheres in an actor by virtue of the actor's structural location within an over-arching social system. Power is at least partly emergent, in the sense of being an *outcome* of social interactions: power, to paraphrase Law's (1986a: 5) definition, is in part an *effect*, not *cause* of strategic success achieved by actors during the course of their interactions with other actors in particular situations or in a series of situations. Actors, including individual human actors and social ("organizational") actors in the public policy field, may become more powerful, or less powerful; this is because their power, their capacity to shape events or to obtain their objectives, is not a structurally bestowed, predetermined or "fixed" capacity. In power terms, actors contingently grow, remain the same size, or become smaller; they have no structurally fixed or predetermined "size" (Callon and Latour 1981: 280). The strategic, performative and variable nature of power is described by Clegg (1989: 33): "Power is not any thing nor is it inherent in any one; it is a tenuously produced and reproduced effect which is contingent upon the strategic competencies and skills of actors who would be powerful." Two illuminating empirical case studies of the acquisition and loss of power are provided by Callon and Latour (1981) and Callon (1986). These studies, which are conducted by "translation" researchers, suggest that strategic success in the acquisition of power is always potentially reversible. It is because power is not structurally predetermined that there are usually formidable strategic problems to be overcome if currently "ascending" or "powerful" actors are to be able to stabilize their situation for very long periods by means of *irreversibly* enrolling and "consigning" (making *durable*, temporally and spatially) a large number of related ideas, policies, practices and resources (Callon and Latour 1981: 293). Some strategically successful ("ascending") actors may be able to achieve and sustain relatively long-lasting asymmetries in "size" between themselves and other actors (ibid. 286), but these temporally and spatially stabilized asymmetries (Gregory 1989: 188), if and where they occur, are contingently and strategically reproduced (Clegg 1989: 6–7): they are not "necessary affects" of some overarching social totality and nor, for reasons that will be explored in chapter three with reference to governance, can they be said to be products of a supposedly unified and independent state (Miller and Rose 1988: 173–4).

Foucault and the question of whether power can be stored

Foucault's (1972, 1980a, 1980b, 1982) relational conception of power is in many ways similar to that outlined in the preceding section with reference to the idea that power is a contingent *outcome* of social relations, rather than a "prior" or structurally predetermined capacity. Power in Foucault's theoretical scheme is not something that is already (pre)constituted ("stored") in macro-social wholes. Power *emerges* through networks of social relations, and is a contingent *effect* of the operation of "discourses" (medical discourses, legal discourses, religious discourses, political discourses, etc). As well, power is so diffuse and unconcentrated that, for Foucault, it is "everywhere" (Hindess 1996: 100). As Thompson (1982: 244–45) observes, in Foucault's post-structuralist and post-modern theoretical scheme, so-called established power structures

> ... guarantee nothing, but only conditionally and contingently arrange a series of possibilities for disputation or action ... power becomes diffused or dispersed into and through the network of relationships operative within the [situation]. It is ... partial, particular, and dependent. It is more the effect of the practices and mechanisms of social interaction and the knowledge lodging within these, rather than something which has a definite "place" where it is held and from which it is deployed ... it ... is, rather, dispersed.

The point being made here is that Foucauldian theorists and empirical researchers regard power as non-unitary, relational, contingent, strategic, and as an *outcome* or product of discourses and of social relations (McNay 1994). This approach has merit in so far as power almost certainly is partly relational and contingent. However, post-structuralist and post-modern images of power have, it can be argued, gone too far in their almost total rejection of "modernist" concerns with *distributions* of power. Foucault, along with translation theorists such as Callon (1986, 1991), Callon and Latour (1981), Callon et al (1983), Callon et al (1986) and Latour (1986, 1987, 1991), pushes his relational and processual conception of power to the point of claiming that power cannot be "stored" in roles nor stored in social systems and networks of social relations. It is in my view important that the sociology of public policy should draw upon post-Foucauldian research (see, for example, the discussion of the policy-oriented work of Miller and Rose (1988, 1993) and Rose and Miller (1992) in the next chapter). Theoretically and methodologically speaking, and bearing in mind the earlier criticisms of theories of structural predetermination, it is useful to retain the typically Foucauldian insight that "nothing becomes real to the point of it not needing a network in which to upkeep its existence" (Latour 1991: 118). However, this does not mean that we have to endorse the whole of Foucault's theoretical position; in particular, there are good reasons for challenging his insistence that power can never be stored.

On the important question of power storage, Foucault seems to ignore not only that agents "possess" power but also that some agents possess more power than others (Best and Kellner 1991: 70), and that part of the reason for this is that some aspects of power are stored in roles and in social institutions and social systems. For example, everyone knows that the prime minister generally has "more power" than a backbencher. Here we have the structurally and systemically preconstituted face of power; in this example, power is secreted (stored) in the pre-existing role of prime minister and in the pre-existing institution of prime ministership. At the same time, we also know that prime ministers' positions are sometimes only precariously sustained (or not sustained at all). Thus, as Law (1991b: 170) put it, *power can be stored, even if not always securely.* Law's conclusion (ibid. 183) is that it is legitimate to say that an actor "has" power (this invokes the idea of power storage), provided we *also* ask (along with Foucault) how that power is constituted and reproduced relationally.

Law's contribution to the debate concerning power storage is in some respects helpful. He highlights the point that we can combine Foucauldian and non-Foucauldian conceptions of power. We are not, that is to say, speaking of an either/or situation: it is not a question of Foucault *or* reductionist macro-structural theories of structural predetermination. Power is partly preconstituted and stored (in roles, systems and social institutions) and partly relational, emergent and contingent, the extent to which it is "systemic" or else "relational" being an empirical variable that is likely to vary from one social situation to another. I suggest, however, that Law, who remains attached to a largely post-structuralist theoretical framework (1991b, 1994), does not move close enough towards the idea of social systems as developed in, for example, the work of Mouzelis (1991, 1995); and Law also fails to explore the idea of social system/social network *recursion* in terms of an integrated anti-reductionist conception of agency/structure, micro-macro, and time-space. In particular, Law's (1991b: 173–4) conception of agency is highly problematical: "an agent is a structured set of relations with a series of (power) effects ... Thus, unlike Hindess, my primary definition of agency refers to relations and their power-relevant effects, rather than to strategies and intentions". Law's definition of an actor as a "set of relations" (ibid. 172) rests on a claim that social networks/social systems are actors. This, as we saw in the previous chapter, is a reified way of thinking that is also associated with Luhmann's neo-functionalist theory of social systems.

There are, too, problems in Foucault's conception of *agency*. In his early work, the actor does not come into view. Foucault's determinism (Best and Kellner 1991: 60–61) is bound up with his view that discourses (forms of thought and practices) are in themselves "power". The problem here, viewed in non-reified terms, is that there is a sense in which discourses are a form of material that must be mobilized and applied by *actors* before the discourse(s) can be said to have any social consequences or effects. Discourses affect (though do not determine) actors, and are a part of the "conditions of action" (this is discussed later); but discourses as such, are not actors. It is true that Foucault's later work attempted to "bring in" agency at least in so far as the causal powers of individual actors was recognized, but this recognition of agency emphasized individuality in a way that (in common with post-structuralist and post-modern theory in general) did not offer a theory of *inter*subjectivity as distinct from subjectivity (Best and Kellner 1991: 66) and this served to highlight Foucault's failure to appreciate the significance of the micro-situational (interactional) dimension of agency and power (Layder 1994: 110–13).

The relational nature of interests and of power

For reasons that I introduced earlier, it is reductionist to suppose that the interests of state actors – whether individual actors or social ("organizational") actors such as government departments – can be reduced to something called "the interests of capitalism" (see Skocpol 1980: 172). Of course, governments invariably want a healthy economy and there is doubtless a general predisposition among state actors to seek to avoid policies that are regarded as likely to damage the economy. However, and as M J Smith (1993) shows in his excellent analysis of policy networks in such fields as agriculture, health, and industrial and trade policy in Britain and the United States, the influence of business groups on state actors is variable and "it is simplistic to see the state acting in the interests of capital in either the short or long term" (ibid. 8). Individual state actors – officials and politicians – have personal interests to do with career advancement (Weir and Skocpol 1985: 118), and they also have political, administrative, or professional perspectives and objectives which shape their involvements in the policy process. These interests, perspectives, and objectives are not reducible to a single reductionist principle of explanation, such as "the interests of capitalism", or "the interests of neo-colonialism", or "the interests of patriarchy". Nor can they be reduced to a combination of these reduction-isms. (Any such combination would merely compound the separate constitutive reductionisms, and would be hopelessly incoherent). The interests and perspectives formulated by state actors (whether individual or organizational actors) are not reducible, whether in the short term or in the long run, to the interests of merely taxonomic collectivities such as "capitalists", "white people", or "men". Nor, as happens in reductionist versions of structural-functionalism that rest on reified and teleological theories, is it legitimate to reduce state or non-state actors' power and interests to so-called social system "needs" or "functional prerequisites". Reductionist theories of whatever kind have no useful explanatory role, and the point I wish to emphasize here is that the interests of state (and of non-state) actors are developed *relationally*. This very often occurs, as M J Smith (1993: 11) notes, in the context of state actors' relations with non-state actors in policy networks: "Interests are not predetermined but develop within the context of social and economic arrangements and relationships between groups and state actors. Therefore, both the interests of the state and of groups develop within the context of networks. Often they cannot be clearly defined as state interests or group interests". Implicit in Smith's statement, incidentally, is a view that the state/civil society distinction is often blurred; this is taken up later in the chapter.

Having established that interests (by which I mean *actor-formulated* interests as distinct from so-called "objective" or "real" interests) are relational and emergent *during* the course of interaction, rather than structurally "given", let us not forget that – as already noted – *power* is also to some extent a relational outcome of social relations. What an actor will want to do and what an actor is able to do, are not structurally predetermined phenomena; agency, power, and interests are, at least in part, relatively contingent outcomes of variable social conditions, social processes, and social relations. It should also be observed that when state actors enter into exchange relationships with non-state actors in policy networks, this need not necessarily involve any "loss" of power on the state actors' part. To the contrary, entering into a relation of negotiation and collaboration with non-state actors may increase the "infrastructural power" of the state (Mann 1984: 188). For the moment, it is sufficient to observe that actors do not have a structurally pre-given amount of power: to some extent, power is emergent, strategic, relational, and contingent. Power is almost always in some measure an outcome or effect of strategy, interaction, and shifting social conditions rather than a wholly systemically predetermined capacity. We have observed, however, that despite Foucault's view to the contrary, elements of power may sometimes be "stored" in social institutions and in roles and social systems/social networks, in part as a corollary of recursive tendencies that, as we saw in the first chapter, are features of social systems and social networks.

Actors: Some Issues for Consideration

In the first chapter, I outlined Hindess's (1986a: 115) and Harre's (1981: 150–52) anti-reductionist and non-reified conceptions of actors as entities that, in principle, have the means of formulating and taking decisions, and of acting on those decisions. Hence in anti-reductionist sociology there are two types of actors: individual human actors (which I call *individual actors*) and *social actors* such as organizations, committees, and micro groups. I pointed out in the first chapter that in terms of the above conception of agency, taxonomic collectivities such as "men", "women", "black people", "white people", "young people", social classes, etc, are not actors. I also suggested that despite claims to the contrary by theorists such as Munck (1995), social movements are not actors. These entities are not actors for the reason that they do not have the means of formulating and acting upon decisions. Nor, therefore, are they entities that can be said to have causal responsibility for existing social conditions, and nor, I suggested in the first chapter, are they entities that can engage in actions designed to reproduce or alter those conditions. These are theoretical topics that, like every other theoretical topic discussed in this book, have methodological and empirical implications; that is, they have implications for the design of empirical studies and for the interpretation of empirical data. Theoretical issues relating to agency are also linked in various ways to public policy as an academic discipline. For example, the idea that agency is associated with causal responsibility for policy outcomes is implicit in Richardson and Lindleys's (1994: 3, emphases added) reference to "possibly the *ultimate* question for all of us concerned with public policy i.e. *who is accountable and responsible for public policy?*" As we shall see, this question is by no means an easy one to answer.

The state is not an actor

Later, I shall observe that in anti-reductionist terms it can be argued that social actors – including organizations in the public, voluntary and private sectors, and international actors such as the European Union – have two related properties. Firstly, they have an ontological status as actors (that is, in principle they are able to formulate and take decisions and act upon those decisions), but secondly, this may be an *intermittent* status that does not obtain in all circumstances. In the case of "the state", however, it can be argued that it is an entity that in no circumstances is an actor. In certain situations it might be legitimate to refer to "the government" as an actor, although there will be circumstances when it is more accurate to say that it is specific governmental committees such as the cabinet or specific organizations (such as a central government department) that are actors: but it is difficult to think of *any* circumstances in which, if we want to avoid reification, "the state" could be said to be an agent. Even if we were to accept that the state has sufficient cohesion to be described as an identifiable entity, we are still left with the implications of the fact that – when compared with social actors – the state has an extremely high level of internal differentiation. The state, to put the matter at its simplest, consists of central and local government departments; quasi-government organizations such as quangos; Parliament; the armed forces; the police; the judiciary; and policy networks of various kinds. These entities are not sufficiently integrated to be regarded as a single, unitary actor (Ponting 1986: 43).

Moran (1990: 48), a political scientist, comments: "It is a useful shorthand to write of 'the state' in action ... but it is no more than a convenient shorthand. Everywhere, state intervention is governed by a complex administrative division of labour". Moran's (48–49) particular interest is public policy pertaining to the regulation and operation of financial markets: "Not only is it impossible to find an instance where an integrated state acts towards the financial markets in a unified manner; even individual state agencies are often riddled with internal rivalries". In their analysis of politics and government in Britain, Gray and Jenkins (1985: 71) argue that there is no evidence to support a "monolithic view" of the state. Central government departments are elements within networks of influence (ibid. 79), and in describing the workings of administrative politics (70–77) the authors observe that there are quite often differences of orientation and of interests within departments and as between departments. Richards (1988: 38), a writer on British government and politics, comments: "contemporary British government is highly complex, with many power centres". The same point is made by Smith and Stanyer (1976/1980: 79) in their text on government and administrative politics. M J Smith (1993) links the idea of internal differentiation to his view that the state is not an agent: "*It is not the state that acts,* but state actors within particular parts of the state" (50, emphasis added). Smith writes (49–50, emphases added):

> The state is neither unified *nor does it have an ability to act*. The state is nothing but a collection of institutions and rules. The term "state actions" is a shorthand for individuals within particular agencies or institutions acting . . . It is ultimately *individuals within these agencies*, acting within their institutional roles that make decisions and take actions.

In the second part of this statement Smith wrongly assumes that only individuals are actors and he therefore ignores the crucial part that social ("organizational") actors play in politics and policy; however, there are ample grounds for endorsing the first part of Smith's statement, in which he observes that the state is not an agent. For some purposes it is convenient and legitimate to use such expressions as "the state" or "the state apparatus": but to suppose that the state is an *actor* is to engage in reification. Whether, however, it can also be said that policy networks are not agents is, as we shall see in the following section, rather more problematical.

Policy networks and agency

I referred in the introductory chapter to social networks. There are various sociological approaches to the study of networks. In translation sociology, for example, Callon's (1986: xvi) ideas on actor-networks and on network configurations (1991) are useful, subject to the qualifications concerning translation sociology that I referred to earlier. I shall shortly return to sociological conceptions of the significance of social networks. For the moment I want only to emphasize that, despite Law's (1991b: 172, 173–4) opposed approach which was briefly mentioned in the first chapter, it can be argued that networks of social relations cannot on the basis of Law's theory be regarded as actors. It is unsafe to assume that a social network, or a "structured set of relations" (ibid. 173), is an actor. As a non-reified rule of thumb, it is better to lean towards the general proposition that social networks are *not* actors; that is, they are not entities with decision-making capabilities and intentional causal powers. However, we should expect that this general rule may occasionally need to be put aside. In the absence of a non-reified conception of agency, Luhmann's (1982: 265) claim that social systems are actors, is a reification. It would, nevertheless, be premature to dismiss every claim (such as Mayntz's 1993: 17–19) that, *under certain circumstances*, networks may be regarded as entities that are actors in the non-reified sense to which I have just referred.

In this section of the chapter I am mostly interested in policy networks, rather than social networks in general. Some policy networks are not integrated policy communities, but loose issue networks that are to a considerable extent fragmented. An example of an issue network is the urban renewal policy network in Britain. The urban policy network has a large number of actors that over the years have included the Department of the Environment, the Department of Trade and Industry, the Department of Education and Employment, the Urban Development Corporations, and Local Authorities. At the local level, as well as the involvement of various departments of local authorities (planning, engineering and transport, social services, etc) there have been numerous "initiatives" and urban regeneration projects. These include BIC (Business in the Community), the NEDP (Neighbourhood Economic Development Programme), BATs (Business Action Teams), LEAs (Local Enterprise Agencies), CATs (City Action Teams), TECs (Training and Enterprise Councils) and various other policy initiatives and policy actors. Lewis (1992: 28–49) argues that the sheer number of actors involved, and the complex, fragmented, and un-coordinated nature of the urban renewal policy network has been a significant factor in policy failure. A similar argument is outlined by Couch (1990: 95). There is little overall planning, audit, or monitoring, and little is done to ensure that "learning from experience" is systematic and that there are sufficient mechanisms to ensure that examples of "good" practice are disseminated for evaluation by other actors in the network.

Such cases lend a measure of support to the idea that policy networks are not – in terms of access to the means of taking decisions and of acting upon decisions – sufficiently unitary to be regarded as *actors*. It may well be that certain types of networks – a consortium of firms, for example – can legitimately be regarded as an entity that has agency, at least in regard to some particular field of action. In general, however, most policy networks are not actors; they are assemblages of actors who, to a greater or lesser extent, interact with each other. I noted earlier that no policy network, not even if it is a relatively highly integrated policy community, can automatically be assumed to be an actor. It is important, also, not to confuse agency with the idea of *recursion* which was discussed in the first chapter.

Recent work in political science and public policy on the topics of governance and "governability" (Kooiman 1993b) is beginning to touch upon aspects of the conception of agency associated with anti-reductionist sociology. Consider, for example, the work of Mayntz (1993: 19): she is interested in

> policy areas that are structured as "aree di movimento" (in the terminology of Melucci 1984), i.e. extensive networks consisting of some institutions (such as service centres), small informal groups and loose interweavings of personal acquaintances fostered by meeting in certain places. Such networks oscillate between latency and activism and they will organize themselves to become collective actors only occasionally and will fall apart again afterwards.

In this statement Mayntz observes that the shape of a network is not necessarily static. This should come as no surprise, once reductionist theories of structural predetermination are relinquished. Mayntz, like Melucci, also raises the question of agency, although the concept of recursiveness (the idea that networks may have self-sustaining tendencies that contingently persist for short or long periods) is pushed by Mayntz to the point of suggesting that networks may under certain circumstances be actors. The problem here is that Mayntz, like most political science writers on government, politics and policy, provides us with no explicitly non-reified conception of agency that might allow us to judge whether any particular policy network located in a given set of time-space circumstances, is or is not an actor. A similar problem exists in the otherwise useful analysis of policy networks undertaken by M J Smith (1993). Smith, having on the one hand claimed (ibid. 49–50) that there are only individual human actors, contradictorily assumes that policy networks are actors equipped with a sense of purposiveness and with causal powers (ibid. 124, 126, 131, 134): in neither case does he have an adequately theorized conception of agency, and he seems unaware of the contradiction to which I have just referred. It will be necessary to return to these and related matters later in the chapter.

Organizational actors

It was observed in the first chapter that *reification* is an illegitimate form of analysis that imputes agency to phenomena that are not actors/agents. Some critics of reification, as already noted, believe that only human individuals can be actors. The assumption here is that to say entities "larger" than individuals may be actors, is to engage in reification. That assumption is not justified. The arguments developed by, for example, Clegg (1989: 187–88), Hindess (1986a: 115, 124, 1990: 25–29), Harre (1981: 144, 150–52), and Holzner (1978: 294–305) amount to a convincing case in favour of the proposition that no reification is involved in the claim that, as well as individual actors, there are also social actors such as organizations, committees, and various micro groups. As noted in the first chapter, *social actors have emergent properties including decision-making and causal powers of a kind that are not reducible to the level of human individuals considered in aggregate.* That having been said, however, it *also* has to be recognized that organizations are internally differentiated, and that organizational policy decisions and organizational actions are sometimes the indeterminate and contingent outcome of conflict and struggle among the individuals, groups or departments that constitute the organization (Clegg 1989: 197). This indirectly raises a theoretical question with methodological implications that have been rather neglected in the social sciences. The question is this: should we assume that the status of a social actor *qua* actor is a fixed and "once and for all" affair, or might it be that an entity that is an actor in *some* circumstances is not necessarily an actor in *all* circumstances? Earlier in the chapter, we looked at the proposition that actors may become more or less powerful. But we have not yet established the quite different proposition that actors may contingently acquire the status of actor in one set of circumstances or in relation to particular issues, and lose the status of actor in other circumstances or in relation to a different set of issues. This is a perfectly sound proposition. Agency, that is to say, is to some extent relational, as also, as we saw earlier, are power and interests. Like power, agency is in some measure "stored" in social systems, in positions/roles, and in social networks: but agency is also partly relational, being an outcome of social relations which in turn are affected by social conditions and the circumstances surrounding action. I shall return to the relational face of agency shortly, but before doing so it will be helpful if we push this discussion of the problematics of agency a little further by means of an inspection of the ontological status of international policy actors, one of the better known of which is the European Union.

International actors: the European Union

Roche (1992: 193) does not address the question of agency but he implies that "world-regional groupings" (these are politico-economic blocs such as the European Union) are actors, in so far as he says that such blocs "engage" in protectionism and various other forms of intervention in the world economy. In an increasingly globalized world (Waters 1995; Held 1995), questions pertaining to the ontological status of international actors are important topics in the sociology of public policy. As with some other questions to do with agency, the part played by international (or transnational) actors in the creation and implementation of public policy is something that in future will require further conceptual clarification as well as empirical research. This is discussed in the final chapter. Here I intend only to briefly sketch a few pointers to the kinds of issues that will require closer attention in the future.

It was observed earlier that it is not legitimate to attribute agency to "the state". Nor, if we wish to avoid reification, should we attempt to attribute agency to "society" or to "the nation". The cabinet, the prime minister, central government departments, private firms, professional associations and trades unions, organized pressure-groups, etc, may be said to be actors; but "nation states" cannot legitimately be regarded as agents. However, the governments of a group of nation states may for whatever reasons decide that it is desirable to create a supra-national organization (such as the European Union) that is empowered to take decisions and act on the collective behalf of its member states. When this happens, the participating national governments will have created a transnational (or "international") actor. Certainly it can legitimately be said that the European Union (EU) is in some respects an actor. It is an entity with causal powers; it has the capacity to formulate decisions, to take decisions, and to act upon them. The fact that the shape of the EU has evolved and changed over the years amidst changing social conditions and in response to changes in actors' perceptions and decisions, does not alter the EU's ontological status as an entity that, in a non-reified and anti-reductionist sense, can be said to be an actor. However, this statement requires considerable qualification. Like most other large international actors, the EU has a very complex and highly differentiated internal structure. Indeed, some of its constituent organs – such as the European Parliament, the Court, the Council of Ministers, the Commission, and the General Assembly – may be regarded, at least in relation to certain political, administrative, or judicial fields of action, as *actors in their own right*. They are, that is to say, entities – social ("organizational") actors – that are capable of formulating and acting upon interests and goals of their own (Peters 1994: 10, 19–20).

In the years following the Rome Treaties, the responsibilities and balances of power among the four major EU actors – the Commission, the Parliament, the Council, and the Court – has in general shifted, and power and influence also varies according to the nature of policy issues and the political and administrative circumstances surrounding the issue in question (Nugent 1994a: 53). Sometimes the Commission is able to exercise a great deal of power, sometimes not. This introduces certain complexities and contingencies that are to do with agency and the policy process. The EU policy process is further complicated by the existence of a large number of administrative units and sub-units that, although not directly associated with the EU's four main organs, are nevertheless involved in policy-making and decision-taking (ibid.)

> Prominent amongst other actors who have inserted, or have attempted to insert, themselves into decision-making processes are the many national and transnational sectoral interests and pressures that have come to cluster round the main institutions in order to monitor developments and, where possible, to advise or pressurize decision-makers.

The formal policy machinery of the EU is, then, subject to considerable variation and contingency in the way that it operates (Judge et al 1994: 28, 31, 49). Nugent (1994a: 53) notes that an additional set of contingencies is associated with *informal* relations and informal patterns of influence: "Which processes and channels operate in particular cases, and what types of interactions occur therein, varies considerably from sector to sector, and can even do so from decision to decision". There are also transnational European policy networks to consider. (These will be discussed in chapter five). In such fields as education and training, industrial development, tourism, transportation and ecology, European-wide policy networks comprised of state and non-state actors have a significant impact upon the EU policy process (Bew and Meehan 1994: 96, 100–105).

In the light of these various factors, it seems legitimate to retain my earlier observation that the EU is an actor in the non-reductive and non-reified terms described previously. However, it is also evident that there are here some complex issues pertaining to agency, and in future these will require close attention on the part of theorists and empirical researchers. In particular, it may be that the EU by virtue of its high level of internal differentiation and systemic complexity (Pollack 1994) is an actor only in certain circumstances or in relation to particular issues or types of policies. In some respects, the EU resembles not so much a large organizational actor as a policy network. A not entirely dissimilar conception is implied in Peters's (1994: 10–11) view of the EU as a type of "political system". Political systems, it should be noted, are part of the conditions of action (see later), but they are not actors. However, and it is to this wider question that I shall turn in the next section, it should not automatically be assumed that policy networks and international actors are either actors or non-actors; they may be actors under certain conditions, but not in others. To say this is, as I have already noted, to say that agency is partly relational and contingent. It is also to say that trying to ascertain in a large number of instances the parts played by both the systemically "stored" and the situationally specific and relationally emergent faces of agency is an important methodological step in addressing the difficulty posed earlier by Richardson and Lindley (1994: 3) who suggested that at the core of the study of public policy is the question: who is accountable and responsible for public policy?

Agency and social actors

I have repeatedly emphasized that, to avoid reductionism and reification, actors (whether individual actors or social actors) should be defined as entities that, in principle, are capable of formulating and taking decisions and of acting on those decisions. Despite what other writers may have claimed or assumed, I have suggested that there are some entities that cannot under any conceivable circumstances be or become actors. These include: taxonomic collectivities such as "women", "men", "black people', "white people", "heterosexuals", "young people", etc; social classes; social movements; "society", "the state", and "political systems"; and also objects such as money, written materials, diseases, natural disasters, computing systems and so on. None of these categories of phenomena can be or become agents. However, we also saw earlier that there are other kinds of phenomena that may be agents in some circumstances, but not in others. Some entities – including organizations, especially large and complex organizations such as the European Union – are social actors whose ontological status as actors may be intermittent. I suggested, too, that a similar observation can be applied to policy networks, with the proviso that it seems better to employ a presumption that most policy networks are not actors. It is this question of intermittency that I propose to concentrate on here.

In regard to the earlier definition of what constitutes an actor, intermittency is bound up with the question of whether an actor, as defined in Hindess's (1986a: 115) explicitly non-reified formulation, can be an entity that is an actor for only a part of its life-span or in relation to only some situations or activities. Notice that this is not the same thing as asking whether actors may acquire or lose amounts of "power" (see the earlier discussion of power): an entity in terms of power can be a strong then a weak actor, but still an actor. Rather, the point I am making here is that some entities may acquire or lose the status of *actor*. If, say, a social ("organizational") actor happens – in some sphere of its activities in which it had hitherto exercised agency – to lose the means of formulating and taking decisions and of acting on decisions (that is, loses the means of engaging in intra-organizational collective decision-formulation, decision-taking and collective action) then that organization will not necessarily cease to exist but will cease to be an actor, or at least, will temporarily or perhaps permanently cease to be an actor in regard to certain issues or certain situations in which it would otherwise have been an actor. Much the same might be said of a hitherto very tightly integrated policy community or of, say, a household or a consortium of private firms.

Policy researchers investigating the question of agency should, then, acknowledge the existence of certain kinds of complexity and contingency in the case of some social actors. Large organizations and international actors such as the European Union are actors made up of constituent units that are in themselves actors. In relation to particular policies, practices, pieces of legislation etc, it may be legitimate to view the European Union (EU) as a large social actor with emergent and distinct properties and powers (including powers of deliberation and decision-taking leading to action) of a kind that are "more than" and which are therefore not reducible to the properties and powers of its constituent actors such as the Commission, the Parliament, individual actors, and so on. For other analytical purposes or in relation to specific policy issues or political situations, it may be more appropriate to regard the EU as a "political system" (Peters 1994: 10–11) rather than as a social actor. For example, Pollack (1994) observes that EU policies can be divided into three "policy types" (regulative, redistributive, and distributive) and each of these have their own institutional histories and distinct political arenas with their own actors and specific decision rules. Other types of agency-related contingency are to be found in the EU. For example, Bennington and Taylor (1993) examine transnational European networks composed of state and non-state actors, these being phenomena that relate not only to the centralizing tendencies of the EU but also to the de-centralizing tendencies that are part of the EU policy process (Bennington and Harvey 1994: 22). And although systemic or role/positional agency ("stored" agency) is always likely to be present to a greater or lesser extent, the relational, processual and emergent forms of agency are sometimes of particular importance. Large social actors such as the European Union and, for example, their internal constitution in relation to transient or enduring differentials in their own and their "sub-actors" access to particular means and conditions of action, are, as I have briefly indicated, empirically complex forms of agency and of agency/structure. This complicates the task of policy researchers who wish to engage in non-reified analysis of the operation of agency: hence as part of the work involved in the construction of a new sociology of public policy, there are grounds for suggesting that the development of a policy-related sociology of agency and of agency/structure will in future require close collaborative attention on the part of theorists and empirical researchers.

Forms of Thought

Another important strand in my theoretical framework is a focus on actors' forms of thought. In Bergerian constructivist sociology, language is regarded as a generalized material that plays a key part in shaping actors' ways of thinking. Language is involved in socialization processes and in the time-space dissemination of meanings; the reason for this is that "language is capable of becoming the objective repository of vast accumulations of meaning and experience, which it can then preserve in time and transmit to the following generations" (Berger and Luckmann 1972: 52). Various philosophers and sociologists have regarded language as the central element in the social construction of reality. Consider, for example, the following conceptions of language and reality construction.

> Language is a guide to social reality ... [language] ... powerfully conditions all our thinking ... the "real world" is to a large extent built on the language habits of ... [our] ... group ... We see and hear and otherwise experience very largely as we do because the language habits of our community predispose certain choices of interpretation (Sapir 1966: 68–9).

> We dissect nature along lines laid down by our native language. The categories and types that we isolate from the world of phenomena we do not find there because they stare every observer in the face; on the contrary, the world is presented in a kaleidoscopic flux of impressions which has to be organized by our minds – and this means largely by the linguistic system in our minds. We cut nature up, organize it into concepts, and ascribe significance as we do largely because we are parties to an agreement to organize it in this way – an agreement that holds throughout our speech community and is codified in the patterns of our language (Whorf 1956: 6).

The institutionalization or "sedimentation" of ways of thinking in the form of discourses (such as technical, religious, political, or professional-occupational discourses) is a theme that is prominent in Foucauldian sociology. However, the notion that meanings may become institutionalized ("tacit") and therefore drawn upon by actors in an automatic, unreflective way, is hardly unique to Foucault; it is a theme developed by sociologists associated with a range of differing theoretical perspectives (see, for example, Berger and Luckmann 1972: 36–38; Giddens 1982; 9, and Hindess 1988: 48). And as we observed in the first chapter, post-modern theorists emphasize the reality-shaping properties of language, although they push this to the extreme and argue that society is *no more than* a product of language and discourse. In that chapter I suggested a more adequate conception is to view the relation of discourses to their social contexts as a dialectical relation in which discourses shape and are shaped by their social contexts. It can be argued that it is this dialectical conception that should inform the study of the relation of public policy discourses to their social contexts.

Hindess (1988) argues that actors' forms of thought are not structurally predetermined (that is, are not determined by actors' structural locations within the social totality). He emphasizes (ibid. 68) the importance of investigating actors' ways of deliberating and the techniques and methods that they employ for assessing situations. A broadly similar emphasis, although from a rather different theoretical standpoint, is to be found in Law (1991b: 183). It is only relatively recently that policy analysts have recognized the significance of language and discourse in the policy process. Thrift (1994: 22–23) in a paper on international monetary networks makes the point that particular forms of thought tend to become institutionalized in policy networks. In more general terms, the significance of the study of policy actors' forms of thought is recognized by Hoppe (1993: 77).

> Policy-making becomes the capacity to define the nature of shared meanings; it is a never ending series of communications and strategic moves by which various policy actors in loosely coupled forums of public deliberation construct intersubjective meanings. These meanings are continually translated into collective projects, plans, actions and artifacts, that become the issue in the next cycle of political judgements and meaning constructions.

Actors' forms of thought in general, but also systems of thought of the kind that may be found in occupations, professions and policy communities, are not necessarily internally coherent and highly crystallized. To the contrary, discourses may be internally splintered (Harrison White 1992: 305). There are also a number of other related matters that are worthy of note although I do not have the space to explore them in detail here. These include the idea that perspectives and ideologies may be mediated at different levels of crystallization, explicitness and internal conceptual consistency (Rootes 1981); Berger and Luckmann's (1972) and Bernardes's (1985) thesis that ideologies and cultural beliefs in modern society frequently embody multiple realities and a plurality of contradictory meanings; and Levitas's (1976) work on the ways in which adoption and rejection of ideas may, in some instances, rest less upon logical consistency than upon emotional consistency or (as in the case of "cognitive dissonance") upon a positive orientation towards the source of an idea. Of significance, too, is the notion that theories, perspectives, and ideologies have "publics" (the mass media, professional groups, the government, consumer or client groups, etc) to which ideologies have to relate. An insightful review of the range of types of relationships that may develop between ideologies and their "publics" is provided by Bouchier (1977) who examines empirically the way in which ideologies for their survival may require pragmatic flexibility and plasticity in relating to the demands of different "publics". The part played by "situational contingencies" is another highly salient research topic in the sociology of public policy. Situations arise, for example, where politicians and policy actors are unable or unwilling to implement their policy ideas, assumptions, and preferences. This can happen for a variety of contingent reasons to do with power, resources, organizational functions, legislation, public opinion, pressure group activity, and so on. For these various reasons, it is desirable that non-reductive empirical investigation of policy actors' forms of thought viewed in relation to the contexts of action, should be regarded as an integral part of the new sociology of public policy.

The Conditions of Action

At various points in the earlier discussion I flagged the importance of the
agency/structure debate. The point I now want to emphasize is that to reject
theories of structural predetermination is not the same thing as overemphasiz-
ing agency at the expense of structure. It is not, in other words, to embrace an
idealist, voluntaristic image of actors as unconstrained beings. To the
contrary, anti-reductionist sociology recognizes that actors are influenced,
constrained, or enabled by the *conditions of action* (Betts 1986: 41), or put
more simply, by *social conditions* (Hindess 1986a: 120–21). The conditions
of action/social conditions, which may be thought of as the element of
"structure" in the agency/structure debate, are not structurally predetermined;
they are not necessary effects of the social totality or of some systemic
"need" or exigency, and they do not require reductionist explanation of the
kind associated with methodological collectivism (Hindess 1988: 95–97). To
say that the conditions of action are not structurally predetermined is to say
that they are not the unfolding of a macro-structural script: they are not so-
called structural (or historical) "necessities". Social conditions are contingently produced and contingently reproduced, eliminated, or transformed.
Viewed from an anti-reductionist perspective, neither methodological individualism nor methodological collectivism can adequately explain social
action and the conditions of action. This rejection of both methodological
individualism and methodological collectivism has theoretical, methodological, and empirical implications for anti-reductionist sociology (Hindess
1982: 498–99, emphases added).

> [theoretical] ... *positions are reductionist in the sense that social
> conditions of diverse kinds are thought to be reducible to phenomena of
> one specific kind*, viz. the creative actions of individuals, the action of the
> structure or the state of the economy. To avoid reductionism it is
> necessary to recognize that social phenomena are always dependent on
> definite and specifiable conditions *which are themselves not reducible to
> any single general principle of explanation*. This means, in particular, that
> outcomes cannot be conceived of as necessitated outside of the particular
> conditions in which they are produced, that we need to take seriously the
> practices of agents and struggles between them. To insist that phenomena
> are dependent on definite and specifiable conditions is to reject ...
> reduction to human creativity ... [or to] ... the action of structures.

In the sense described in the introductory chapter, the ontologically flexible
approach favoured by Hindess is anti-reductionist and interpretively "open"
in the handling of empirical data. For Hindess (1986a: 120), social conditions
refer not to the functional exigencies of society, but nor are social conditions
reducible to the creative actions of individuals; rather, they emerge from "the
complex intersection of a variety of specific practices, policies and actors"
(ibid.).

Social conditions, which are in some sense the outcome of social chance and of the intended and unintended consequences of social action, are neither structurally predetermined nor static (Betts 1986; Callon 1986, 1991; Clegg 1989). They are empirically contingent and very often fluid, shifting conditions; and if social conditions are stabilized across large stretches of time-space, this is regarded in anti-reductionist sociology as a contingent process of reproduction rather than a matter of historical or structural necessity.

Social conditions/the conditions of action may be constraining or facilitative factors, but either way they have implications for actors in the situations in which the actors in question are involved (Barbalet 1985: 543–44). The conditions of action facing policy actors and practitioners in, let us say, the fields of health and social services, consist of other individual and social actors; particular situations and one-off events; intended and unintended policy outcomes; routinized formal and informal practices; legislation; organizational frameworks and conventions; institutionalized discourses of various kinds (administrative, political, professional, etc); service-user and public perceptions (and mass media perceptions) and expectations of health and social services; resource distributions; and networks that are involved in the spatial and temporal flow of policy materials across locales that relate to the policy field in question. As should be clear from this and the earlier observations, an anti-reductionist sociology of public policy suggests that neither social action nor the conditions of action are structurally predetermined, but this does not mean that the conditions of action are insignificant elements in the policy process. Public policy is shaped – though not wholly determined – by social conditions. What policy actors will want to do, what they decide to do, and what they are able to do, are in various ways influenced by the conditions of action.

Contingency

Although questions to do with contingency and indeterminacy have loomed large in recent social theory associated with, for example, ethnomethodology, post-modernism, translation sociology (Callon 1986, 1991; Latour 1986, 1991) and Law's (1994) sociology of ordering, such questions are not entirely recent. One of the leading post-war sociologists, Aron (1967: 27), stated that "social reality is neither a completely integrated whole nor an incoherent mass". He observed that the social fabric "contains innumerable semi-organized parts, but not obvious total order". Anti-reductionist sociology portrays social life as relatively processual, fluid, and indeterminate; or at least, as *potentially* indeterminate unless and until particular segments of social life are spatially and temporally stabilized, "firmed-up", and institutionalized for long or short periods of time. This raises an important matter. There are no good reasons for constructing an either/or theoretical dichotomy between, on the one hand, a structural conception of rigid system determination and predictability and, on the other, a conception of the social fabric as a process of endless flux, indeterminacy and purely random change. As Callon and Latour (1981: 282) put it: "There is no chaos, but no rigid system either". Elias's (1978) figurational sociology theoretically constructs an image of a continuously processual, indeterminate social reality as a series of "figurations in constant flux with neither beginning nor end" (ibid. 162). Layder (1986: 378) is critical of this model of social life: "Elias seems to be operating with an illicit dichotomy between *complete statis* and *complete flux*; there are no intermediary 'states' or combinations of elements". Layder's criticism is that Elias constructs a theoretical dichotomy consisting of "complete statis" and "complete flux", then opts for the latter. Anti-reductionist sociology transcends this dichotomy through the empirical application of a postulate which recognizes that social life is always potentially open to change and variability, the extent to which stability and continuity, or else discontinuity and change, actually occurs being treated as an empirical variable for investigation. That is to say, time-space continuities and discontinuities are regarded as matters for empirical investigation, not for theoretical predetermination: in the social sciences there are no valid theoretical grounds for presuming, in advance of empirical enquiry, the existence of either continuities or discontinuities. And as already noted, if relatively stable conditions persist for long periods, this does not mean that the conditions in question are structurally predetermined (Hindess 1986a: 123). In anti-reductionist sociology, social conditions are held to be contingently produced and reproduced, partly as an effect of the recursive tendency – a self-reproducing tendency associated with institutionalized meanings and practices – of social systems and social networks; and partly as a consequence of actors' decisions and actions. The social fabric, because not structurally predetermined, is always potentially variable and indeterminate: but it also regularly happens that various segments of social life became stabilized in what is otherwise unstable and shifting terrain (Clegg 1989:17). Whether, in the world of politics and policy, any particular institutionalized materials (ideas, policies, practices, laws, organizational frameworks, service-delivery patterns, etc) do become stabilized for long periods, is an empirically open question and not something that can be theoretically predetermined in terms of an *a priori* theoretical commitment to one or the other polar opposites ("complete statis" or "complete flux") in an either/or dichotomy.

Unintended Consequences

As Giddens (1993: 84) observes, the concept *unintended consequences* is of great significance to social theory. A similar observation which addresses not only unintended consequences but also the dialectical linkages that may develop between actors and social contexts (a dialectical conception that is congruent with anti-reductionist sociology) is to be found in Burns's (1986) theory of "actor-structure dynamics". He writes (ibid. 9):

> agents – individuals as well as organized groups, organizations . . . are subject to material, political and cultural constraints on their actions. At the same time, they are active, often creative, forces, shaping and reshaping social structures and institutions and their material circumstances. They thereby change, intentionally and unintentionally (often through mistakes and failures), the conditions of their own activities and transactions.

The conditions of action in which actors operate, are in part the outcome of intended and *unintended* consequences of actions taken by historically previous actors, and by the current actors at an earlier time. The currently most powerful actors in a scenario may, should they perceive that an unintended outcome fortuitously coincides with their self-formulated interests, be able to "retain" the outcome, institutionalize it, and disseminate it far across a range of sites that are widely scattered in space and time. This is but one way by which particular actors and particular ideas become influential. Another possibility is that if the unintended outcome is experienced as threatening by some actors, those actors may be able to exercise a "veto" and "damp down" or perhaps kill off the undesired unintended outcome. In these and other ways, unintended consequences, which may be regarded as a complicating factor in the dialectics of micro-macro and agency/structure, sometimes play a crucial part in the social reproduction or change of social contexts. No structural predetermination is involved in these processes. As Betts (1986: 40) puts it: "Contexts may be built up by a series of unintended outcomes, and an unintended outcome may have the effect of constraining, or enabling, future behaviour, but these are contingent questions". In government, politics and public policy it is possible to conceive of situations where an enduring policy material – despite its apparent longevity – initially came into existence as an unplanned effect of a response to a particular circumstance or event, that emergent effect then being reproduced as an unintended outcome of the operation of interlocking agencies, events, and conditions (Miller and Rose 1993: 77–79). In such cases, the political or policy material in question, though originally planned by no-one, becomes established as a constituent part of the current conditions of action and thus as an element in the dialectics of agency and structure.

Time-Space

In the first chapter, in the section on locales, materials and social networks, I referred to *time-space*. This is a concept to which I will return in later chapters with reference to the policy process. Here I shall confine myself to a brief statement that will help to put into context my earlier observation that time-space is a relevant concept in the new sociology of public policy. Cohen (1989: 127) writes:

> Systemic relations are maintained and reproduced as these results of social conduct are transmitted or transported to other agents who may be situated in the same spatio-temporal setting, or who may be situated in the same setting at a later time, or who may be situated in another systemic locale across some interval of time-space. These agents, in turn, may engage in further transformations of the outcomes of activities which have been transmitted/transported to them. Each transformation in some way changes the content of events and/or material objects.

One of anti-reductionist sociology's assumptions is that material which travels in time must also travel spatially; and that spatial dissemination necessarily has a temporal dimension. Cohen (1989: 77) in his analysis of structuration, observes: "If social patterns are embedded in the reality of social activity, then a concern for time and space becomes difficult to avoid. Social conduct, after all, is always situated in specific settings, and it takes time to engage even in the most fleeting practices, let alone sustained sequences and series of interactions". Cohen's observation serves to highlight the point that temporality is a significant variable among competing sociological paradigms. As Clegg (1989: 212) notes: "Different theoretical perspectives diverge on the temporality within which the conceptualization of action is conceived". The two most obviously contrasting examples of this are ethnomethodology, which focuses on the immediate temporal context of action, and institutional analysis which investigates social processes that stretch across decades or perhaps even centuries (ibid.).

The spatial dimension of time-space was referred to in the first chapter and we shall look at some sociological aspects of this in the following section on network analysis. As well as in sociology, there is in political science some evidence of recent interest in the idea of spatiality. Among political scientists there are, for example, signs of increased attention being given to data which indicate that national (and transnational) social, political and economic patterns of change have not impacted upon localities in a uniform way. This is an important theme in Duncan and Goodwin's (1988) *The Local State and Uneven Development*. The authors comment (275–6): "Post-war consensus, constructed around a fairly uniform geography as well as a uniform society, has given way to diversity and disjuncture. Places, as well as people and social groups, have become less alike and there is a greater disparity between various parts of the country". An instance of the increased interest that surrounds spatial differentiation in the policy process is Bonnett's (1993) investigation of the significance of spatiality in the social construction and application of equal opportunities policies (EOPs). Bonnett's empirical study of anti-racist policies and practices among public sector professionals in two localities (London and Tyneside) led him to emphasize "the salience of a geographically sensitive approach to the analysis of public professional radical consciousness" (ibid.281). Public policy material to do with EOPs is, says Bonnett, significantly different in Tyneside when compared with London. He found large differences in policy content, organization and style. Bonnett's general conclusion (295) is that "radical ideologies vary geographically . . . the examination of public professional radical commitment needs to be sensitive to the existence of a geography as well as a history of its subject matter. To ignore or marginalize the spatial complexity of social processes is to neglect the diversity of human experience". In passing, it is worth noting that this conclusion refers to micro-macro as well as to time-space. Bonnett focused on differences *between* localities (London and Tyneside) in actors' construction and handling of EOP policy materials. A more micro research orientation also shows variation in the forms taken by EOP materials *within* localities, that is, at the organizational and micro-situational levels. (On this aspect, see Jewson and Mason 1992). Thus, as will become clear in the following chapters, *time-space* is an important concept that – together with the major conceptual motifs of agency/structure, social chance, and micro-macro – serves to direct policy researchers' attention to spatial and temporal aspects of both micro-situational and transituational policy dynamics.

Network Analysis

In the first chapter I indicated that network analysis has a part to play in the sociology of public policy. Scott (1988: 109) argues that network analysis should be regarded not as a specialized technique or sub-field of sociology but, rather, as sociology's theoretical and methodological foundation stone: "the roots of . . . [network analysis] . . . are as old as sociology itself. This perspective, centred on the image of the intertwining of social relations, offers not so much a specialized method as a formulation of the fundamental concepts of the sociological enterprise". Network analysis, Scott observes, is concerned with links between actors; the intersection of chains of action and their consequences; and the emergent structural properties of networks of social relations (ibid.). A focus on networks raises important and interesting questions, including those introduced in the first chapter where it was noted that the idea of networks is relevant to: the study of recursive processes; the problem of reification (as in Luhmann's claim that social systems and social networks are actors); the concept *time-space*; and material diffusion processes. There are differing sociological approaches to the study of networks and, for reasons discussed earlier, I prefer to steer clear of structuralist theoretical approaches to network analysis of the kind referred to by Rubinstein (1988: 81–82) and Ritzer (1992b: 628–9): such approaches, which neglect what Lockwood (1956), Mouzelis (1991, 1995) and others call a *social integration* perspective, consist of forms of analysis that do not give sufficient attention to agency in terms of actors' forms of thought and actors' formulation of intentions. To avoid this neglect of agency and to do so in a balanced way that does not go to the other extreme and neglect the systemic dimension of social action, it is necessary that network analysis should, as described in the first chapter, include an emphasis on *system integration* (relationships among parts of a system, such as social institutions, roles/ positions and rules) and on *social integration* (an emphasis on agency and on relations, whether conflictual or co-operative, among actors). I am thus not suggesting that an emphasis on actors and on agency and social integration should dominate social scientific analysis. System integration is also important, a point that is neatly illustrated in Knoke and Kuklinkski's (1991: 179) observation that

> a network's *positions* are conceptually distinct from any specific incum-
> bents. For example, in a hospital system the positions defined by patterns
> of relations between actors – given such conventional labels as doctor,
> patient, nurse, administrator, paraprofessional, and so forth – persist
> despite frequent changes in the unique individuals occupying these
> positions.

I have already referred to translation sociology and to Callon's (1991) work on network analysis. He observes that the extent to which social networks are routinized/institutionalized, is a variable factor (ibid. 154).

> The less convergent a network, the less it is irreversibilized and the more
> the actors composing it can be understood in terms of concepts such as
> strategy, the negotiation and variation of aims, revisable projects, and
> changing coalitions. Under such circumstances analysis has to start with
> the actors and chart their fluctuating interactions. The trail is still hot . . .
> Uncertainty rules the day.

> At the other extreme, a completely convergent and irreversibilized
> network, the actors become agents with precise objectives and instru-
> ments . . . The trail is cold, and the story is economized. The states of the
> world – that is to say, the states of the network – are known for each point
> at each instant . . . the network is known and predictable . . . Controversy
> and disinteressment (to use the language of translation sociology) is highly
> unlikely.

> There are many intermediate positions between these two extremes.

Callon argues that translation sociology's approach to network analysis is capable of "opening up an entirely new space in the social sciences" (ibid.). I am inclined to the view that there is something in Callon's claim, subject to the qualifications concerning translation sociology that I referred to earlier.

In less theoretical and more policy-related vein, an interesting typology is provided by Thompson et al (1991a) in their *Markets, Hierarchies and*

Networks: The Co-ordination of Social Life. Markets, which are, of course, based on the price mechanism, have since the early 1980s become an increasingly significant component of politics and public policy provision; *hierarchy* includes state bureaucracy that in one form or another continues to be involved in public policy and in the delivery of services; *networks*, which involve more or less patterned interactions among state and non-state actors, are an increasingly important mode of modern governance. The view of networks taken by Thompson et al (1991b) tends to give too much emphasis to trust, loyalty and co-operation as defining features of networks (ibid. 15–16). To regard these as defining features of networks is misleading. For example, in reality some actors have very little choice but to remain within a network and their continued membership may be a condition of their survival, as in those instances where the government *directs* public organizations and personnel to collaborate in joint programmes and to engage in joint activities that would not ordinarily occur on a voluntary basis (Hudson 1993: 374). In general, however, the "markets, hierarchies, and networks" approach to the study of politics and policy (Thompson et al 1991a; Maidment and Thompson 1993) is an interesting conceptual framework that will underpin at least a part of my discussion of governance in the next chapter.

Material Diffusion

In the first chapter I introduced the idea that social materials – broadly defined to include a range of phenomena such as values, ways of thinking, laws, policies, guiding principles and assumptions, forms of knowledge, criteria used for assessing situations, practice conventions, etc – travel across time-space. In that chapter I briefly referred to variations in the *mobility* and *durability* of materials (Law 1986a); questions of this kind are to do with the extent to which policy materials may be transmitted across time-space in more or less unchanged form, as distinct from the transformation (or perhaps the destruction) of the materials as they move across locales that are scattered across social space and time (Lidz 1981; Duster 1981; Latour 1986, 1991; Callon 1991; Fararo 1992; Braithwaite 1994). These theoretical considerations were illustrated in the first chapter with reference to housing policy materials and the housing policy network.

An interesting approach to social network analysis and material dissemination processes, is Fararo's (1992: 320) "generative structuralism". There are problems in Fararo's overall theoretical position: his perspective, which relies on mathematical modelling of network and system processes, is prone to the reification of social systems. However, the processual elements in his theoretical scheme (ibid. 48) are worth retaining. Provided that they are, so to speak, detached from his own paradigmatic contextualization of them, his formulations on material dissemination within and across social networks can readily be incorporated into anti-reductionist sociology. One of Fararo's interests is the "process of flow or spread of something through a network" (261). This is associated with his proposition that *social structure* can be regarded as "a social network within which various diffusion processes may occur" (266). In Fararo's theoretical scheme, it is "social relations that function as the linkages along which the cultural object can flow and be inhibited or not in its spread through a population" (274). For Fararo, diffusion is very closely associated with processes of *institutionalization*.

> Diffusion processes, which can be understood as processes in networks, are more important for general sociology than is often recognized. Institutionalization, in the sense of a scheme of typifications (and corresponding interaction generators), can be construed as diffusion from local subnetwork to local subnetwork using paths of integrative ties (340).

> A theoretical model of the local process by which the institution is adopted or not would be possible but the main structural interest would lie in the global process by which it is spread throughout the network of local embodiments so as to ultimately constitute an institutional procedure in the social system of which each local network is a part (274).

> . . . global integration means connectivity, the extent to which paths of ties permit information, attitudes, and other entities – including emerging typification schemes constituting aspects of institutions – to diffuse widely through the system (306–7).

Depending on the nature of the particular analytical task in hand, the term *materials* can refer to general cultural meanings which circulate on a widespread basis across a nation state (Harrison White 1992: 5, 294), or from one nation state to another (Braithwaite 1994); or for other analytical purposes the term can refer to specialized material of the kind that tends to be largely concentrated within a particular institutional domain such as an academic, administrative, or professional community. Miller and Rose's (1993) useful extension of Foucault's work on governmentality has a bearing upon these matters. In effect, Miller and Rose's thesis is that contingently reproduced materials play a vital part in processes of governance (ibid. 81) including the time-space dissemination of discourses which result in the emergence of policy networks (84). It is necessary to recognize that some policy materials, or aspects of materials, may remain unaltered as the material moves across time-space, whereas other materials, or aspects of them, may be modified or transformed during their passage across time-space. And some materials perish, perhaps at the same time as new materials are created. That these are usually interwoven and *overlapping* processes has an empirical importance that is recognized by some policy researchers. For example, in his study of the historical development of urban regeneration policy in England, Stewart (1994: 136) observes: "Successive stages of urban policy are not totally discrete; each successive stage incorporates elements of earlier policy cultures. Equally, however, each new stage adds its own distinctive dimension". The more general point arising from Stewart's study is that the configuration of the flow of materials across time-space, and also the relative durabilities of different kinds of materials in policy locales, very often presents an empirically complex picture.

In the light of the theoretical arguments developed earlier in the chapter and in the first chapter, it can be argued that analysis of the construction and diffusion of policy materials is not reducible to explanations of the kind associated with methodological individualism. But nor can methodological collectivism offer any suitable methods of analysis. As I have already observed more than once, reified and methodological collectivist forms of analysis have no empirical explanatory value. The creation, diffusion/ reproduction or transformation of materials are not structurally predetermined processes; materials are not reflections of any "deep" cultural logic, or of structural "necessities" or structurally-given ("objective") "interests". There is no single or "primary" underlying structural mechanism (the economy, patriarchy, system needs, or whatever) that can predetermine social life. The properties of social materials and of their spatial and temporal contexts are not, in other words, reducible to any single general principle of explanation. To suppose otherwise is reductionist. And in regard to the exercise of agency we have already seen that to attribute agency to entities that are not actors, is a form of reification. So as to avoid theoretical reduction and reification and to achieve an ontologically flexible ("open") interpretive mode of empirical analysis, close empirical investigation of processes involved in the construction of policy materials and investigation of their contents and contexts, and of actors' forms of thought, intentions, strategies and use of media (oral, written, electronic) for disseminating and in various ways acting upon materials, are regarded in the new sociology of public policy as crucial topics of empirical enquiry.

Role/Positional, Dispositional, and Situational – Interactional Dimensions of Social Action

In the preceding discussion I touched upon aspects of a useful typology of social action that lends itself to incorporation into the new sociology of public policy. In his important conceptual scheme pertaining to sociological theory and method, Mouzelis (1993b: 579) states that "every interaction entails three analytically distinct dimensions: these are a role/positional, a dispositional, and a situational-interactional dimension". Taken together, these allow us to focus on system integration (an emphasis on role/positional factors) and on social integration (an emphasis on actors as beings who are not determined by their role/positional locations in the social totality) (Mouzelis 1991: 106).

Analysis which gives emphasis to the *role/positional* dimension is, following the Durkheimian/Parsonian tradition, a form of analysis that is mainly concerned with investigation of the ways in which social statuses (positions) and predefined role-scripts are significant factors that shape interaction. Mouzelis's illustration (ibid.) is drawn from a situation of face-to-face interaction. He notes that the pattern of interaction that occurs between a teacher and a student is partly shaped by the respective *positions/ roles* of each; role-scripts specify the appropriate behaviours for the actors, and also specify in general terms how the actors should relate to each other. These scripts are preconstituted: they exist prior to and are "over and above" the actual sequence(s) of interaction in which these two particular role incumbents happen to be involved. The generalized role scripts of pupil and teacher will also continue in existence even after this instance of pupil-teacher interaction is discontinued (when, let us say, the pupil has left school and the teacher has retired). Role-scripts, then, though they do not necessarily remain unchanged over the course of time, nevertheless have an existence that predates and postdates any particular instances of their enactment by actors in specific settings or micro-situations. Undoubtedly, role/positional factors have some influence on social interaction; it makes sense, for example, to speak of "the role of a teacher". I should add that although I have no difficulty with Mouzelis's example, I would want to add social ("organizational") actors to his illustration. For instance, in a policy network, particularly in tightly-coupled policy communities such as British health policy and agricultural policy, social relations and inter-organizational exchanges to some extent reflect institutionalized conceptions of the proper parts ("roles") to be played by the various social ("organizational") actors, and reflect institutionalized procedures and ideas concerning the question of how the various state and non-state actors in the network should relate to each other in terms of rights, duties, and patterns of social exchange. These may be regarded as social-actor equivalents of the role/positional factor that tends to be more commonly associated with individual actors but which, for the reason I have just given, should not be restricted to individual actors.

The *dispositional* dimension of social life, the second dimension in Mouzelis's typology, borrows from Bourdieu's (1977, 1990) concept of "habitus". This refers to actors' general "dispositions" (attitudes, skills, norms, etc) that do not derive from the specific roles in question – the roles of teacher and student in Mouzelis's example – but rather, from the actor's wider experiences of life in regard to social class, ethnicity, religion, gender, attendance at specific educational establishments, etc. The actor brings to any specific encounter (for example, teacher-student) those acquired generalized aspects of self which, though not derived from the specific roles involved in the encounter, nevertheless partly shape the pattern of interaction that develops among the participants. This makes good analytical sense: *general* life experiences affect how we act in any *particular* situations and the dispositional dimension helps us understand why it is, for example, that no two teachers ever perform the role of teacher in exactly the same way. Once again, I would want to extend the dispositional dimension to include inter-organizational relations. For instance, in policy networks some state and non-state organizational actors may be steeped in historical traditions (ranging from civil service or departmental traditions, to the ethos that permeates certain voluntary organizations or professional bodies), and these traditions may mean that the actors have acquired a generalized "disposition" that influences the way in which they approach any particular situations or relationships.

The third dimension of interaction, the *situational-interactional* dimension, refers to features of the interactional situation itself, and in particular to emergent and situated meanings that come into existence *during*, and as an outcome of, the process of interaction within the micro setting. Included here are emergent and situated forms of thought, meanings, intentionalities, practices, etc that to some extent reflect the personalities and biographies of the participants involved: and that, crucially so, also derive from the situational particularities of meaning, power, and interests that emerge out of the process of actor-actor *interaction* within the particular micro setting. The setting might be, for example, a situation involving contact between a state official and a member of the public; or an informal meeting of policy actors; or a formal policy-making committee. Interactive processes, as Mouzelis (1993b: 579) notes, may enable actors to "mobilize facilities/resources that are primarily *situational* – in the sense that they derive neither from roles nor from dispositions". Here the expression "situational" refers to the micro level of analysis (that is, face-to-face relationships within micro settings). At the mezo level of analysis, which includes social network analysis and inter-organizational relations, the equivalent relational and emergent phenomena refer to "new" (emergent) configurations of power and of new self-formulated conceptions of interests and meanings, these having arisen *relationally* during the course of social relations and social exchange within the network.

There is much to be said in favour of Mouzelis's typology of role/positional, dispositional, and situational-interactional dimensions of social action (for a fuller discussion, see Mouzelis 1991: 106, 112, 168, 196–200; 1993a: 5; 1993b: 579; 1995: 136–37). In, for example, a central government department, the institutionalized *positions/roles* associated with ministers, senior civil servants, junior staff, outside experts and policy consultants, etc, are relevant to an understanding of the policy process. But so also are the *dispositional* dimension (dispositions that the actors will have acquired over the years in various contexts outside the government department), and the *situational* dimension which implies that at least some aspects of the meanings and happenings in the situation are relationally emergent from within the situation itself. In determinist macro-structural theories of social action, the situational-interactional ("micro") element tends to be overlooked. A balanced view of this matter suggests that "although the meanings of particular actions are quite obviously related to social positions and dispositions, they are not moulded by them entirely. They take their final shape in the process of interaction itself" (Mouzelis 1991: 198). Which of these three dimensions predominate in social life, is something that varies empirically (Mouzelis 1993b: 580). That having been said, it is possible to make cautious generalizations about the extent to which one or the other of these dimensions is likely to be paramount in particular types of situations. For example, Moulzelis states (ibid):

> In highly ritualized ... [situations] ... (such as Catholic mass, say) the norms and resources pertaining to roles are much more important than those pertaining to the dispositional and situational dimensions. In cases, on the other hand, where role structures are weak or weakening (as during the demise of traditional status hierarchies in periods of rapid economic change) situational norms and resources come to the fore.

It is desirable that Mouzelis's typology be integrated with the previously described anti-reductionist conceptions of actors and social action, power, interests, social networks, the handling of policy materials *within* micro-situational settings, and the diffusion, reproduction or transformation of policy materials as they travel *across* policy settings that are scattered in social space and time. At the most general level, Mouzelis's classification of the role/positional, dispositional, and situational-interactional dimensions of action is a reminder that, as I have tried to show in this and the earlier chapter, *agency/structure* and *micro-macro* are core underlying concerns of social scientific theory and methodology; hence they are also key underlying concerns in the conceptual and methodological development of the new sociology of public policy.

The State/Civil Society, Postindustrialism, and Citizenship

In the following chapters it will occasionally be necessary to make reference to three inter-disciplinary themes that in recent years have interested sociologists, political scientists, and policy academics. These themes, which I propose to outline in this final section of the present chapter, are: the state/civil society distinction; postindustrialism; and the idea of citizenship. In discussing these it will once again be appropriate to also draw out a number of general theoretical matters that underpin the sociology of public policy.

The state/civil society distinction

The formulation of a distinction between the state and civil society has in recent years attracted increased attention in the social sciences and in political life. An emphasis on civil society is often associated with anti-state right-wing politics. However, it should be noted that the collapse of state socialism in Eastern Europe at the end of the 1980s was welcomed by the new left, while in the United Kingdom attacks by the Thatcher Government on civil society (trades unions, the media, voluntary associations, and even the church came under government fire) were resisted by the political left. Left-wing emphasis on "new social movements" (relating to, for example, women, ethnicity, ecology, and gay rights) and on the decentralization and democratization of state services, are additional indications that the 1980s witnessed growing interest in "civil society" and that this interest emanated from almost all sections of the political spectrum. It is perhaps not surprising that this escalation in political preoccupation with the idea of civil society, was reflected in academic discourse.

Taylor-Gooby (1991: 19) suggests that civil society includes the market, and "kinship, family and community systems"; also included are new social movements, and "the education system, the union movement, local govern-ment, the media, voluntary organizations and . . . the church" (ibid.). This definition, however, is somewhat confused in so far as it includes local government and education, which are normally regarded as parts of the state apparatus. Keane observes (1988: 14, emphasis added): "Civil society can be conceived as an aggregate of institutions whose members are engaged primarily in a complex of *non-state* activities – economic and cultural production, household life and voluntary associations". The distinction between state and civil society has become, however, increasingly complex; social, economic, and political change has generated shifts in "the very *form* of the state, the *form* of civil society, and the forms of relationship between them" (Bagguley 1994: 74). Chapter three will be concerned with, among other things, the institutional framework of the state, government, and politics. For the moment I want only to bring out the point that the state/civil society distinction is becoming increasingly blurred. It was noted earlier that state actors' and non-state actors' power, and their formulations of their interests, emerge in a *relational* way in, very often, policy networks consisting of state and non-state participants. Against a background of increased blurring of the state/civil society distinction, Kickert (1993: 191) refers to the recent interest in the idea of governance and the relation of governance to the operation of policy networks: "Public management is mainly the governance of complex networks by many different participants, such as government organizations, political and social groups, institutions, private and business organizations, etc". In their discussion of governance and associationism, Amin and Thrift (1995: 55) comment on the shift away from binary thinking (state/society, plan/market, public/private) and the increasing significance of governance networks which blur the traditional state/civil society distinction (ibid. 55). And as we shall see in chapter five, although it can be argued that the nation-state is a significant player in governance networks and this is likely to continue (Roche 1992: 231), sub-national (for example, regional) and transnational networks are increasingly significant components of contemporary governance. Perhaps inevitably, these developments mean that traditional formulations of the state/civil society distinction are increasingly called into question.

Postindustrialism

In the 1960s a number of sociologists – Daniel Bell, Raymond Aron, Ralph Dahrendorf and others – reacted against structural-functionalists' and Marxists' alleged failure to adequately grasp the significance of social, economic and political changes associated with movement towards a *postindustrial society* (Bell 1973; Touraine 1974). It was argued that the key organizing features of industrial society were industrial capitalism and the manufacture of material goods; and social class interests and class conflict. In contrast, postindustrial society, sometimes referred to as the "information society" (Webster 1995) or "post-modern society" (Kumar 1995), is said to be characterized by the centrality of information and knowledge and by a decline in the importance of manufacturing activity. In postindustrial society there is a relative decrease in the numbers employed in manufacturing industry and an expansion of service occupations; the clerical and professional sectors have increased in size. In the theory of postindustrialism, what Bell (1973) calls "codified knowledge" (systematized bodies of knowledge and information) becomes one of the most crucial resources for society, and a new "knowledge class", those involved in the creation and dissemination of information – academics, scientists, professionals, computer specialists, economists, and technical experts of all kinds – become powerful groupings who supercede the industrialists and entrepreneurs who had been associated with the older, "industrial" form of society. Consequently, the centres of power and policy-making in postindustrial society are not business firms, but educational, scientific, professional, and governmental organizations that deal in knowledge and information. In this new postindustrial scenario, policy-making is said to be increasingly based on expert knowledge and scientific rationality, rather than on intuitions and "judgements".

Though one of the characteristics of postindustrial society is said to be consumerism, some writers have pointed out that the ability to "consume" is not equally open to all citizens. Postindustrial trends, including the movement towards highly automated, robotic methods of production are associated with de-industrialization, rising unemployment, poverty, urban decline, and a highly disadvantaged "underclass" (Kasarda 1989; Judd and Parkinson 1990). Also, the movement towards the flexibilization of labour (Standing 1986) has resulted in increased job insecurity and low wages for unskilled workers and for many part-time workers. The changes in labour-market conditions to which I have just referred, coincided with government initiatives in the United Kingdom in the 1980s to de-regulate working conditions and reduce trade union power. These features of postindustrialism are sometimes overlooked in the more "upbeat" descriptions of a new social order based on the idea of a postindustrial society, and on closely associated notions such as "the information society", "the post-capitalist society", or the "technological society".

Although the thesis of postindustrialism refers to a number of undoubtedly important social and economic trends in contemporary society, it is a thesis that has been criticized (Kumar 1978; Williams 1985). Theorists of postindustrialism, post-Fordism etc, quite often accurately identify certain patterns of change, but they tend to exaggerate the nature and scale of change. For example, many service occupations are manual and unskilled, and do not involve handling of the complex information upon which some postindustrial/information society theorists lay such emphasis. And many white collar jobs have become computerized, routine and in various ways mechanized. Another relevant factor is that quite a number of computer experts and "service" professionals are in fact employed in manufacturing industries. Moreover, the notion of "information" and "codified knowledge" as a central organizing principle of society, is far from clear (Lyon 1987). The information society is a contested rather than self-evident concept: "While everyone agrees that there is more information and that this has increased in pertinence nowadays, thereafter all is disputation and disagreement" (Webster 1995: 215). Part of the difficulty in accepting the postindustrial thesis is its tendency towards oversimplification and reductionism. As Waters (1995: 18) observes: "In Bell the emerging society is governed by a single axial principle (the use of theoretical knowledge to produce services) and it is specified as the only possible principle of future social organization ... all the societies on the planet march resolutely forward to a singular post-industrial future".

Theorists of postindustrial society propound a singular and *general* substantive theory of social change. General theories of social change are, however, inherently problematical (Giddens 1984: 227–28). In theories of postindustrial society, too much is laid at the door of something labelled "postindustrialism". The problem here, and with all general theories of social change, is described by Giddens (ibid. 243, emphasis added): "In explaining social change, *no single and sovereign mechanism can be specified*; there are no keys that will unlock the mysteries of human social development, reducing them to a unitary formula, or that will account for the major transitions between societal types". In the theory of postindustrialism, social change in general is largely attributed to economic change and there is more than a touch of economic determinism (and therefore reductionism) in the approach. Moreover, as noted earlier, it is assumed that there is a near-inevitability surrounding the changes predicted by Bell and others; it is almost as though the earlier reductionist type of theory associated with the "logic of industrialism" thesis has been replaced by an equally determinist and mechanical theory involving a so-called "logic of postindustrialism". A more adequate conception of social change would recognize that the impact of macro-social processes to do with de-industrialization, technological change, the growth of service occupations and professions, the expansion of information technology, etc, are likely to be variable and differentially shaped by a variety of cultural, economic, and political factors at the subnational, national, and transnational levels of social process. It is also important to recognize the part played by *agency*: patterns of social life, and their reproduction or change, are in various ways influenced by the activities of *actors* whose forms of thought and formulations of interests and purposes are not structurally predetermined nor guided inexorably in a single direction by something called "postindustrialism". Actors involved in politics and public policy are undoubtedly affected by some of the macro processes described by theorists of postindustrialism: but events in the various policy sectors – health, education, agriculture, trade and industry, foreign policy, urban renewal, and so on – are not determined in a singular or universal way by "postindustrialism" nor by any other macro-social phenomenon (Marsh and Rhodes 1992a, 1992b; Wilsford 1994, Dunn and Perl 1994: 312). It can be argued that public policy exhibits a great deal more time-space diversity and discontinuity than can be explained by the notion of "postindustrial" economic and social change. And in those cases where policy material exhibits stability and time-space continuity, it is unlikely that grand theories of social change – such as the theory of postindustrialism – will ever be capable of providing an adequate explanatory account of policy reproduction processes. These observations relate to a more general sociological precept that I have already discussed and which will recur throughout the following chapters. That is, the world of public policy, like the social world in general, is relatively contingent. The social world is not driven by a determinant macro-structural motor such as postindustrialism, or whatever; the message from anti-reductionist sociology is that there are no such prime movers.

Citizenship

The idea of citizenship has a long history in social and political theory (Barbalet 1988: 2). However, academic interest in the concept declined in Britain in the post-war years. The reasons for this are not entirely clear. Probably an important factor was the creation of a welfare state with universal benefits and services that perhaps caused many to assume that citizenship was not problematic, but something that could be taken for granted. This is not to say that the notion of citizenship dropped out of sight altogether. In a variety of political struggles – for example, the anti-Stalinist and anti-fascist movements and the civil rights movement in the United States in the 1960s – there were appeals to "human rights" that in one way or another invoked ideas of citizenship. In general, however, it was the case that in post-war Britain and elsewhere academic debates about citizenship lost much of their impetus (Oliver and Heater 1994: 1).

Since the mid-1980s there has been a marked revival of interest in the concept. This has been associated with academic and political perceptions of problems of unemployment, poverty and an underclass (Lister 1990; Moynihan 1989) associated with economic decline and de-industrialization. Other relevant factors include: ecological concerns and the idea that citizens have both rights and duties in regard to the natural world; a concern that right-wing governments in the 1980s were adopting individualist political philosophies that eroded notions of community and citizenship; and a growing awareness that not only social class but also gender and ethnicity are relevant to the idea that citizenship implies full participation in, or membership of, a community or society. At a more general theoretical level, writers such as Hall and Held (1989), Taylor-Gooby (1994) and Thompson and Hoggett (1996) have examined what many perceive to be a major tension between, on the one hand, the idea of citizenship (which is traditionally associated with equality and universality) and, on the other, the idea of post-modern society and postmodern theory which emphasize not equality and universality but diversity, difference, and particularities of identities, values, and needs (Nicholson and Seidman 1995). For these various reasons, an escalating intellectual interest in "citizenship" had by the early 1990s become evident across a range of social science disciplines including sociology, social theory, political science, and public policy (Roche 1992: 2).

The dominant post-war social science paradigm of citizenship was derived, in the main, from Marshall's (1950/1963) influential essay, "Citizenship and social class". Marshall identified three components of citizenship – civil, political, and social – which he believed emerged in historical sequence (Marshall 1963: 76): civil rights emerged in the 18th century, political rights in the 19th century, and social rights in the 20th century (ibid.). It was argued that each set of rights – civil, political, social – are serviced by matching institutions (Marshall 1963: 74, emphases added).

> The *civil element* is composed of the rights necessary for individual freedom – liberty of the person, freedom of speech, thought and faith, the right to own property and to conclude valid contracts, and the right to justice. The last is of a different order from the others because it is the right to defend and assert all one's rights on terms of equality with others and by due process of law. This shows us that the institutions most directly associated with civil rights are the courts of justice. By the *political element* I mean the right to participate in the exercise of political power, as a member of a body invested with political authority or as an elector of the members of such a body. The corresponding institutions are Parliament and councils of local government. By the *social element* I mean the whole range from the right to a modicum of economic welfare and security to the right to share to the full in the social heritage and to live the life of a

civilized being according to the standards prevailing in the society. The institutions most closely connected with it are the education system and the social services.

The message contained in Marshall's essay, which was originally published in 1950, suited the "welfare statist" post-war political climate, and his conception became – sometimes tacitly, sometimes explicitly – the dominant academic and political paradigm of citizenship. It is noteworthy that the paradigm, as Roche (1992) observes, had very little to say about *civil society*; and little to say about citizen *duties*. The emphasis was "statist"; and there was also a concern for individuals' rights, these being rights that were to be serviced by the state. Roche (1992) charts some of the factors that served to challenge Marshall's paradigm of citizenship. Firstly, the paradigm rested on the geopolitical idea of nation-state, an idea that is increasingly challenged under conditions of globalization and globalized policy (see chapter five). Secondly, the paradigm assumed a healthy capitalist economy to fund an expanding Beveridge-type welfare state that would ensure "social citizenship" rights for all. However, de-industrialization, demographic and other factors mean that today the notion of an expanding welfare state is problematical. Thirdly, the dominant paradigm was ideologically challenged by the new right, and by the "new social movements" that focused on, for example, peace, feminism and ecology (Scott 1990). Although the New Right and the new social movements are not ideologically similar, they have at least two things in common: (a) the New Right and the new social movements emphasize civil society as opposed to the dominant (centre-left) paradigm of citizenship and the traditional left paradigm, both of which are statist; and (b) both the New Right and the new social movements emphasize not only citizens' rights but also citizens' duties and responsibilities, in contrast to the views of Marshall, and of the left, whose notions of citizenship focused almost entirely on rights.

It is difficult to predict the probable course of future debate concerning conceptions of citizenship. However, it seems likely that at least four areas of debate, some of which are interconnected, will increasingly challenge the dominant paradigm. Firstly, the contemporary focus on citizenship duties and responsibilities will probably gain further momentum and lead to attempts to combine recent theories of "duties" with the traditional post-war Marshall-type discourse of "rights". Secondly, growing recognition of social diversity of a kind that, as well as social class, includes, in particular, "race", ethnicity and gender, has prompted a wider debate about the extent to which a singular and universal category of citizenship is capable of enhancing the citizenship rights of diverse social groups such as women, black people, gays, and disabled people. Two excellent sociological discussions of this complex question, written largely – but not exclusively – in terms of the debate over gender and citizenship, are Lister (1995) and Walby (1994). Thirdly, the growing interest in civil society, and in the blurring of the state/civil society distinction as described earlier, is likely to figure increasingly in debates about citizenship. Some of these debates link into parallel work on the development of a "new" political economy of governance (Jenson 1995; Thrift 1994; Amin and Thrift 1995; Held 1995), and the growing interest in power and governmentality (Hindess 1996). Fourthly, the recognition that social, economic, and political problems and ecological issues are increasingly perceived and responded to at subnational, national, and transnational levels of governance, has profound implications for the idea of the nation-state and for the state-centred assumptions that are scripted into the conventional paradigm of citizenship. For instance, the question of the relation of citizenship to personal and political identities (Calhoun 1994) is made more complex by the existence of not only the nation-state as a source of identity and citizenship, but also multiple and overlapping identities and citizenship rights associated with differing units or "layers" of governance. British people, for example, have rights (and perhaps "identities") that refer to the nation-state; but they also have transnational "European" citizenship rights by virtue of legislation enacted at the level of the European Union. In these respects Europe is not unique and, as Roche (1992: 193) observes, it may be that future world-regional blocs (as in the case of the increasingly closer links that are developing between Japan, Taiwan, and South Korea) will become increasingly significant factors in academic and political debates surrounding the idea of citizenship.

CHAPTER THREE

THE INSTITUTIONAL FRAMEWORK OF GOVERNMENT AND POLITICS

Theoretical knowledge of an *explicit* kind is a crucial part of social science; for as I pointed out in the introductory chapter, theory inevitably affects our perception of the social world and influences the way in which we set about the task of investigating that world. There is no such thing as a theoryless description, whether the theory in question be formal, or based on informal "commonsense". Thus, in seeking to develop a contemporary sociology of public policy, wherever appropriate in each of the chapters I have drawn attention to the sometimes inadequate and often inexplicit theoretical and methodological assumptions that have influenced social scientific accounts of public policy. However, in a book of this kind it is also necessary to provide some empirical descriptive analysis of those features of the social world – such as the state, and systems of central and local government – that are closely enmeshed with the policy process.

The earlier chapters established in a fairly comprehensive way the conceptual and methodological groundwork for the construction of a contemporary sociology of public policy. In what follows the intention is to partly shift the focus of attention away from theory, and towards descriptive analysis. For example, I provide below a mainly empirical description of aspects of the institutional framework – such as central and local government – through which public policy is mediated. In some places in this and the later chapters I shall, however, need to make explicit reference to the earlier theoretical material, and sometimes I will extend in new directions the theoretical ideas that were introduced earlier. There will be times when, as in the first half of the present chapter, the emphasis will be primarily descriptive. Even here, though, it should be borne in mind that, as I have just indicated, every description of the world contains underlying ontological assumptions. The assumptions that will apply in what follows are those that were introduced in the earlier chapters. For instance, in the following descriptive account it is not assumed that systems of national or local government are structurally predetermined; nor, for example, that the "new public management" that emerged in the 1980s is an expression of "real" ("objective") interests imputed to taxonomic collectivities such as social classes. And in a more general anti-reductionist sense, it is not assumed that the state and governmental institutions can be accounted for in terms of any single general principle of substantive explanation.

The first part of the chapter is an outline – with particular reference to Britain – of the institutional framework of government. This begins with a brief overview of the nature of parliamentary democracy, followed by a description of key institutional aspects of the policy process. These are: central and local government; the new public management; and the growing institutional significance of the European Union for British public policy. In the second part of the chapter, which focuses on the idea of *the state* and its relation to the policy process, I shall describe and evaluate conventional social scientific theories of the state and also examine analytical problems and possibilities raised by post-Foucauldian conceptions of the state and governance.

The Institutional Framework Through Which Public Policy is Mediated

In what follows I do not intend to provide a highly-detailed treatment of the institutional framework of government and politics, since there is no point in duplicating material that is readily available elsewhere. There are numerous empirically informative political science texts that describe British government in some detail. Among the better ones are Coxall and Robins (1994), Jones and Kavanagh (1994), Peele (1995), and Pyper and Robins (1995a). It should be noted that my purpose in what follows is to examine only those features of the British system of government that relate closely to the policy process.

The principle of parliamentary democracy

Parliamentary democracy implies a separation of powers consisting of a law-making body (a *legislature* or parliament) that is freely elected by the people; an *executive* (a government) that is responsible to parliament as in the United Kingdom, or, as in the American system, an elected president who is more directly accountable to the people (the electorate) than to elected representatives sitting in Congress; and an independent *judiciary* that is free from political control. Parliamentary democracy also implies the rule of law (this is to do with, in particular, freedom from arbitrary arrest), and the existence of two or more political parties – if there is only one political party, this is not democracy in the usual sense of the term.

The principle of a separation of powers associated with parliamentary democracy requires that the law-makers as policy-makers should be elected by the people, leaving the *implementation* of policy to non-elected professionals, administrators, and technical experts. The assumption here is that politics (policy-making) and administration (policy-execution) can be clearly separated: this separation is widely referred to as the politics/ administration dichotomy. Relatedly, parliamentary democracy in the United Kingdom rests on the idea of *ministerial responsibility*; government departments are headed by ministers who are responsible to Parliament for decisions taken by themselves and their staff. Parliament is charged with the task of scrutinizing the activities of departments and of the various semi-autonomous organizations (Her Majesty's Prison Service, the Benefits Agency, the Employment Service, etc) that are linked to departments. In discharging this function, the mechanisms available to Parliament include Parliamentary Questions (both oral and written), select committee enquiries, and investigation by the Parliamentary Commissioner or Ombudsman. A related point that is sometimes emphasized by writers on parliamentary democracy and government is that the matters to which I have just referred go a long way towards providing an explanation of why it is that government departments are organized along bureaucratic lines (Greenwood and Wilson 1989: 25–26). That is, it is assumed that in order to ensure departmental officials (civil servants) are accountable to the minister, who in turn can be held accountable to Parliament for the decisions and activities of his or her officials, a hierarchical, bureaucratic system of organizational control is necessary so as to limit the discretion of officials. The line of reasoning here is that without a bureaucratic system of rules, clearly prescribed civil-servant roles and clear-cut lines of communication, and hierarchical tiers of responsibility and accountability, it is hard to see how any minister could be expected to be accountable to Parliament for the activities of departmental staff. That is, *bureaucracy* is the mechanism for ensuring that departmental officials are accountable to ministers, and in turn, *ministerial responsibility* is the mechanism for ensuring that ministers are held accountable to Parliament in respect of departmental affairs. Whether this means that the "post-bureaucratic" forms of organization associated with the new public management are therefore undemocratic, is a question that I shall return to later in the chapter.

As the description above has demonstrated, there is a relationship between the principle of parliamentary democracy and various constitutional and organizational arrangements to do with policy-making and policy-implementation. The above description provides a formal constitutional picture of government, politics and policy. Whether, however, political and policy processes actually function in the way described above is a question to which I will return at various points in the following discussion.

Central government

Some years ago, Smith and Stanyer (1976/1980: 135) referred to government departments as the main organizational form of the executive branch of the state. This remains true to some extent, subject to some important provisos that I will introduce in the later section on the new public management and the creation of the "Next Steps" Executive Agencies. The main departments are the Treasury, the Home Office, the Foreign and Commonwealth Office, Defence, Trade and Industry, Environment, Health, Social Security, Education and Employment, Transport, Agriculture, the Scottish Office, the Welsh Office, and the Northern Ireland Office. Departments vary in size, function, and in the nature of their powers, and there are also numerous other government organizations of various kinds. This structural diversity was a factor that led Jordan (1994: 2) to argue that the British system of government is characterized by "uncertainty, inconsistency, disorder".

In a formal constitutional sense, departmental officials are supposed to be impartial and anonymous civil servants who implement policy with no involvement in policy-making, and who are protected by the doctrine of ministerial responsibility; it is, as I have already noted, the minister who is answerable to Parliament for the conduct of departmental affairs. Parliament is by no means entirely marginal in regard to the policy process: the comprehensive system of select committees introduced in 1979 has, if anything, strengthened Parliament's role in the policy process (Barberis 1996: 17). Select committees can question ministers, civil servants and the chief executives of semi-autonomous agencies, and the committees are often vigorous in their questioning (Jones and Kavanagh 1994: 187). However, the formal constitutional image of Parliament at the centre of policy-making is not an accurate reflection of how things work in practice. Some writers, for example, have pointed to the involvement of civil servants in policy-making (Lawton and Rose 1991: 13). There is no simple or straightforward pattern in regard to such involvement (ibid. 12–16). Some officials are engaged almost exclusively in activities that could not be called policy-making. Others may be involved in either defensive bureaucratic obstruction (the "Yes, Minister" civil servant) or proactively engaged in policy formulation (in local government, for example, professional staff are sometimes very closely involved in policy-making). Another factor at the central level is the part played in the policy process by Downing Street Policy Unit members and various other advisers to the prime minister. These individuals and groups may in some circumstances be influential in shaping policy. For instance, there is some evidence (Hencke 1996) that education policy in the 1990s was influenced by right-wing think tanks (in particular the Adam Smith Institute, the Institute for Economic Affairs, and the Social Affairs Unit) or, at least, by certain of their members who had close connections with officials and advisers attached to No 10 Downing Street.

Another topic to which attention should be drawn, is the role of the prime minister in the policy process. In the political science literature on British government there is an ongoing debate as to whether the power of modern prime ministers has increased to such an extent that there has been a shift away from cabinet government to "prime-ministerial government". In part, this debate was heightened by the forceful personal style of the former Prime Minister, Mrs Margaret Thatcher. It is probably true that prime ministers' power has increased in recent years. But the extent of this should not be exaggerated. Such is the volume and complexity of government activity that most policy decisions nowadays are made in departments, not in No 10 (Jones and Kavangh 1994: 165). Nor should it be assumed that cabinet government no longer exists as a meaningful political institution (ibid. 166, 169). And nor should the constraints imposed by political party be underplayed (ibid. 166): the need for a prime minister to retain the support of his or her political party in the House of Commons is a constraint on prime-ministerial power, as Mrs Thatcher discovered to her cost in 1990.

Central/local relations

A controversial topic in the political science literature on government is the suggestion that central/local relations have shifted: it is sometimes claimed that the influence of local government in recent years has declined while the power of central government has increased. In the 1980s, central government took on new powers to intervene in local affairs. The amount of national funding to local authorities declined and, through the mechanism of "capping", the amounts that local authorities could raise for themselves were subjected to tighter central controls. In addition, the introduction of compulsory competitive tendering meant that each local authority had to put out to tender a range of activities that previously would automatically have been carried out by the authority's own workforce. Political commentators have also pointed out that, quite apart from these centralizing tendencies of the 1980s, Britain was already a relatively centralized state when compared with some other European countries (Coxall and Robins 1994: 93). However, the pattern of central/local relations is far from clear-cut. In the case of education policy, for example, Pyper and Robins (1995b: 3–4) are probably correct in saying there has been some shift of power from local government to central government: it is true that there has been a shift of power from local Education Authorities to school governors, but the National Curriculum and active encouragement of schools to opt out of local government control together represent a potentially significant accretion of power to central government (ibid. 4). Glennerster et al (1992) fear that in such services as education, housing, and social services, the decentralization of power from local authorities to small management units (schools, community centres, housing estates, colleges, etc) might lead to a weakening of the "middle-tier" of government (local government) and an enlargement of central government power over small, relatively weak decentralized management units. The fear is that there will be no effective power base standing between these small, decentralized units, and the state. As Glennerster et al put it (413): "Local authorities now provide some counter-balance to central power. What we may face is the problem of the excluded middle in the hierarchy of political power". It is important, however, to note that while the state at local government level and national level is becoming less involved as a direct provider of services, it is nevertheless the case that the role of government as an "enabler, a contractor, and a regulator" has expanded (Pyper and Robins 1995b: 4). Local government is increasingly becoming an "enabler" and regulator of services contracted from the voluntary and private sectors, rather than a direct provider of services. This is not the absence of any role at all, though it is a changed role when compared with the traditional model of local government. More generally, the pattern of central/local relations is not a structurally fixed pattern. It varies according to the service or issue in question (Peele 1995: 369): "to speak of a single central-local government relationship is in many respects misleading because of the high degree of fragmentation within the central and local government structures and within the policy communities working through those structures." In theoretical terms we can see here an affinity between recent political science writing on government and policy, and the sociological understandings referred to in earlier chapters where I argued that the policy environment is not a unified social totality driven by an analytical prime mover: there are many foci of power in society and although not "chaotic", the social fabric nevertheless is always potentially discontinuous across time and social space. Thus we should not be surprised that while it may be that Britain is a relatively centralized state, there is, none the less, considerable variation in the overall configuration of central/local relations (Wilson 1995: 245–46).

Local government

Local government is, of course, an integral part of the institutional framework of government, politics and policy. The recent history of local government can for our purposes be divided into three periods, each of which is characterized by a particular style of organization and management. The 1970s may be described as the era of corporate planning/corporate management; the 1980s saw the rise of the so-called "excellence" movement which focused on the search for improvement in the quality of local government services; the 1990s have been described as the "beyond excellence" era in which, it is argued, efforts should be made to achieve improvements not only in the quality of service but also in the quality of government. This is a fairly rough and ready classification, not least in regard to periodicity and overlap between these three organizational, managerial and political styles. Moreover, it would be wrong to imply that these styles were fully implemented, or implemented in the same way, in all local authorities. Nevertheless, the classification is sufficiently accurate to be a heuristically useful indicator of some key developments in the recent history of local government in Britain.

The corporate planning approach (or corporate management as some call it) became part of the local government scene in the 1970s. The impetus for the approach came partly from academics, and in particular, from Professor John Stewart and his colleagues at the Institute of Local Government Studies at Birmingham University. Of relevance to the theoretical framework described in the earlier chapters is Clapham's (1986) rejection of the reified and reductionist idea that the part played in the local state by corporate management in the 1970s was an expression of class interests. In fact, a broad range of actors became involved in the corporate management movement and in responses to it; these involvements occurred for a variety of reasons that cannot be reduced to a "class interests" explanation. Books, journal articles, conferences, workshops and training courses were used to disseminate the idea of corporate management among local government administrators, training officers and academics, and the approach soon became a symbol of progressive local government organization and management. The corporate planning/corporate management movement is described by Smith and Stanyer (1976/1980: 249–51). Its main features can be summarized as follows.

- Improve the quantity and quality of data on community needs.
- Ascertain whether existing local authority programmes meet needs, and ensure that alternative programmes are being examined.
- Cost the local authority's programmes in terms of results achieved and value for money.
- Evaluate the impact of the local authority's activities on community problems and needs.
- Avoid a rigid departmentalism and as far as possible avoid professional rivalries between staff in the various departments (education, social services, planning, transport, community development, libraries, environmental protection, etc).
- Avoid a proliferation of departments and committees – keep these to a minimum.
- Have a managing body (a central policy unit) for the local authority as a whole, additional to the managing committees that are responsible for particular departments/services.

A few of the features of corporate management were carried over into the public sector "excellence" movement of the 1980s. This movement had a major impact on local government, central government, the National Health Service, and on semi-autonomous organizations and quangos. The so-called "excellence" movement was stimulated by an influential book, Peters and Waterman's (1982) *In Search of Excellence*. Their book argued for non-

hierarchical and non-bureaucratic organizational structures that might stimulate organizational cultures of a dynamic and innovative kind. Peters and
Waterman's prescriptions arose from a study in which they identified
common characteristics among highly successful ("excellent") private
corporations such as Boeing, IBM and McDonalds. It was argued by those
involved in the "excellence" movement that in the public sector there should
be more delegation than there had been in the past, and increased efforts
should be made to tap the skill and creative talents of staff. And crucially, the
public sector should be more responsive to its customers and service-users.
Lawton and Rose (1991: 7–8) describe the approach as action-orientated; as
involving a reduction of bureaucratic controls and fewer hierarchical levels;
and as an attempt to strike a balance between, on the one hand, core values
formulated at the organization centre, and on the other, a less centralized
structure that entails delegation and allows autonomy to sub-units so long as
their behaviour conforms to the core values specified by the centre. The
approach was, it may be noted, a fairly radical departure from traditional
hierarchical and professional norms that, notwithstanding the corporate
management ideas of the 1970s, had tended to dominate public sector
organization, management and service-delivery.

The "beyond excellence" approach of the 1990s is described in Hambleton
and Hoggett's (1990) *Beyond Excellence: Quality Local Government in the
1990s*. The "excellence" movement of the 1980s was about quality of
service. But it can be argued that local government is, unlike private sector
enterprises, more than a management unit for the efficient delivery of
services; it is also about local political democracy, about local *government*.
Hambleton and Hoggett's expression "beyond excellence" is intended to
convey the growing acceptance of a view that modern local government
should strive to improve quality of services *and* quality of local government.
In regard to quality of government, Hambleton and Hoggett outline various
ways in which both representative democracy and participative democracy
might be improved at the local level. In essence, the case advanced by
Hambleton and Hoggett and by others is that local government in the 1990s
should be more responsive to service-users as *consumers* (the "excellence" or
"quality of service" emphasis), but also more accountable and responsive to
citizens (the "beyond excellence" or "quality of government" emphasis).

In local government, the 1970s, the 1980s and 1990s have undoubtedly
been a period of challenge and change. As well as the shifting organizational,
managerial and political cultures implied in the approaches described above,
there were other developments. There have been structural changes. In 1974
there was a major re-organization of local government; in 1986 the Greater
London Council and six English metropolitan counties ceased to exist; and
currently a major structural review of local government is underway. It
should also be noted that running alongside the excellence/beyond excellence
developments of the 1980s and 1990s there has been, on the one hand, a
growing right-wing challenge of traditional public sector practices (and some

would say of the idea of local government itself), and on the other hand, particularly in the 1980s, left-wing orientations involving municipal social- ism and the "new urban left". All in all, there has been a considerably increased politicization of local government in the 1980s and 1990s. Nor should we overlook the general significance of the previously discussed question of central/local relations. Here the future is uncertain. In regard to the balance of power between central and local government, no structural predetermination is involved and it is impossible to predict with any certainty the future shape of local government. "Everything will depend on the balance of power between central government, producer organizations (local govern- ment trade unions and professional associations), voters and local politicians" (Pickvance 1990: 18). Once again, this statement should come as no surprise; the general thrust of the theoretical material discussed in the earlier chapters is that the social world is a relatively contingent outcome of dynamic processes and social conditions that are not structurally or historically predetermined.

The "new public management"

I referred earlier to central government departments. I also mentioned that some writers regard the traditional form of the British state as relatively centralized. Post-war British government, however, has also assumed a decentralized and delegated form, which is variously described by political scientists as "quasi-government", "indirect government", or "arm's length government" (Coxall and Robins 1994: 169). There are numerous non- departmental organizations; these are very often called quangos ("quasi- autonomous non-governmental organizations"). Organizations of this kind are special-purpose organizations that, so it is argued, can discharge their functions more efficiently and effectively than a larger and functionally more diverse organization such as a department. Quasi-government includes the former nationalized industries, and a large number of other special-purpose organizations such as the Commission for Racial Equality, The Arts Council, the University Funding Council, the General Nursing Council, the BBC, the Nature Conservancy, the Apple and Pear Development Council, and a host of other organizations including well over a thousand advisory bodies such as the Food Hygiene Advisory Board. In the 1980s, however, the long- established principle of quasi-government was given a new and radical twist. This involved a major reform of the civil service and a process of transferring to new semi-autonomous organizations a range of policy functions that hitherto had been seen as an integral and necessary part of the role of central government departments.

The Ibbs Report of 1988, or to give it its proper title, the Efficiency Unit Report *Improving Management in Government: The Next Steps*, was delivered by Sir Robin Ibbs, a former industrial manager who became head of the Government's Efficiency Unit. The then Prime Minister, Margaret

Thatcher, hailed the Ibbs reforms as a "revolution" and the "biggest shake-up of the civil service in a century" (Butcher 1995: 67). The Ibbs reforms were designed to achieve increased efficiency and effectiveness in public administration. Tasks formerly performed by departments were "hived off" to new semi-autonomous agencies that were to be free to operate with no ministerial interference in operational affairs. The chief executives of the new agencies, some of whom were recruited from industry and commerce, were to have relatively unfettered freedom to exercise commercial and managerial expertise. A number of "Next Steps" agencies were quickly established: the list of agencies, which is now a long one, includes the Job Centre network, the Passport Office, Her Majesty's Stationery Office, the Benefits Agency, the Employment Service, and Her Majesty's Prison Service. It should be noted that the "Next Steps" agencies are an example of organizational "contingency theory" applied to the process of government (Lawton and Rose 1991: 161–62). That is, the Ibbs approach is based on the idea that rather than employ a common organizational blueprint for the civil service as a whole, the structure of an organization should be tailored to suit the particular problems facing the organization and the particular tasks and functions given to it. Hence semi-autonomous organizations are financed in a variety of ways: these include normal parliamentary funding, funds raised from the organization's own resources (from the sale of services), special grants, and levies from clients (Smith and Stanyer 1976/80: 56). Staffing arrangements can also vary. Rather than have identical arrangements for the whole of the civil service, Ibbs recommended the abolition of uniform civil service grades and pay structures that applied across all departments and units. Staffing arrangements, Ibbs argued, should vary according to the particular needs and function of each unit of management.

By 1993 about 60 per cent of the British civil service was located in Next Steps organizations or in organizations that operate on Next Step lines under chief executives who are set performance targets and given considerably more managerial and financial freedom than occurs in the conventional civil service. The intention is that by the beginning of the next century the bulk of civil service work will be performed in semi-autonomous organizations (Butcher 1995: 61). The Next Steps philosophy involves *control by contract*, rather than bureaucratic control. The chief executives are encouraged to be innovative and creative and to devise their own managerial strategies for attaining performance targets. This managerial philosophy is reflected in contracts between Next Steps organizations and the main department, contracts which emphasize performance targets and performance monitoring. These developments are underpinned by the Ibbs Report's argument for separating policy work from management. The idea here is that the managerial and operational side of government should be "hived off" to Next Steps organizations, leaving ministers and senior civil servants in departments to concentrate on policy development and overall strategic planning (Barberis 1996: 8).

As Dowding (1995: 2) observes, in the 1990s the civil service has been radically transformed: it has been "altered from a straightforward hierarchical line structure to a complex form with a core of policy-making civil servants in Whitehall surrounded by a periphery of policy-executing agencies". Furthermore, the changes described above are part of a larger shift of direction that includes compulsory competitive tendering and the privatization of many civil service activities. While contracting out of cleaning, catering and related support services had been a feature of the civil service for some years, the Government in its 1991 White Paper "Competing for Quality" set out proposals for market-testing that could result in the privatization of other civil service functions such as clerical services, and professional services. *The Civil Service Yearbook 1994* (HMSO, Cabinet Office, 1994: iii) summarized the Government's intentions for the future of public management: there should be a reduction in government activities, this to be achieved via compulsory competitive tendering and privatization; and those remaining activities that have to be state-provided should as far as possible be provided not via traditional civil service methods but by executive agencies. Pyper and Robins's (1995a: 4) assessment is that:

> The interventionist state is by no means at an end, and the role of government as a provider remains valid in some spheres at least ... However, put simply, the choice facing the UK government in the 1990s is really between different modes of governing. Increasingly, the government eschews the option of continuing as a large-scale direct provider except where this remains unavoidable, and moves instead into a new governing mode as an enabler, a contractor, and a regulator. The enabling government sees its primary role in terms of facilitating service provision by non-state bodies or partly autonomous state bodies.

Pyper and Robins (ibid. 5) go on to comment that "the precise balance to be struck between the government's role as provider, enabler, contractor and regulator is, of course, a matter of policy". It has been argued that the policy is flawed. The Ibbs assumption that a separation can be made between policy development/strategic planning, and the policy-execution and administration functions performed by Next Steps agencies, is challenged by critics. In some respects, this is part of a larger debate surrounding the question of whether a clear distinction can be made between policy-making and policy-implementation. Ham and Hill (1993) argue that the politics/administration dichotomy is misleading. They argue that "policy will often continue to evolve within what is conventionally described as the implementation phase rather than the policy-making phase of the policy process" (12), and "there may be difficulty in determining where policy-making stops and implementation begins" (107). For Ham and Hill, the concretization of policy (translating general objectives into specific goals and activities) very often results in a "seamless web" (107) that fuses "policy" and administration/implementation together (105–6). If

Ham and Hill's arguments are accepted, it is reasonable to conclude that the Next Steps organizations are engaging in policy development rather than only policy-execution. This links in with the more general criticism that semi-autonomous agencies weaken the principle of ministerial responsibility and weaken accountability in general. The Ibbs Report had stated that in order to ensure political accountability, the relevant ministers must have overall responsibility for the budget and broad policy direction of executive agencies. However, the Ibbs Report also suggested each semi-autonomous agency should evolve its own form of accountability, and some years ago Greenwood and Wilson (1989: 32) observed that this might produce a confusing system comprised of differing mechanisms of accountability. Some have argued that the new agencies, because of their quasi-autonomous nature, will be less accountable to ministers than are departments (Peele 1995: 118). Even though it is true that, for example, parliamentary select committees can question the chief executives of Next Steps agencies, some critics argue that it is difficult for ministers to be accountable to Parliament for the operation of agencies if the Next Steps chief executives are expected to exercise managerial control free from ministerial "interference" (Butcher 1995: 75). O'Toole (1994: 29) believes the new arrangements merely pay lip service to established methods of political accountability; he points out that the executive agencies operate "at a distance" from ministers, and that executive agencies, like departments, also have increasingly close links with private contractors. O'Toole argues (ibid.) that when it comes to securing citizens' redress for individual grievances (grievances to do with confidentiality, equality of treatment, etc) the traditional system is far better because it is built around a unified structure of authority and accountability. A plurality of systems of accountability involving departments, Next Step Agencies, and private contractors, will in O'Toole's view create major problems of political accountability. Not that all of the critics of Next Steps want to retain the status quo. Some have advocated major reform of Whitehall, but argue that Next Steps is not the right kind of reform. For example, Hutton (1995), two years after having left civil service employment, described the civil service as having outmoded traditions and very little expertise (and few management systems) of the kind necessary for undertaking good quality policy analysis and policy development. He argues, however, that the Next Steps initiative is no solution to the problems of the civil service because the Next Steps programme is leading towards a fragmentation of the civil service and this is preventing the introduction of civil service-wide reforms based on improved professional standards.

The new public management is not, of course, restricted to reform of central government and the civil service: it is also a feature of the NHS; of the way in which quangos and executive agencies are organised; and of local government. One of the better treatments of the new public management in local government, is Hoggett's (1991). He describes in some detail the shift towards flexible "post-bureaucratic" organizational forms: in effect, this is a shift from hierarchical "mechanistic" structures to loose "organistic" structures. In what follows I shall draw on Hoggett's unusually comprehensive paper. He refers to the 1980s trend towards devolved management in the NHS, and in local government in such fields as housing, education, social services, and recreation. The expression "Decentralized Service Units" (DSUs) refers to decentralized units of management (schools, social service area teams, housing estate management teams, etc). The new public management in local government is predicated on the idea that instead of senior management employing bureaucratic methods to control DSUs, the latter should be free to operate in a creative and flexible manner without centralized, hierarchical controls. There is here a rough parallel with the previously described changes at central government level. The changes in local government involve a separation of *strategic planning/strategic control*, these being functions which remain with senior management and the elected representatives (councillors), and *operational control*, a function which is delegated to the semi-autonomous DSUs. The notion of "control by contract" replaces hierarchical, bureaucratic control. The centre defines the organization's core values, and, in the form of a contract, sets performance targets ("the kinds of results to be expected") for the DSUs. The DSUs negotiate with the centre on the forms of central support (such as centrally provided finances, personnel and training services, legal and accountancy services) that the DSUs require in order to achieve their performance targets. Hoggett emphasizes (249–50) that what is involved here is a switch from control by bureaucratic regulation to control by contract, that is, control in terms of the outcomes expected (expected performance and expected effectiveness as specified in the contract between each DSU and the centre).

Criticisms of these arrangements have concentrated, once again, on the question of political accountability. Earlier, in discussing parliamentary democracy and central government, I noted that the need for political accountability via the principle of ministerial responsibility is sometimes cited as *a reason for preserving bureaucracy and hierarchy in the public sector*. O'Toole (1994: 33), for example, in rejecting the Next Steps semi-autonomous agencies, argues that bureaucracy is necessary to sustain ministers' accountability to Parliament. Hoggett (1991) raises a similar question, but in relation to political accountability at the local government level. In Hogget's opinion (251), however, the movement towards post-bureaucratic structures, which is, in effect, an attempt to de-bureaucratize the public sector, poses no threat to democracy or to the principle of political accountability. He argues that devolved management frees top management for the task of strategic control, a task that is undertaken in conjunction with councillors. Strategic planning and strategic control relates to *general* policies, values, and objectives. Neither top management nor politicians can possibly control the details of policy and management (operational control), and this is especially so in an age when the tasks of government are becoming increasingly complex. The "new wave" post-bureaucratic top management is freed of operational responsibilities and this means top management can concentrate on strategic-control functions in a way that makes senior managers more, not less, accountable to politicians. That is, senior managers become involved, under the new arrangements, in working closely with elected politicians in order to help translate politicians' aspirations into policies and to develop strategic goals, targets and objectives; to provide support services (legal, financial, personnel, etc) to the DSUs; and to monitor the DSUs performance against the strategic "mission statement" that is formulated at the centre by councillors working alongside senior local authority managers. Moreover, and as my earlier reference to the "beyond excellence" movement (Hambleton and Hogget 1990) will have indicated, it has been argued that a devolved operational management system (a focus on "quality of service") is in no way incompatible with a simultaneous focus on "quality of government". In regard to the latter, Hambleton and Hoggett point (12–13) to a range of possible measures for strengthening representative democracy: these include providing better support services for councillors such as improved secretarial, information, and research facilities (17). At the same time, direct democracy can be strengthened by means of such measures as establishing user-groups for parks, libraries, leisure centres, community centres, and so on.

As already noted, the new public management is controversial. At both central and local government levels, compulsory competitive tendering signifies the Government's wish to reduce civil servants' and local government staffs' involvement in direct service provision. Increasingly, central and local government organizations are being cast in the role of "enablers", planners, and regulators. And such services as are directly provided by government are, in the ways that I have described, being organized along lines that will, it is claimed, ensure flexible, devolved management, efficiency, and responsiveness to service-users. Since no structural predetermination is involved in these developments, it remains to be seen how the new public management will develop in the years ahead. As Butcher (1995: 80) put it in his analysis of these matters: "The future is unclear".

The European Union

No description of the institutional framework of public policy would be complete without an account of the European Union (EU), which today has major consequences for British parliamentary sovereignty, government, politics and policy (Nugent 1994a; Peters 1994). The European Community became the European Union in 1993: in what follows I will use the latter term (some writers prefer to use the expression European Community when describing events prior to 1993). In chapter two, I made reference to the European Union in order to illustrate some theoretical complications surrounding the concept of agency: it was argued that in certain fields of action it makes sense to describe the EU as an actor, but that there may be circumstances or fields of action where it is better for analytical purposes to view the European Union as a context of action, or else as a collection of actors who are part of a policy system. In the present chapter, my interest in the European Union is primarily descriptive. To begin with I will look at the structure of the EU, paying particular attention to its main actors and to the ways in which the EU's formal decision-making machinery involves patterned relationships among these actors. Later, I shall focus on contingency and variation within the EU policy process, and refer to the tension that exists between intergovernmental and supranational orientations towards the European Union.

The *European Commission* consists of 20 Commissioners appointed by their respective governments, with the number of Commissioners decided on a formula based on the size of states. All Commission employees, including the Commissioners, must represent the EU rather than their member states; Commission staff are required to formally declare allegiance to the EU. In this respect, the Commission is quite unlike the Council of Ministers (see later) whose members are invariably orientated towards the protection of national interests. The Commission, which has a large administration staff, is divided into sections (the Directorates General) which specialize in particular policy areas such as agriculture, environment, energy, transport, and regional policy. The Commission is a powerful part of the EU, as is the Commission's president (formerly Jacque Delors) who is appointed by the European Council. It should be noted that the Commission has no equivalent in the British system. Peele (1995: 489) observes: "The Commission is, on the one hand, the bureaucracy of the European Community, but it is not a bureaucracy in the sense of a simple administrative organization. It exercises substantial powers of policy initiation and is indeed the permanent government of the Community". Hence although the Commission is often regarded as the civil service of the EU, such a description is not entirely accurate. Nugent (1994b: 127) makes the point that in some key respects the Commission is *more than* a civil service (the Commission proposes EU laws and policies, acts as a watchdog to ensure EU laws are correctly applied in member states, and represents the EU in external relations); he also notes that in some other respects the Commission is *less than* a civil service, for although it undertakes some implementation work, much of the direct administration of EU policies is delegated to the member states. The Commission, should it decide that any of the member states is not correctly applying EU legislation, is empowered to take that member state to the European Court of Justice. The Commission also drafts and, after it is approved, manages the EU budget. And crucially, as I have already indicated, the Commission initiates legislation. That is, the Commission proposes legislation to the Council of Ministers (described below). The Commission is the sole source of legislation proposals to the Council; the Council cannot itself initiate or draft legislation. Moreover, if the Council of Ministers wants to amend a proposal from the Commission, the Commission's agreement to this is required; and if the Commission refuses to give its agreement, the Commission can be overruled by the Council of Ministers only if the latter's vote on the matter is unanimous (Coxall and Robins 1994: 111). Clearly, then, the European Commission is much more than a "civil service", even though it performs some civil service functions as part of its wide-ranging role within the European Union.

The *Council of Ministers*, which meets on a fairly regular basis, has one member from each of the member states; the membership shifts according to the particular policy area under consideration (when EU transport policy is under discussion national transport ministers will attend the Council, national agricultural ministers will attend Council discussion of agricultural policy, and so on). The Council has its own bureaucracy divided into sections that specialize in particular policy areas, and a General Secretariat that currently has some 2,000 staff. The Committee of Permanent Representatives – sometimes identified by its French abbreviation, COREPER – is an especially important branch of the Council's administrative structure. The Committee comprises national ambassadors from the member states, diplomatic advisers and civil servants. Unlike the European Commission which has an EU supranational identity, members of the Council of Ministers are orientated towards the protection of their individual state's interests. Voting mechanisms, which vary according to the kind of issue under deliberation, may be based on unanimity; on simple majority voting; or on qualified majority voting, a system which allocates a certain number of votes to each member state based on a formula that, for example, gives ten votes each to France, Germany, Italy and Britain, five votes to Belgium, and two votes to Luxembourg. Any member state can exercise a veto, though this in practice is not an easy course of action to follow, not least for political reasons (to be seen as isolationist brings its own political costs in EU terms and countries that want to block legislation usually try to arrange blocking coalitions with other member states). The function of the Council of Ministers is to accept, reject or modify legislative proposals sent to it by the Commission, and the Council is the final voice in the legislative process of the European Union (Peele 1995: 490). In formal constitutional terms, the Council of Ministers cannot initiate legislation; its function being to consider proposals initiated and drafted by the Commission, although in reality the Council is often able to exert influence on the kind of proposals sent to it by the Commission (Coxall and Robins 1994: 114). Thus the Council of Ministers is, in effect, the legislature of the European Union (Nugent 1994b: 128) and it is widely regarded as the EU's main decision-making body (Jones and Kavanagh 1994: 251).

As implied in the above, the *European Parliament*, despite its name, has only a very limited and largely consultative legislative role: to all intents and purposes, it is the Council of Ministers that is the EU's legislature. The European Parliament (EP) has over 600 members (MEPs): these are directly elected in each of the member states. I have already described part of the EU legislative process, whereby the Commission sends proposals to the Council of Ministers. The European Parliament is asked to express an opinion on proposals. If the EP approves a proposal, legislation is enacted by the Council; any EP amendments to a proposal are returned to the Commission and then to the Council, which has the final say; EP rejections of a proposal can also be overturned by the Council. Though made more complex by the existence of different voting procedures (absolute majority, unanimity, and qualified majority voting) at the various stags of the process, the basic features of the legislative process are as I have just described. The European Parliament can, it is true, exercise the power of veto, though this can be used with reference only to a limited amount of legislation; and the Parliament has the formal right to dismiss the Commission, although this right has never been exercised. As Coxall and Robins (1994: 115) note, the fact that these are "all or nothing" powers deters from their usage. Exceptionally, the European Parliament does have considerable power in regard to the EU's Annual Budget. The budget process, which is described in detail by Nugent (1994a: 347–60), involves preparation of a draft budget by the Commission; this goes to a first-reading stage in the Council of Ministers. The budget then goes for its first reading in the European Parliament, after which it is returned to the Council for the Council's second-reading. Finally, it is submitted to the European Parliament for a second reading, and here the EP may decide to reject the budget. This is unlikely in practice because at the previous stages there will have been opportunity for the various parties to negotiate and amend the draft budget. There is as yet no formal mechanism to handle Parliamentary rejection of the budget when it comes to the final stage of the process (second-reading in the EP). On the rare occasions that this happens, the matter is settled through further negotiation amongst the various parties. Aside from the Annual Budget, however, the EP has relatively little power within the European Union. This is not to say that the EP is entirely without ability to influence legislation. Some EP amendments to legislation are accepted by Council and by the Commission; and the EP is sometimes able to exert influence through informal contacts with the Commission and the Council. Nevertheless, it will be clear from my earlier description of the legislative process that the EP's power to affect legislation is limited. As Coxall and Robins (1994: 115) put it, there are areas of European Union action where the EP has no right to be consulted, and where it does have the right to be consulted, its approval is not required. Commentators have pointed out that, unlike members of the Commission and of the Council of Ministers, members of the European Parliament are directly elected, and some critics have argued that to enhance democracy at the European Union level it will in future be necessary to enhance the capacity of the EP to influence the legislative process. However, any future moves to strengthen the European Parliament's role in legislation would be highly controversial: any such move would be seen by some national governments as a further erosion of national sovereignty and as a further step towards a supranational and federal conception of Europe (Nugent 1994b: 130).

The *European Court of Justice* comprises a judge from each member state, together with a supporting administrative apparatus. The main function of the European Court of Justice (ECJ) is to interpret European Union law and enforce its consistent application within the member states. The Court is the highest judicial authority in respect of EU law (Nugent 1994b: 129) and there is no appeal against ECJ judgments. Cases are referred to the ECJ by a variety of routes: judges in national courts of law can refer cases, and cases are also referred by the Commission. The ECJ has the power to impose fines on member states, and to determine the legality or otherwise of actions taken by the Commission and by the Council of Ministers. European Union law is superior to national law in the sense that EU law applies in national courts, and if there is any conflict between national law and European law it is the ECJ that adjudicates. There can be no doubt that the ECJ exercises considerable power, although it should be remembered that the role of the ECJ only applies to policy areas (such as trade, agriculture, and product standards) where there is a framework of laws: some EU policy areas (for example health, education) are transacted not in terms of a set of EU laws, but through inter-governmental cooperation (Nugent 1994b: 132).

The *European Council* meets twice a year (the so-called six-monthly "summits"). Though not at the heart of the more detailed European Union decision-making process in the way that the Commission and the Council of Ministers are, it is nevertheless an influential actor. The seniority of its membership is a factor here: the members are the Heads of Governments, Foreign Ministers, together with the President and Vice-President of the Commission. At its six-monthly "summits" the European Council engages in a general overview of European Union affairs, though particular problems and issues also find their way on to the Council's agenda. The European Council often takes wide-ranging political decisions to do with the general direction of EU policy, and also to do with institutional reforms. Any such decisions, however, are political, not legal decisions: to be given legal effect, European Council decisions have to go through the previously described legislative process and be formally approved by the Council of Ministers (Nugent 1994b: 128).

Having identified the principal organizational actors in the European Union, there are some other, more general, matters that merit attention. These relate to the policy process. In terms of the dynamics of EU policy-making and implementation, the European Union is a complex political system (Peters 1994). In the EU system there are, as we have seen, formal rules, procedures, and patterned relationships between the actors (the Commission, the Council of Ministers, etc). There is also a sense in which the EU policy process, whereby policy is shaped (struggled over, negotiated, amended, etc) as it moves between various EU policy actors, illustrates the theoretical observations in chapters one and two concerning the "new" or "emergent" structural properties of social systems, properties which indicate that the system in question is "more than" the sum of its constituent parts. It is this "more than" property of systems which shapes (though does not wholly determine) system "outputs" (or which shapes policy outcomes, in the case of the European Union as a social system). In certain circumstances the EU can be regarded as an actor, but in virtually all circumstances it is also a social system. Provided we recognize the importance of both *system integration* and *social integration* perspectives (Mouzelis 1995) as described in the first chapter, it is appropriate to view the EU as a social system. Also relevant here is the proposition that social systems are not structurally predetermined. Systems are contingently reproduced, or contingently modified or transformed.

Employing the conceptual and methodological tools developed in the earlier chapters, it seems clear that research into the European policy process should not presuppose a mono-causal or uni-linear developmental path in the emergence and subsequent handling of EU policy proposals: policy development and implementation is a relatively variable, "untidy" and contingent process in which agency, structure/social conditions ("the conditions of action") and social chance, each play a part. Although political scientists and policy researchers very rarely articulate underlying theoretical assumptions of the kind just mentioned, a number of political science researchers have produced valuable data and data-interpretations that relate to the theoretical and methodological constructs that I outlined in the earlier chapters. For instance, Bulmer (1993: 353, 356) observes that within the European Union there are policy-specific or issue-specific "governance regimes". That is to say, patterns of governance within the EU may vary from one policy sector to another, or vary according to circumstances and changes in actors' perceptions of circumstances. Such patterns are not part of a predetermined or unified social totality. Their reproduction, or their transformation, relies on their being continuously worked upon by actors, although, as we have seen, social conditions and social chance/contingency also play a part. Research reported by Judge et al (1994) indicates that the EU policy process is highly contingent and variable across time-space, and much also depends on the nature of the policy issue. For instance, which EU actors have most influence on policy, is itself a variable factor. Judge et al examined intra-EU negotiations and interactions in such areas as research and technological development policy (38–41) and environmental policy (32–38), and under the broad heading of environmental policy the authors referred to case studies of the European Environment Agency, to biotechnology policy, and to policy for municipal waste water treatment. The authors were particularly interested in exploring the ways in which the European Parliament appears to be a weak actor in some policy areas and a fairly influential actors in others. Without going into detail here, the author's conclusion (41) is worth noting. "From the case studies it is apparent that the EP has been able to exert influence within the areas of environmental policy and technological development. It is also clear that *within* these areas influence is variable and contingent". As already noted, an important aspect of the contingency that is associated with the European Union policy process is the relationally constructed and in some sense "emergent" nature of EU policy involving interaction between the Commission, the Council of Ministers, the European Parliament, and the European Council, not to mention interactions among sub-groups. In effect, the EU policy process involves negotiation and exchange among a multiplicity of policy actors. It is also, incidentally, precisely these features which led Nugent (1994b: 130) to suggest that the EU policy process is inefficient. The process is, he suggests, "protracted, cumbersome, and very susceptible to the necessity of compromise".

Another dimension of variation in the EU policy process relates to intergovernmental and supranational orientations towards the European Union. Coxall and Robins (1994: 121) note that the EU is increasingly a supranational concept, whereas the British government has preferred intergovernmental cooperation as a basis for greater European unity. The latter orientation is described by Salmon (1995: 189): "Intergovernmentalism is a mode of action which preserves the authority of the member states by providing each with the right to say no and stop a measure of which they disapprove, and where agreement is consensual or non-existent". Another writer, Nugent (1994b: 132) defines these orientations as follows: an *intergovernmental* orientation implies that "no member state is obliged to do anything against its will and policy activity is focused primarily on encouraging exchanges of information, facilitating liaison, and generally promoting co-operation", whereas a *supranational* orientation is such that "the status of decisions amount not just to understandings which it is hoped the Member States will act upon, but laws which they are obliged to apply and uphold". Supranationalism, then, involves transfer of national sovereignty to a supranational actor (here the European Union) which is thereby empowered to make decisions "on behalf of" its constituent member states. While the Commission is, so to speak, more supranational than the Council of Ministers, there is no doubt that the European Union as a whole is moving towards a supranational orientation (an orientation sometimes referred to as a federalist conception of Europe). This statement, however, requires qualification if we are to do justice to the different forms of variation that are to be found within the EU policy process. The status of EU involvement in member states' policy activities varies according to the policy area in question. In some policy areas (notably agriculture, and trade) the EU's involvement is supranational (the style of involvement is formal, regulatory, and legally binding) (Nugent 1994b: 132). In other areas (ibid.), such as education, health, and law and order, EU involvement in nation states' policy affairs is intergovernmental (that is, the EU's involvement is "loose", informal, and voluntaristic). There is, as I observed earlier, tension between intergovernmental and supranational orientations, and some national governments, Britain in particular, have adopted a rather hostile stance towards supranational conceptions of the European Union. The EU principle of "subsidiarity" – the idea that EU policy decisions should be made at the centre but that decisions concerning how the policies are to be implemented should be made at national or subnational (for example, regional) levels of governance – is an attempt to reconcile the very real differences of viewpoint associated with intergovernmental and supranational political perspectives (Pilkington 1995: 4). Whether and how these political differences can in the long term be reconciled, particularly in view of the fact that the number of states gaining entry to the EU is likely to increase and this may complicate the intergovernmental/supranational debate, is not something that can at present be reliably predicted.

The State and Public Policy

In the second chapter I referred to sociological arguments that suggest the state is not an actor; it is not an entity that has the means of formulating and of acting upon decisions. I also noted that this is not, of course, to say that the machinery of the state is unimportant in the policy process. Giddens (1989a: 301) defines the state in these terms: "A state exists where there is a political apparatus (governmental institutions, such as a court, parliament or congress, plus civil-service officials), ruling over a given territory, whose authority is backed by a legal system and by the capacity to use force to implement its policies". The point that I want to emphasize here is that there are differing theoretical conceptions of the state. Below, I will briefly outline some of the main conventional theories of the state (these are theories which figure in numerous political science texts, and also in sociological writing); this is followed by a review of a rather less well-known body of sociological work that involves an attempt to formulate post-Foucauldian sociological understandings of the state and governance processes.

Conventional theories of the state

There is an extensive introductory political science literature on theories of the state and the relation of these theories to conceptions of the policy process. Particularly useful accounts are to be found in Adams (1993), Dunleavy and O'Leary (1987), Eccleshall et al (1994), Schwarzmantel (1994), and Vincent (1992). The most widely employed theories of the state in post-war social science have been pluralism, elite theory, corporatism, and Marxism. My purpose here is not to enter into discussion of the varieties of each of these theories, but simply to provide a brief overview of them. Though these are theories of the state, it will emerge in what follows that there is a wider sense in which they are also theories of society.

Viewed in historical perspective, *pluralism* has sometimes been associated with the writings of Alexis de Tocqueville (1805–1859), in particular his political treatise entitled "Democracy in America". Tocqueville was struck by the plurality of organizations (organized groups, voluntary associations, civic bodies, etc) in nineteenth century America. He argued that participation in the groups and associations of civil society provides citizens with an experience of politics and citizen participation; gives expression to competing interests; helps ensure a plurality of power sources, which act as a counter against any tendencies towards the centralization of power in the state; and by giving voice to majority but also minority interests, the existence of multiple associations and groups helps to avoid a "tyranny of the majority". As far as possible in social science we should try to distinguish value statements which are primarily intended to be "ought" statements, from "is" statements which claim to describe the world as it is. The basic assumption of pluralism is that power does in fact tend to be spread fairly widely across society, rather than concentrated in the state or in one or two dominant interest groups. In this view, power is relatively diffuse, fragmented, and widespread: no one group or entity, not even the state, is wholly dominant and no group is wholly powerless. One of the most widely cited pieces of research in the pluralist tradition is Dahl's (1961) *Who Governs?*, a study of politics and policy in an American town called New Haven. Dahl's conclusion in regard to, for example, education and urban redevelopment policies was that no single group was wholly dominant in the policy process. Different groups were dominant on different occasions or in relation to particular issues, and shifting coalitions together with changing patterns of inter-group relations affected policy outcomes in New Haven. Many pluralists believe that findings such as Dahl's are reflections of pluralism in the wider society. Some pluralists regard the state as a relatively neutral mediator, a kind of referee among competing interest groups, while other pluralists, such as Dahl, see the state (or the government) not so much as a neutral arbiter but more as one actor in a network of interacting actors each pursuing their own objectives and none of whom (not even the government) has complete dominance or, at least, not lasting dominance. Notice that pluralists do not claim that power is always equally distributed, though it is claimed that there is a tendency for power to be spread fairly widely among different groups, and that no group is always dominant or always wholly powerless. There is also present in pluralist thinking a relatively processual conception of power in so far as pluralists believe that power can and very often does shift from one group to another. In terms of the policy process, pluralist theorists do not see the state as all-powerful: power is dispersed, though not necessarily equally so, across a range of interest groups and pressure groups (voluntary bodies, trades unions, employers' federations, professional associations, etc) and state actors negotiate with these groups in order to gain their support and cooperation in the development and implementation of policies. It should also be noted that although pluralists hold the view that within a society there are likely to be a plurality of cultural beliefs, values and interests, it is assumed that there is, nevertheless, usually sufficient overall commonality of values, purposes, and interests to hold the society together.

Elite theory, which is sometimes referred to as neo-pluralist theory, rests on a view that power is held by a relatively small number of interest groups, that is, by fewer groups than pluralists suppose. Elite theorists also regard the groups in question as being relatively highly integrated. Clegg (1989: 9) comments: "It is not that pluralists deny the existence of elites: they simply see them as more dispersed, more specialized and less co-ordinated than would elite theorists." The classical theorists of elitism, such as Mosca and Pareto, argued that in all societies there is a fundamental division between *elite* and *mass*: the elite possess some characteristic or resource – such as military skills, leadership qualities, wealth, organizational skills, or powers of political manipulation – which the mass do not possess. Marxists believe society is dominated by an elite (for Marxists this is the capitalist class), a dominant strata whose power stems from the economic structure of society. However, elite theorists, although they see the division of society into dominant and subordinate groups as something that is inevitable in all kinds of society, take the view that elites' power can stem from various non-economic factors of the kind to which I have just referred. It is instructive to compare elite theories not only with Marxism, but with other theories of the state. The differences, briefly referred to above, between classical elite theories and pluralist theories, are highlighted by Schwarzmantel (1994: 69).

> Elite theory emphasizes the single versus the many: the co-ordinated and integrated elite versus the passive, fragmented and disorganized mass. Pluralism, by contrast, is a theory of diversity and the role of the many, who organize in groups and associations to influence the power-holders and to compete for power. In contrast to the pluralist picture of dispersion and diffusion of power, and the related concept of multiple sources of power, the elitist hypothesis is one of power concentration, of a single power elite that dominates a mass.

More recent theories of elitism are concerned with the relation of elitism to democracy. The existence of elites might seem to pose a threat to democracy. However, Schumpeter (1965) in his conception of "democratic elitism" takes a different view; the existence of elites does not threaten democracy so long as there are a number of competing elites, and providing the people have the opportunity to choose between those elites at election time. C Wright Mills (1956) in *The Power Elite* took another line. Mills, like others in the radical tradition of writers on elitism, argued that those at the top of the economic, political, and military institutional hierarchies constitute a relatively homogeneous power elite that takes decisions of national importance, and that this is anti-democratic. It need hardly be said that the debates set in train by

Schumpeter and by Mills are far from resolved. The wider point for emphasis here, however, has already been touched upon. That is, it was mentioned earlier that elite theory and pluralism hold in common a view that the power base of dominant groups might be rooted in one or more of a range of possible economic or non-economic sources; whereas Marxists argue that the power of the dominant group is directly or indirectly the product of a "deep power structure", the source of which lies within the economic system.

Marxism, and here I am referring to classical Marxism, invokes a model of capitalist society that presupposes a basic division between a substructure and a superstructure. The substructure is the economic base of society: this consists of the means of production (land, tools, machinery, etc); the modes of production (for example, agriculture, or cottage industry or, with the arrival of the Industrial Revolution, the factory system); and the relations of production (in industrial society based on the factory system, the relations of production are capitalist-worker relations). The superstructure consists of the state, including the welfare state, culture, religion, the family as a social institutions, mass media, education, the law, and various other social institutions. It has been claimed that Marx was a crude economic determinist; that he believed that what he regarded as the economic base of society (the substructure) determines the superstructure. More recent versions of Marxism rest on the idea that the superstructure has "relative autonomy" from the substructure, although the substructure (economy) is seen as determining the superstructure "in the last instance". Class ownership or control of the means of production, and the relations of production, are in Marxism regarded as key factors in the constitution of the state as an instrument of class domination: the state and state policies function to allow the capitalist class to exploit and dominate the working class. The notion that the state functions to reproduce "the interests of capitalism" is, as I have just noted, underpinned by the idea that the economic base of society is ultimately determinant. It is argued that while the state may have temporary "relative autonomy" from the economic base, economic production is determinant in the end. Thus, for Marx, "the parliamentary state is . . . a class state which perpetuates the interests of the dominant, economically defined, class" (Judge 1993: 60). Marxist theory has been widely criticized. Judge (65) refers to some of the main features of "post-Marxist" conceptions of the state: "first, the state does not function unambiguously in the interests of a single class; second, it is not a centralized-unified actor; thirdly, there can be no satisfactory general analysis of the capitalist state". These features of post-Marxist theories of the state are, it is worth noting, broadly compatible with the anti-reductionist and non-reified postulates in chapters one and two; they also have a certain amount of affinity with post-Foucauldian conceptions of governance, which are discussed later in the chapter. Theories which suppose that the state functions on behalf of "the interests of capitalism", are reductionist. Revised Marxist theory suggests that the state – even if it does not at every moment perform the function of reproducing capitalism – does so in the long term ("in the last instance"). This, however, does not remove the inherent reductionism that lies at the heart of Marxist conceptions of the state and public policy. As M J Smith (1993: 162) rightly observes: "the impact . . . of variables on policy means that the policy process is not always going to suit the interests of capitalism even in the long term". It is true that modern governments want, among other things, a healthy economy, and that this predisposes state actors to favour policies that seem likely to preserve or stimulate economic growth. But any such predispositions are contingently sustained, or not sustained as the case may be: they are not necessary effects of the social totality or the playing out of some "deep" structural script.

The final conventional theory of the state that I want to consider here, is *corporatism*. Put at its simplest, corporatism describes a social system that is jointly ruled by the state and by large corporate groups. The groups in question are usually representatives of labour interests and employer interests, though other organizations (such as professional associations, or voluntary bodies) may also be part of corporate arrangements. Put another way, a corporatist state is one where a small number of large organized interest groups are incorporated into state policy-making. This is not the same scenario as elitism. Under elitism, groups may exercise power *per se* rather than, as happens in a corporatist arrangement, in conjunction with government. As society becomes more complex and differentiated and as power becomes dispersed across civil society rather than concentrated in the state, states (or governments, as I would prefer to say) increasingly have to enter into bargaining and negotiation arrangements with non-state groups: incorporating large and influential groups into state policy-making is, it has been argued, a good way for the government to consult on complex issues of policy and a good way to pave the way both for the introduction of new policies and for policy-implementation. One aspect of this is that corporate associations, in exchange for resources from the state and joint involvement in the policy process, agree to exercise control over their members.

Some corporatist states have been dictatorships (included here are former regimes in Portugal, and the regimes of Fascist Italy and Nazi Germany) but there is, of course, a distinction between these examples of authoritarian "state corporatism" and the "societal corporatism" that some writers claim is to be found in Western Europe and elsewhere. In a Western European context some have argued that corporatist arrangements increase the power of the state and make for a strong state; an opposing view is that corporatism is an indication of a weak state that has been colonized by powerful interests. It has been said that corporatism existed in Britain in the mid-1970s when the Labour Government formulated policy with the trades unions and the Confederation of British Industry (CBI) so as to construct a "social contract" whereby the trades unions agreed to restrain wage demands, in return for which the government initiated "egalitarian" legislation on employment and welfare. While corporatist tendencies can be found, these should not be exaggerated. Johnson (1991) doubts if corporatism exists to any great extent in the West and he argues (223) that there was no corporatism in Britain in the 1970s: the reality was that the trades unions were divided among themselves, as were the employers, and in this situation the government was unable to "compel" support from the Trades Union Congress (TUC) and from the CBI. In the early 1970s the Conservative Government led by Edward Heath had also tried to involve trade unions and employers' associations in policy formulation but nothing like a corporatist state emerged from this, in part because the unions were unable to control their members in regard to strikes and wage demands. It has, however, been claimed that corporatism exists at the level of local government: this is said to centre mainly on close connections between local authorities and local business interests, and is assumed to have increased in recent years as the public/ private sector distinction becomes increasingly blurred as part of the idea of public/private partnership in urban redevelopment programmes. Stoker (1991) found very little evidence to support such claims. He pointed to the increasing diversity of society; and in the 1980s the emergence at the local level of a variety of proactive and assertive lobby groups that press demands to do with women's issues, anti-racism, energy and pollution, animal rights, sexual orientation, homelessness, and other matters (121–39). It is therefore not accurate to say that modern local authorities typically have "corporatist" arrangements with one or two large local businesses or with business pressure groups: rather, in the increasingly socially diverse and politicized climate of the 1980s and 1990s, local authorities are having to relate to a wide spectrum of groups. This has, it may be noted, been reinforced by the new public management described earlier. One of the keynotes of the "excellence" and "beyond excellence" movements is responsiveness to the self-defined needs and interests of consumers and citizens, including local authority responsiveness to and involvement with groups that give voice to consumer and citizen interests.

A major problem with conventional theories of the state is that all of them – pluralism, elitism, Marxism and corporatism – are *general* theories, each of which is predicated on a single unifying principle of explanation. It is, for theoretical reasons that I discussed at length in the earlier chapters, reductionist to suppose that government, politics and policy can be reduced to a single substantive principle of explanation. There are no good reasons for supposing that policies and practices in the various policy sectors – health, education, agriculture and so on – are predetermined in any singular or universal fashion in the way implied by pluralist, elite, Marxist, and corporatist theories. These theories of the state have a tendency towards ontological inflexibility; they are general theories that make *a priori* assumptions about the nature of the state, civil society, and political and policy dynamics. Such theories oversimplify complex relations among individual and social actors in civil society, as well as relations between those actors and state actors. A more processual, relational approach to the study of the state and policy is afforded by post-Foucauldian sociology which offers a useful analytical entry point in regard to investigation of the blurring of the state/civil society distinction and also in regard to the idea of contingency in the policy process.

A post-Foucauldian sociology of governance

In the disciplines of political science and public policy there have recently been attempts to develop a theoretically and empirically formulated conception of *governance*. Governance may be defined as the management of networks, but more in the sense of a negotiable and interactive process of "steering" than of top-down management control exercised from a central position (Kickert 1993: 193; Amin and Thrift 1995: 50, 54). Kickert's (1993: 191–92) observations on governance and public policy are worthy of note:

> Public management is mainly the governance of complex networks of many different participants, such as governmental organizations, political and social groups, institutions, private and business organizations, etc . . . there is no single monolithic actor but many various actors all of which have their own interests, goals and positions. None of the actors is dominant, none has the power to unilaterally force others . . . Decision-making is a negotiating process. In this view it is better to use the broader concept "governance" than the concept of "management" which is interpreted more narrowly in business administration.

A number of factors combined in the 1980s to produce a scenario conducive to the emergence of the idea of governance. These included a general climate of public, political and academic questioning of the legitimacy of the state; the increasing interest in new social movements and in "the associational networks of civil society" (Waltzer 1992: 99); and a growing awareness among public administration academics of the limitations of conventional forms of government in the face of changing socio-economic and political conditions. These factors help to explain why it is that, as I have just indicated, political science approaches to the study of governance are an expanding area of the literature on public policy (Kooiman 1993a, 1993b). Some interesting future developments are likely in this field. However, there is another, more sociological approach to the study of the state and governance, and it is to this that I shall now turn.

There is, it should be noted, a certain amount of similarity between political scientists' interest in governance, and post-Foucauldian sociology of governance. For example, Rose and Miller's (1992: 184) sociological reference to "Loose and flexible linkages . . . made between those who are separated spatially and temporally" could equally well have been written by political scientists such as Kooiman or Kickert. Nevertheless, we must be aware of the implications of taking theoretical statements out of context: the intended meanings of such statements are shaped by the larger theoretical frameworks of which they form a part and there can be no doubt that post-Foucauldian concepts of the state and governance have, as we shall see below, a distinctive style of their own. Two key writers in this field of study are Miller and Rose (1988, 1993: Rose and Miller 1992) and in the following account I shall refer frequently to their work. In so doing my intention is not to seek to replace political science approaches but, rather, to argue for a synthesis of the differing approaches.

The state, it was observed in chapter two, is not a unitary actor nor an integrated social system controlled from some single vantage point or centre, and nor is it an expression of structurally given interests: rather, the state is "a result not of intended action, a realization of some other, real interests, but of complex, contingent, strategic action in constituting networks of power for many diverse but sometimes explicable reasons" (Clegg 1989: 242). Here Clegg is alluding to a Foucauldian view of the state, a view which differs markedly from the conventional theories of the state described earlier (Gane and Johnson 1993: 7). This relates to the concept *power*, which was discussed in chapter two. Miller and Rose derive from Foucault a conception of power that is closer to Machiavelli than to Hobbes: that is, Miller and Rose regard power as a shifting and precariously sustained outcome of networks and alliances and of the operation of discourses, and not an expression of a monolithic or unitary source of power such as "the sovereign", "the state", "the government", or whatever. In Foucault's theoretical scheme, power is an effect of discursive practices (in politics, administration, law, medicine, psychiatry, criminal justice, etc). Contained within these discourses are definitions of the objects or "problems" that are to be the subject of intervention; and discourses also specify solutions or responses (in the form of therapies, guidance, or controls) to those problems. Discourses, it may be noted, are widely disseminated across time-space and Foucault argues that discursive practices are not the intentional effects of the will of any individual actors nor of the state; and nor, Foucault insists, should discourses – whether of government, of administration, or professional discourses – be regarded as expressions of structurally given ("objective") interests.

The idea of self-control and self-regulation, and the related notion of "action at a distance", are of significance. In political science, Kickert (1993: 195) rejects an image of government as a unitary social system controlled from a single centre. Public governance involves actors engaging in what might be called "self-control" and in exerting control or influence on other actors. Kickert argues (ibid.) that "control in a complex network is not something of a 'third' party, an influence from outside and above, but an influence which the actors exert on each other and themselves". In Foucault's scheme this is taken further and also given a special theoretical meaning (Gane and Johnson 1993: 9):

Foucault's conception implies that power cannot be reduced to an act of domination or intervention; rather, the relationship of power peculiar to modern liberal democracies emerged with the shift from divine to popular legitimacy. That is to say, in the modern era the legitimate political power has resided in the obedience of subjects, and it is Foucault's central concern with formation of the obedient subject that explains his focus on the role of discipline (disciplines/knowledges) in his analysis of modernity.

Rose and Miller (1992: 187: Miller and Rose 1993: 89) discuss self-regulation and discourses which lead to factories, government organizations, families, individuals and various other entities engaging in "self-government" (Miller and Rose 1993: 102). For Miller and Rose, self-regulation is bound up with what might be called "action at a distance" (Miller and Rose 1993: 83; Rose and Miller 1992: 180), a term which the authors borrow from Callon (1986), Callon et al (1986), and Callon and Latour (1981) who had employed it in their accounts of the ways in which governments foster the self-organizing capacities of civil society. Take, for instance, health and social care. Here an effect of the spread of expertise and professional discourse has been to promote the idea of self-regulation so that, for example, the home becomes "a machine for constructing hygiene, not coercively, but by inspiring in individuals the wish to be healthy" (Miller and Rose 1988: 177).

In chapter two in the section on actors' forms of thought, I referred to theoretical issues surrounding the idea of language and reality construction. Knowledge, language, and expertise are significant components of governance. Like Foucault, Miller and Rose (1988: 174) emphasize the constitutive role of knowledge, and they note: "for something to be manageable it must first be knowable", and "knowledge is . . . central to government and to the very formation of its objects, for government is a domain of cognition, calculation, experimentation and evaluation" (Rose and Miller 1992: 175). Methodologically speaking, research into governance should therefore include investigation of policy actors' forms of thought, their use of techniques for assessing or evaluating problems or situations, their occupational and professional perspectives, their political values, and so on (Miller and Rose 1992: 183). For Foucault, the topics of social policy – social needs, rights, dependency, human welfare, and more specialized topics such as poverty, homelessness, or child abuse – are not "given" or preconstituted, but rather, are formed by political, professional, and welfare discourses that "construct" their own topics and imbue them with particular meanings. Given the theoretical discussions of language and reality construction in more than one place in the previous chapters, I need not elaborate here the conceptual underpinning for Foucault's and Miller and Rose's position. Langauge is performative (Rose and Miller 1992: 177) and discourses in some sense create their subjects (actors) and their objects (phenomena to be acted upon). The socially and politically constructed nature of the objects of government and policy ("the family", "the economy", and so on) is a factor in the construction not only of the objects but also of ways of acting upon those objects (Rose and Miller 1992: 182, 186); put another way, political and policy discourse constructs an object – crime, marriage, the welfare state, or whatever – in such a way that it can be "governed" (Miller and Rose 1993: 79).

The discussions of social networks, materials, and material diffusion in the first chapter and again in chapter two, are of relevance here. Miller and Rose's work, which, as already noted, draws on Foucault and on Callon and Latour's translation sociology, is of interest to anti-reductionist sociology for the reason that their approach shows an awareness of the analytical significance of the discursive character of actors' perspectives, and an awareness of the operation of governance, languages and discourses across time-space and across social networks (Miller and Rose 1993: 84):

> Persons, organizations, entities and locales which remain differentiated by space, time and formal boundaries can be brought into a loose and approximate, and always mobile and indeterminate alignment.

> Language ... plays a key role in establishing these loosely aligned networks ... It is, in part, through adopting shared vocabularies, theories, and explanations, that loose and flexible associations may be established between agents across time and space – Departments of State, pressure groups, academics, managers, employers ...

Thus, a degree of continuity (a degree of "order") may emerge across the policy domain, or at least across particular policy sectors (housing, social services, health, etc), though any such continuities and alignments are contingent and subject to change. That said, those policy actors who succeed in mobilizing and relating previously separated actors, discourses, resources, and programmes may become powerful (Rose and Miller 1992: 183), although whether they remain so for long is not something that can be guaranteed. Also of interest here is Rose and Miller's (1992) contention that information, especially in the form of written materials (circulars, policy documents, statistics, etc) is compiled, assessed and translated into public policy in part through the establishment of a "network of conduits for the detailed and systematic flow of information" (187); in part via the use of linked "centres of calculation" (185) such as the cabinet, public sector organizations, regional committees, local managers' offices, case conferences, etc; and in part, bearing in mind the previously noted idea of "action at a distance", through the use of various mechanisms by which "authorities can act upon and *enrol* those distant from them in space and time in the pursuit of social, political, or economic objectives" (ibid.).

Before ending this discussion I should like to reiterate and also extend some of the earlier observations concerning the idea that the state and frameworks of governance are contingently reproduced (or contingently modified or transformed) and are also much "looser", more disorganized and more processual than implied by conventional theories of the state. Implicit in some of my earlier remarks is the notion that the networks that constitute the state and public policy are multiple, and they intersect. For example, professional networks and discourses (education or social services, say) relate in various ways – some of which may be conflictual and not all of which will be intended or planned – to other professional networks and discourses (for example psychiatry, or criminal justice) and to various other cultural, political, and administrative discourses. What emerges from these intersections of discourses, and from the discourses themselves, are, very often, contingent and at least partly unplanned outcomes (Miller and Rose 1993: 77, 82) that may be further modified by other dimensions of the governance process. These other dimensions include: the relation of national policy actors to subnational actors (for example, local authorities) or to transnational actors (such as the European Union); and singular events such as a dramatic and unexpected rise in road accidents, or a shift in world commodity prices. Thus, for Foucault and for Miller and Rose and for translation theorists such as Callon and Latour, the policy world is not seen as a structurally given or static entity that is highly integrated: instead, policy domains are seen as contingent, processual and performative outcomes of interactions between actors, institutions, discourses, procedures, conflicts, unplanned events, etc (Miller and Rose 1993: 84). There is no single sovereign source of power; policy is not an unambiguous series of controlled and co-ordinated responses to commands issued from a "centre". And nor, for the reasons just referred to and for wider theoretical reasons discussed in the earlier chapters, should we give credence to reductionist and reified theories that portray the state and policy as an exercise in "social control" on behalf of a set of "real" ("objective") interests (Miller and Rose 1988: 172). Governance, which in post-Foucauldian terms is viewed as a fairly "messy" and uncertain affair, is a complex and shifting nexus of actors, discourses, resources, moral impulses, practical politics, personal ambitions, intra- and inter-professional conflicts, the unintended consequences of programmes, singular happenings, and much else besides. This is a far cry from theories of structural predetermination or historical inevitability; and a far cry also from conventional theories of the state and of public policy.

The post-Foucauldian approach to the study of governance is, as I have indicated, quite unlike the approaches associated with conventional theories of the state such as pluralism, elitism, corporatism, and Marxism. In some respects, the theoretical assumptions and methodology of post-Foucauldians are an improvement on conventional theories. This stems from the former theorists' understandings of contingency, non-unitariness, and the performative and relational features of governance. In comparison, conventional theories of the state seem ontologically rigid and inflexible, this being something that I will return to in the section on policy networks in the next chapter. However, it also has to be said that in the light of the theoretical material introduced in the earlier chapters, post-Foucauldian conceptions of the state and governance are not entirely satisfactory: they tend, on the one hand, to lack an explicit, non-reified conception of agency, and on the other, to neglect what Mouzelis (1991, 1995) describes as system integration. An instance of the neglect of system integration – which refers to the study of institutionalized relations between social institutions and positions/roles – is the tendency to underestimate the significance for the policy process of systemic aspects of the institutional framework of government and politics (such as the organizational structures of central and local government and of the EU as outlined earlier in the chapter). Related to this is an unhelpful tendency to blur the agency/structure distinction, and an unwillingness to employ the micro-macro distinction. These are not arguments for rejecting post-Foucauldian sociology of the state and governance but, rather, reasons for suggesting that the post-Foucauldian approach represented by Miller and Rose be reworked for inclusion in a new synthesis that focuses not only on relational and processual aspects of social life, but on systemic features including relations between social institutions and between roles/positions; and that focuses on micro-macro and agency/structure and social chance, these being important social scientific concepts that I introduced earlier and which it will be necessary to explore further in the next chapter.

CHAPTER FOUR

THE POLICY PROCESS

I intend in this chapter to amplify, with reference to the policy process, part of the earlier material concerned with key theoretical postulates that underpin the new sociology of public policy; these are to do with agency (Archer 1988: ix-x), social chance (Smith 1993), and the micro-macro distinction (Knorr-Cetina 1981: 2; Munch and Smelser 1987; Ritzer 1990). At the beginning of the first chapter I noted that agency/structure refers to *agency* in terms of intentionality and the causal powers of actors (or agents), whereas *structure* is conventionally defined in terms of constraints upon actors. Later, I broadened the definition of structure to include social conditions which may constrain *or* enable actors, and which in any case influence actors in various ways. *Micro-macro*, it was noted, is to do with differences in the units of and scale of analyses concerned with the investigation of varying extensions of time-space. It was observed in chapters one and two that surrounding these postulates are important subsidiary concepts such as time-space, social networks and social systems, materials, and material diffusion; it was also noted that in anti-reductionist sociology these postulates and concepts are deployed in a way that builds upon anti-reductionist and non-reified conceptions of agency, power, interests, emergent structural properties of social systems, and the idea of recursion. In the first part of the present chapter the point will be made that the conception of agency developed throughout this book is not a form of *idealism* – it is not a conception that overbalances towards agency at the expense of structure. This is, as I will demonstrate, bound up with a recognition that policy actors operate in terms of the discourses available to them, and in terms of the conditions of action. Moreover, it is also recognized that actions may have unintended consequences. It will also be noted, with particular reference to the work of Betts (1986) and Smith (1993), that the idea that agency, structure, and social chance may interrelate has implications that have a close bearing on analysis of the policy process. The second part of the chapter explores theoretical, methodological, and policy-related dimensions of macro, mezo, and micro levels of social process: it will be shown that an integrated conception of these levels is an important methodological tool for policy researchers. The third and final section of the chapter builds on the earlier material and demonstrates that policy network analysis has an important part to play in the construction of a contemporary sociology of public policy.

Agency, Structure, and Social Chance

It was observed in the earlier chapters that social ("organizational") actors are no less significant than individual human actors. Indeed, it can be argued that many of the major political decisions affecting society are made by social actors (organizations and committees) in government and elsewhere. Reed (1985: 185) errs in restricting his conception of agency to individual human actors; but providing the following statement is broadened to include social actors, his summary of the tension between constructivist and objectivist theories is instructive. He refers (ibid.) to a

> basic ontological disagreement ... between a "constructivist" and "objectivist" view of social reality. The former maintains that social reality is constituted through the meaningful social interaction engaged in by pro-active human agents. As such, it has to be continually renewed and reaffirmed through human interaction and has no independent ontological status apart from that conveyed through the cognitive process and interpretive practices necessarily engaged in by human agents. Objectivism is founded on the premise that social reality is an objective structural configuration determined by the material conditions in which it develops irrespective and independent of the interventions of human agents. While the latter may engage in cognitive and interpretive processes of various kinds, these only have ontological significance insofar as they directly reflect the objective structures of material processes and relations that determine social interaction.

In effect, Reed is describing a long-standing tension between theoretical conceptions of agency and of structure. A crucial theoretical and methodological consideration, to which I shall now turn, is that in addressing this tension it is necessary to avoid elevating agency to a position of dominance.

Avoiding idealism: discourses, conditions, and unintended consequences

"Different terms are used to refer to the agency versus structure" theoretical debate. Reed, above, refers to objectivist and constructivist views of social reality. Others, such as Larraine (1979: 38), refer to tension between materialist and idealist conceptions: "While materialism makes consciousness a reflection of external reality, idealism makes reality the product of consciousness". I discussed this matter in the first chapter as part of a critique of post-modern theory, and again in the second chapter in the section on actors' forms of thought where it was suggested that the relation of actors' discourses to their social context(s) is dialectical (a two-way relation in which discourses both shape and are shaped by their contexts). Drawing on the material in the first and second chapters, there are a number of reasons

why an anti-reductionist and non-reified sociology, though critical of
objectivist notions that actors' forms of thought and behaviour are
structurally predetermined, cannot legitimately be accused of going to the
other extreme and endorsing subjectivist, voluntaristic or idealist images of
actors as unconstrained agents who shape society without in any way being
shaped by society. Here I would like to draw attention to three reasons why
this is so, these being generally applicable to individual human actors and to
social actors. I shall outline these reasons in purely theoretical terms to begin
with, following which the discussion of these matters will turn more directly
to the policy process.

Firstly, to reject theories that presume policy actors' forms of thought are
structurally predetermined is not, of course, to deny that actors formulate
interests, objectives, and reasons for acting *in terms of the cognitive materials
available to them*. One aspect of this is the availability to actors of empirical
information. Actors, it need hardly be said, do not "know everything" and
some events that influence public policy and its outcomes may occur "behind
the back" of the actor: an actor may be unaware of historical, demographic,
economic and various other factors that impinge upon the situations in which
the actor may be involved (Duster 1981: 113). This is why, among other
reasons, actors may make "many ... judgements ... which turn out to be
wrong, partial, or ill-informed" (Giddens 1989a: 18–19). Empirical information has to be interpreted ("made sense of") in terms of the discourses
available to the actor: these may be "lay" discourses, academic, professional,
religious, political or any other form of or combination of discourses. Actors,
that is, *formulate ideas and purposes in terms of the discourses available to
them* (Hindess 1988: 89). A related point is that knowledge is not always
fully explicitly and discursively held by policy actors. Knowledge may
become tacit, and unreflectively acted upon. Through its institutionalization
and through various processes of socialization, knowledge in occupations,
professions, politics and public administration, or in any other walks of life
may, by virtue of its regular, repeated everyday use, become taken-for-
granted and deeply sedimented in actors' habitualized, routinized forms of
thought and practices (Berger and Luckmann 1972: 36–38; Giddens 1982: 9;
Hindess 1988: 48). Discourses are institutionalized constellations of meanings and practices that, though not every policy actor will necessarily
interpret and "apply" them in exactly the same way, exist *prior* to the actor
who becomes involved in them. This, though, for all the reasons set out in
chapters one and two, does not mean that policy actors' forms of thought are
structurally predetermined, nor does it mean that in those situations where
actors draw upon discourses in habitualized, tacit ways, that this constitutes a
form of "false consciousness" in the sense connoted in reductionist structural
theories such as Marxism. Rather, pervasive discourses are those discourses
that have become contingently institutionalized.

Secondly, in rejecting determinist and structural theories, anti-reductionist
sociology rests on an understanding that social action *is shaped by the*

conditions of action/social conditions in which the actors in question are involved. The concept "conditions of action" was discussed in chapter two at some length and illustrated in policy terms. In that chapter it was observed that actors are influenced, constrained, or enabled by the conditions of action (Betts 1986: 41), or social conditions as Hindess calls them (1986a: 120–21). It was also noted that social conditions are *contingently* produced and contingently reproduced, modified or transformed; they are not necessary effects of the social totality.

Thirdly, there is another sense in which to reject structural theories is not the same thing as endorsing idealist or subjectivist theories of social action. Non-reductionist sociology, in the ways indicated in the two preceding paragraphs, is based on postulates that direct attention to the empirical investigation of actors' formulations, decisions and actions in terms of the knowledge, discourses, and means of action available to actors and in terms of the conditions of action in which the actors are involved. Anti-reductionist sociology is premised on an understanding that actors' "definitions of the situation" are not always successfully imposed upon the social world to become "structure". A reason for this, additional to those already examined, is that actions may have *unintended consequences*. In chapter two in the section on unintended consequences it was observed that this concept has important empirical explanatory uses. Stated in terms of micro-macro, and in terms of Giddens's (1982) theory of agency/structure and structuration, the existence of unintended outcomes and of actors' strategic responses to those outcomes may be regarded as empirically crucial "complicating factors" (ibid. 10) in the dialectics of agency-structure.

The above factors serve to demonstrate that in addressing agency/structure the analyses developed in this and the other chapters avoid idealism/subjectivism and thus avoid, to put it another way, an overemphasis on agency at the expense of structure. The three sets of factors to which I have just referred can be summed up in three short theoretical postulates. Firstly, when actors formulate reasons for action, they do so in terms of the discourses available to them; secondly, social action and its formulation are influenced by the conditions of action/social conditions in which actors are involved; and thirdly, the concept *unintended consequences* refers to circumstances where actors' "definitions of the situation" are not successfully imposed upon the social world.

Agency, structure, and social chance in the policy process: theory and policy illustrations

Betts (1986: 60) distinguishes between "structure", "fate" (or "event causation"), and "agency causation". She writes (ibid.):

if theory tries to take account of the possibility that conscious human decision making sometimes (though not invariably) plays a part in effecting outcomes, we need to separate out three central concepts: the rules and resources potentially available in given contexts (referred to here as "structure"); processes generating outcomes in the absence of conscious decision making (referred to here as "event causation" or "fate"); and conscious human activity ("agency causation").

Betts underplays the significance of social ("organizational") actors, as does Giddens from whom she derives some of her ideas about structure. Also, like Giddens, she has no explicit non-reified conception of agency. Moreover, it can be argued that to define structure exclusively in terms of "rules" and "resources" is unduly restrictive; most sociologists would concur with my earlier suggestion that "structure" be viewed as the conditions of action/social conditions (see chapter two). Nevertheless, her formulation is useful in that it serves to focus attention on the need to avoid either/or theories of "agency versus structure": in her terminology, agency, structure, and "fate" (or social chance) all play a part in human affairs. She rightly argues that none of these elements should be given automatic or *a priori* prominence over the others; the part that each plays in politics and policy is an empirical matter to be determined in each instance, not a matter that can be theoretically predetermined in advance of empirical enquiry.

Another analytically useful formulation is developed by Smith (1993) who argues that contingency ("social chance" in his terminology) should no longer be seen as a residual or unimportant analytical category. He writes approvingly (527) of a recent tendency among sociologists "to replace residual chance by potentially important chance and to perceive chance as an explanatory element that must be interrelated over time with predisposing conditions and intentional models that explore the indeterminate nature of reality". What this means is that in any particular situation it is perfectly possible that agency, structure/social conditions and social chance will *impact one upon the other*. Smith's description of his conception of synchronic and diachronic connections between agency, structure/conditions, and social chance, is worthy of note (ibid. 528):

> sociological models which include chance avoid assumptions of either total chaos or total regularity. Instead, the three main causal elements of "agency", "chance", and "conditions" are placed within a diachronic relationship where agencies, working within the constraints of ... conditions and chance impacts, in turn, modify these circumstances through a combination of intended outcomes and unforeseen chance consequences. Thus, the acceptance of chance as a sociological concept does not deny the significance of either structure or agency. But neither does it marginalize chance to the status of a residual category. Rather it defines social chance in terms of general characteristics that should be included in flexible models of social development.

In the light of Smith's formulation let us now consider some policy illustrations of the theoretical and methodological principle that it is always appropriate in sociological research to look for possible linkages between agency, structure/conditions, and social chance. The first such illustration concerns the politics/administration dichotomy which I discussed in the preceding chapter with reference to parliamentary democracy and the formal constitutional doctrine of ministerial responsibility. Empirically speaking, there are grounds for supposing that in the real world the politics/ administration distinction is a mixture of agency (such as the intentionality of particular politicians and civil servants), conditions (in particular, parliamentary democracy and ministerial responsibility as long-standing constitutional doctrines), and social chance (or what Smith in the above statement referred to as "unforeseen chance consequences"). A measure of support for this interpretation of the politics/administration dichotomy is provided by Lawton and Rose (1991: 12–16) and also by Norton (1982: 90) who observes: "the argument . . . is not necessarily an argument of extremes . . . The extent to which officials will or will not enjoy a certain mastery over their minister's decisions will vary from minister to minister, depending on the minister himself, his permanent secretary and other officials, the ethos of the department . . . and the political conditions then prevailing". Neither Lawton and Rose nor Norton provide any systematic theoretical rationale for their empirical interpretations, but it would appear that their understandings of the dynamics surrounding the politics/administration dichotomy are based on a tacit theoretical assumption that empirical events are shaped by agency, by structure/conditions, and by social chance.

Another illustration may be found in the field of environmental policy, where social conditions (environmental deterioration over a period of many years) and agency (in the form of changed attitudes in favour of protection of the environment) are significant factors in the development of policy. But so too are contingent factors that were neither planned nor intended by those involved with environmental policy. For example, one-off events such as the Chernobyl nuclear disaster that occurred in Soviet Russia in the mid-1980s and which affected many parts of Europe, or the Gulf War of 1990–91 which was accompanied by world-wide media coverage of burning oil wells, sabotaged oil installations and massive coastline pollution, are contingent events ("social chance") that may shape environmental policy by increasing public and political awareness of environmental issues and by engendering pressure for more emphasis on policy designed to protect the environment. Conversely, a massive rise in unemployment might result in increased pressure for economic growth and job creation, even if this might impact adversely on the environment. As these examples show, contingent happenings ("social chance") may combine with social conditions ("structure") and with agency to in some way influence the policy process and policy outcomes.

Wilsford's (1994: 258–62) investigation of the German health care system is an interesting illustration of the linked operation of agency, social conditions/structure, and contingency/social chance. Wilsford describes how in 1989 the federal Ministry of Health initiated health service reforms intended to reduce health costs. It soon became clear, however, that no significant reduction in costs had been achieved. This was largely because the package of reforms that was eventually implemented was much "weaker" than originally intended. The government (a coalition) had to some extent been divided over the reforms from the start, a factor here being that the Free Democrats in the coalition traditionally had close ties with the medical profession and with the pharmaceutical industry (ibid. 260). A consequence of this was that health-interest groups were able to negotiate a "dilution" of the originally intended package of reforms. In Wilsford's words, the reforms "failed" because of the operation of "structural forces" (ibid.). In 1992, however, a new health reform strategy was launched and this had more success than the earlier policy in reducing health costs. This was in large part the outcome of what Wilsford describes as a "conjuncture", that is, the coming together of a number of contingent factors. Firstly, a new health minister who was appointed in 1992 had a more dynamic political style than the former minister and the new minister was, moreover, able to "learn" from the events of the previous two or three years. Secondly, Germany's fiscal crisis had intensified. The world-wide recession, Germany's high wage costs, and various other factors were having damaging economic effects and this led to a wider consensus on the urgent need to reduce social expenditure. Thirdly, it had by 1992 become clear that, following German unification, the cost of integrating the former East Germany's socialized medical system into (West) Germany's health insurance system, was much higher than had been anticipated. This added to the pressure for change. Not only the government but also the opposition Social Democrats now wanted to see significant cost reduction in health care. Finally, the result of the 1990 elections (the first post-unification elections) strengthened the hand of the Christian Democrat-led coalition. This conjuncture of factors enabled the German government in 1992 to implement a new health care strategy designed to reduce costs in hospital care, in drug prescribing, etc. While it is too early to say what the long-term picture will be, the early indications are that the 1992 reforms, which were to a large extent the outcome of a contingent "conjuncture" of factors, will achieve some reduction in German health care costs (262). Wilsford's study of the development of German health policy in the early 1990s reveals the operation of a combination of "*structure*" (the long standing social conditions referred to earlier – such as the close relation between the Free Democrats and medical interest groups – were factors in the failure of the first policy initiative); "*agency*" (the dynamism and strong intent of the new Minister was of considerable importance); and "*social chance*" (the conjuncture of factors described above contributed to the emergence of the second policy initiative).

The above examples serve to empirically illuminate the theoretical understanding that in politics and policy there are good reasons to expect that there will be many situations in which agency, structure/conditions, and social chance interact one upon the other. Hence the crude dichotomy of agency "versus" structure, despite its long-standing existence in the social sciences (particularly in sociology), is a simplistic formulation that should have no part in contemporary social science. A somewhat different but no less crucial analytical matter remains to be discussed: this is taken up in the following pages where it will be observed that as well as building methodologically on the theoretical conception that agency, structure/conditions and social chance each play a part in the policy process, it is also necessary to formulate policy research strategies which recognize that the world of public policy, and the social world in general, should be investigated at macro, mezo, and micro levels of social process.

Macro, Mezo, and Micro

In the first chapter I observed, firstly, that rational choice theory based on methodological individualism fails to focus on the interactional order (face-to-face relationships in micro settings); and secondly, that rational choice theory thereby overlooks the partly *emergent* nature of meanings, practices, and intentions in micro settings. Implicit , however, in the earlier chapters is the argument that micro-sociological approaches, of which symbolic interactionism is probably the better known, are a necessary but not a "sufficient" part of sociological methodology. That is to say, although microsociology is important, it is not of itself a "sufficient" method of analysis (Giddens 1989a: 701):

> Sociologists influenced by symbolic interactionism usually focus on face-to-face interaction in . . . contexts . . . symbolic interactionism yields many insights into the nature of our actions . . . But symbolic interactionism is open to the criticism that it concentrates too much on the small-scale. Symbolic interactionists have always found difficulty in dealing with more large-scale structures and processes.

Most sociologists would concur that the small-scale and the large-scale processes referred to by Giddens are in some way connected, and that therefore it is theoretically and methodologically necessary to link micro-social and macro-social conceptions of social life. Making such links is not the easiest of tasks. For example, Webb (1991) in a paper on public policy and inter-professional and inter-organizational coordination, argues that spanning *micro* (inter-personal) and *mezo* (organizational and inter-organizational) levels of analysis is an unresolved theoretical and methodological problem in social science: he refers to (ibid. 237, original emphasis)

> a . . . problem of theory: the lack of integration between mezo and micro levels of analysis. The public policy literatures operate on the level of

whole organizations, professions and middle range theory. Yet practitioners consistently highlight the level of interpersonal relations when discussing coordination and collaboration. They give pride of place to the micro. What is needed is both theoretical explanation of collaborative behaviour at this level *and a way of spanning the mezo and micro levels of explanation.* The spanning of levels of analysis is a fundamental challenge to social science.

To some extent Webb has a point, although he is open to the criticism that he tends to ignore such progress as has been made in addressing the theoretical and methodological problem to which he refers. In particular, the theoretical materials set out in my earlier chapters go a considerable way towards identifying conceptual and methodological tools for (a) analyzing micro, mezo, and macro as distinct and relatively autonomous levels of social process, while (b) at the same time searching for possible linkages between these levels.

It should be clear from the theoretical discussion in the earlier chapters that the concept *macro* (by which I mean large time-space extensions of actors, materials, and of social systems and networks) is, providing it is employed in a non-reductionist and non-reified manner, an important analytical construct. In discussing the institutional framework of government and politics in the previous chapter, it was observed that the state is a macro concept; and that so also is the constitutional edifice of parliamentary democracy and the politics/administration dichotomy in so far as these constitutional materials are to be found (though not necessarily in the form prescribed by formal constitutional doctrine) in a large number of political and administrative sites spread out across the UK as a whole and, indeed, spread out across sites of politics and policy in many other nation states. These *macro* constitutional materials do not wholly determine practices at micro and mezo levels (to assume they do would be to ignore the relative autonomy of and the distinctive properties of each level): nevertheless, the macro-social order – though not entirely determinant – undoubtedly has some influence upon interpersonal meanings, relations, and practices in micro settings, and upon inter-organizational (mezo) relations. In this example, we are saying that *macro* constitutional materials influence how politicians and civil servants behave in interpersonal situations (a *micro* effect) and also influence how political organizations and policy organizations behave and how they relate to each other (an effect at the *mezo* level). Another illustration of the significance that the macro-social order has for the operation of the policy process at macro, mezo, and micro levels, is provided by the American political system. To engage in analysis of the US political system as a whole, is to engage in macro analysis. The US has a relatively fragmented political system and, with few exceptions, this engenders a fairly fragmented policy process. At the federal level there are many decision-making centres (the President, executive departments, Congress and congressional committees, and various interest groups that play an influential part in the American political system). Additional macro-level sources of fragmentation of the policy process occur in respect of the division of power and influence among Federal and local (state) governments. This multiplicity of decision-making centres means that a large number of actors often become involved in decisions on a single policy issue. Perhaps inevitably, this has implications for (though does not wholly determine) the policy process at "lower" levels of social process. The more general point being made here is that the macro-social order – which in the above examples consists of constitutional arrangements pertaining to the politics/ administration dichotomy, and the structure of national systems of government and administration – is a factor in its own right and is also significant in so far as it tends to have implications for mezo and micro levels of the policy process.

Micro-situational studies, as already noted, have an important part to play in the sociology of public policy. If we wish to avoid what Mouzelis (1991: 138) calls "downward reductionism", which rests on the *a priori* assumption that micro phenomena have no dynamics of their own and can be explained *entirely* in terms of macro phenomena, it is necessary that micro-situational analysis be incorporated into sociological investigation of the policy process. Macro structural theories which portray policy practitioners' forms of thought and practices as pre-given local expressions of a macro social structure or system of government, or of a macro discourse, are rejected by micro-situational empirical researchers who focus on "creativity" and the *emergence* of meanings *during* the course of face-to-face interaction in micro settings. An example of micro-situational research is Sudnow's (1965) study of the "situated" nature of plea-bargaining in the American criminal justice system. In this judicial system plea-bargaining takes place between the prosecuting counsel (the District Attorney), the defence counsel (the Public Defender), and the accused person. Sudnow shows that whether plea-bargaining can produce agreement leading to a plea of guilty to a less serious charge partly hinges on *negotiation* of the concept of "normal crime": "normal" burglaries, for example, involve no use of weapons, little damage to property, theft of only low-priced items, and an "amateur" as opposed to "professional" *modus operandi* in carrying out the offence (ibid. 260). Wootton (1975), in a commentary on Sudnow's data, makes the point that definition of what in any *particular* instance constitutes an actual example of a "normal crime" cannot be determined with reference to general policies or conventions but, rather, has to be situationally negotiated by the participants on each occasion that the question arises. For this reason Wootton (1975: 19) refers to "expressions *whose meaning relies on the context in which they are used* in such a way that attempts to delineate the meaning of words in some more general way are both misleading and incomplete" (emphasis added). Other ethnographic empirical studies have revealed important interactive processes in the "local" construction of meanings and practices in the policy field. For example, Wootton's contention that language, meanings, and practices are "situational" gains a measure of support in Carlen's (1977) detailed investigation of magistrates' courts where she examined interactions between police officers, probation officers, magistrates, solicitors, and social workers. The situated, particularistic ebb and flow of meanings and negotiations between judicial and welfare professionals in Carlen's study has a contextuality and situated significance that it would be difficult to infer from a knowledge of formal law, abstract rules, official conventions, or from an uncontextual general knowledge of the formal professional and occupational functions and tasks of the participants observed in situ by Carlen. In the light of these empirical illustrations and the earlier theoretical material there are good grounds for suggesting that the importance of situational/ microsociological studies in the sociology of public policy lies in their capacity to provide data which, when *placed alongside other types of data*, contribute to a fuller understanding of *which policy materials are idiosyncratic, site-specific, and interactively emergent, and which materials are local variations or local applications of much "larger" general patterns of material that are temporally and spatially dispersed across a large number of policy sites*. Put another way, the micro-situational approach is a *necessary* but not a *sufficient* perspective in the sociology of public policy; for investigating the larger space-time dimensions of public policies and policy mechanisms, other theoretical perspectives and methodologies and other forms of data are required. To attempt to explain the existence and time-space dissemination of these larger (macro) configurations of material in micro-situational (or situationally "emergent") terms, is reductionist (that is, a micro-to-macro form of reductionism which attempts to explain the macro *in terms of* the micro). As we have already seen, however, it is important that we should not abandon one kind of reductionism only to embrace another. As well as avoiding micro-reductionist accounts of the macro it is also necessary to avoid macro-structural reductionist theories (for example, structural-functionalism, Marxism, or radical feminism) that claim to adequately account for both the existence of larger (macro) patterns and their consequences for micro happenings. These theoretical considerations have methodological implications that were touched upon in the earlier remarks, but which I shall highlight in a more explicit way later in the chapter.

As well as the macro and micro dimensions described above, it is also necessary to recognize the significance of the *mezo* (organizational and inter-organizational) level of social process. The notion that the mezo level is no less important than other levels is argued by Reed (1992: 209) in his text on organizations, in which he refers to three levels of analysis: intra-organizational, inter-organizational, and societal. With reference to the joint involvement of health authorities and local authority social services departments in the provision of Community Care, Webb (1991: 232–34) addresses inter-organizational (mezo) relations, his main interest being the theme of inter-organizational and inter-professional co-ordination and barriers to policy coordination (barriers such as vested interests, structural complexity, and divergent professional and organizational cultures). Webb examines three models of coordination. The first of these is imperative or mandated coordination, based on the exercise of authority where a third party (for example, the government) compels interaction among organizations who would otherwise not choose to mutually plan or synchronize their activities. The rational-altruistic model, the second model considered by Webb, assumes a degree of commonality of method and purpose among organizations, and assumes that in some circumstances actors will sacrifice their self-interests for some general interest such as the "public good". The third model, the bargaining exchange model, assumes that sectional interests are normal and expectable, but that organizations in pursuing their self-interests will exchange resources and engage in bargaining which can itself sometimes be a basis for inter-organizational coordination. Each of these models helps us to understand different aspects of mezo-level social interactions. Broadly similar mezo-level policy analyses which, like Webb's, also explore policy coordination themes, are provided by Challis et al (1994), Degeling (1995) and Hudson (1993). Inter-organizational relations are also, it may be noted, bound up with the idea of policy networks. Indeed, political scientists such as M J Smith regard policy network analysis as an exemplar of a mezo-level approach to the study of the policy process (1993: 7, 233); this is taken up in the final section of the chapter which is concerned specifically with policy networks.

Earlier in the chapter, and at some length in the first chapter, it was observed that the micro-social order (the interactional order) has relative autonomy from the macro-social order; that is to say, the micro is not reducible to nor wholly determined by – though invariably is influenced by – the macro-social order. By the same token, the mezo-social order (the organizational and inter-organizational level of social process) and the macro order (phenomena such as social institutions, social materials that extend widely across time-space, large social systems, trans-national relations, etc) have relative autonomy from the micro-social order; the macro and mezo levels exhibit "new" or *emergent* structural properties and therefore although they may to a greater or lesser extent be influenced by the micro-social order they cannot be said to be wholly produced by (determined by) the micro-social order. These matters were examined in the first chapter where it was noted, in contradistinction to the *macro-to-micro* reduction of structural-functionalism and the *micro-to-macro* reduction of rational choice theory, that it is necessary in anti-reductionist sociology to avoid both these forms of reductionism, which Mouzelis (1991: 138) refers to as "downward reductionism" and "upward reductionism". The relative autonomy and distinct properties of the different "layers" of social reality are good reasons for not endorsing the work of those theorists – such as Elias or Foucault – who *collapse* the micro-macro distinction in such a way that the social world appears to be a seamless web of social relations *with no distinction between micro and macro*. Rather, it can be argued that the micro-social and macro-social orders should be analyzed as interpenetrative but empirically distinct entities (Mouzelis 1991, 1995: Layder 1993, 1994). It is not only that their time-frames are different (micro analysis is concerned with face-to-face relations viewed across relatively short time spans, whereas macro analysis may, for example, be concerned with the development of a society or group of societies viewed across a period of decades or even centuries). It is also the case that large-scale (macro) extensions of materials, resource patterns, cultural styles and power distributions of the kind that persist across large social systems and across large time spans, have distinctive properties of their own that are different in kind to those of the micro-interactional order.

It should be emphasized that to point to the *relative autonomy* of differing levels of social reality, this being something to which I will return later, is not, as I have noted, to say that there are no connections between the levels. To the contrary, there is a sense in which an "integration" of micro and macro variables is a routine actors' accomplishment (Cicourel 1980). When, for example, social workers in their everyday practice in *micro* situations make assessments of their clients' problems, formulate plans of action, write reports, etc, the social workers' forms of thought and practices to a greater or lesser extent embody *macro* cultural materials (cultural meanings and assumptions concerning "family life", child-rearing practices, parental responsibilities, etc). Routine cognitive and practical integration of micro and macro variables also occurs in social science. Sometimes this is done tacitly. A mundane example of this is an observer's or researcher's description of a person walking into a bank and cashing a cheque. The researcher's description of this commonplace micro activity is a description that implicitly invokes macro assumptions; the researcher in his or her account is describing a micro activity (the exchange of money in return for a slip of paper) that would seem bizarre unless the researcher tacitly assumes (s)he and the reader both share a general background ("cultural") knowledge of the workings of the banking system, which is a macro phenomenon. This illustration makes the more general point that agents engaged in routine activities in local sites do not "re-invent the wheel each time": macroscopic (trans-situational) materials such as general cultural meanings are already "in" routine micro happenings. The point of these observations is that the *unavoidable* invoking of assumptions about (the existence of) macroscopic variables in sociological descriptions and interpretations of micro data pertaining to cognitions and practices in local sites should, instead of remaining hidden or latent, be made fully explicit and open to analytical empirical scrutiny in explicitly anti-reductionist terms, as also should the invoking of micro referents in the interpretation and analysis of macroscopic data.

So far I have demonstrated that, on the one hand, the micro-situational perspective is a necessary part of social research but, on the other, it is not a perspective that, as Knorr-Cetina (1981: 28) puts it, can portray non-reductively the *interconnections* between spatially segregated events and the *linkages* between micro settings. Therefore, *a multi-level research strategy is required for investigating the ways in which policy materials are empirically manifest at different levels of social process.* An example of a methodologically multi-layered approach is Duster's study of American medical screening programmes for inherited disorders. Duster's (1981: 133) research objective was to examine empirically the ways in which *the phenomenon under investigation is manifest at different levels of social process.*

> Three levels of entry are (1) direct observation of behaviour in the local setting in which it routinely occurs, the grounding for the "micro" base of the study; (2) observation and analysis of the administrative, bureaucratic, or organizational unit(s) that are interposed between the local scene, and (3) the "macro" trends, rates, or perhaps law, or federal social policy development.

Duster's approach serves to illustrate the more general methodological principle that micro-situational method is appropriate for investigating the social construction and emergence of at least some aspects of "new" policy materials, and for investigating local applications and modifications of, or local resistance against, existing trans-situational materials. But micro sociology is *not* equipped to investigate the mezo or macro levels of the policy process. Let me explain in a little more detail why this is so.

Micro sociology employs such methods as participant observation and other techniques geared to the study of meanings, practices and interpersonal ("face-to-face") relations in small scale settings (for example, a study of interviews between Social Security officials and claimants; direct observation of committees or staff meetings; or, say, investigation of patterns of meanings, intentionalities and interaction in small groups of civil servants studied in a number of locations across a period of some weeks). Macro sociology, in contrast, deals with spatially and temporally much larger units of analysis and therefore macro sociology builds up its empirical data through the use of such techniques as large scale social surveys designed to produce quantifiable data; analysis of existing ("secondary") statistical data pertaining to large social systems or to large configurations of materials (such as cultural beliefs) that extend far across time and space; and analysis of historical or documentary data. These methodological factors, which relate to the theoretical ideas discussed in chapters one and two, have a bearing not only on micro-macro but also, as I briefly noted earlier, on the question of time-space linkages. That is to say, micro-situational research, though an important element in sociological enquiry, is generally not involved in producing data explicitly designed to "address the *interrelation* between situated social events" (Knorr-Cetina 1981: 28). Micro sociology is neither theoretically or methodologically equipped to analyse the inter-situational connections to which Knorr-Cetina refers. This is acknowledged by a number of micro theorists including Charon (1995: 167), himself an enthusiastic advocate of micro sociology: "Symbolic interactionists recognize . . . society

... but they are not able to give this ... its due, simply because the focus is on interaction". Such acknowledgements of the limitations of micro sociology and symbolic interactionism, however, tend to lack substance when in the next breath, like many other symbolic interactionists, Charon claims that "Society ... is ... *individuals in interaction*" (ibid., original emphasis). Here Charon jumps levels of analysis and he goes on to claim that the terms "dyad", "group", "organization", and "society" each refer to interacting individuals and that "therefore" these terms can be used "interchangeably" (ibid.). If anything, this illegitimate jumping of levels of analysis – which results in a *collapsing* of the macro (and mezo) into the micro and a collapsing of the distinction between these levels – reinforces the point that micro sociology, though a necessary element in sociological methodology, is neither theoretically or methodologically equipped for macro social analysis.

What, therefore, is required in the new sociology of public policy is an *integrated multi-level theoretical and methodological approach* that is concerned with: the study of intra-situational *micro* processes and happenings in local policy sites (for example, in local authority social services departments); *inter*-situational and inter-organizational (*mezo*) processes in policy sectors (social services, in this instance) viewed, usually, across a relatively short time frame that, however, is likely to be larger than in the case of micro analysis; and a *macro* focus on, in the present example, macro-social conditions which include the history and recent development of welfare politics and the welfare state viewed in terms of a national and perhaps trans-national time-space frame of reference. As observed earlier, it is important to treat these as distinct and *relatively autonomous* levels of the policy process, and to avoid reductionist theories which attempt to explain the micro *in terms of* the macro, the macro in terms of the micro, the mezo in terms of the macro, and so on. None of these levels wholly determines (though may have some effects upon) the other levels, and to this extent each level should be studied in its own right: this means that policy analysis should include exploration of the ways in which macro phenomena are shaped *by other macro phenomena*, and in which mezo phenomena (for example inter-organizational relations) are shaped at the mezo level by other mezo phenomena; and it is also necessary to explore the ways in which micro happenings are influenced by other micro-level happenings, that is, by ongoing relations and events within the micro locale in question or in other relevant micro locales. At the same time it is also necessary to recognize that, as observed earlier, there are nearly always at least some contingently produced and contingently sustained linkages between micro, mezo, and macro levels – these levels are relatively but not *absolutely* autonomous of each other – and it is important, methodologically speaking, that the policy researcher should look for any such linkages and be equipped to analyze them using non-reductionist and non-reified analytical tools.

Bolderson (1994: 273), a policy academic, argues that recent policy researchers who explicitly address micro-macro are "pioneering an approach which may herald new directions for the study of the policy process". While there is, as I noted in the introductory chapter, much that sociology can learn from political science, Bolderson's observation does I think point to a need for political science and public policy/policy analysis to look to sociological theory and methodology. Unlike political science, sociology has for some considerable time explicitly addressed micro-macro in theoretical and methodological terms, and although it can hardly be claimed that sociologists have fully resolved every theoretical-methodological problem pertaining to the micro-macro distinction, I have tried to show that there are, nevertheless, invaluable sociological insights that are capable of contributing to political science's growing awareness of the significance of *micro-macro* for the study of the policy process.

Policy Network Analysis

The preceding discussion is in various ways relevant to this final section of the chapter, which is focused on policy network analysis. This is a form of analysis that, as we shall see, has a particularly important part to play in sociological investigation of the policy process. M J Smith (1993: 7, 233) observes that policy network research is conducted at a mezo level of analysis, and while my description of the approach is also mainly at the mezo level it is desirable that future work in this area should complement existing methods of policy network analysis by incorporating data relating to the macro and micro levels of the policy process. Despite the existence of a sociological literature on social networks (see the sections on social networks in chapters one and two), very little sociological work has been undertaken on policy networks. I shall wherever appropriate draw on the sociological ideas that were outlined in the earlier chapters. It is, however, political science that has contributed most to our understanding of policy networks and in what follows I shall refer to the work of political scientists who have been involved in this field of study; prominent among these are Richardson and Jordan (1985), Rhodes (1988, 1990), Marsh and Rhodes (1992a, 1992b) and M J Smith (1993).

In terms of the major theoretical issues examined in chapter two, the policy network approach lends itself to the inclusion of both *systemic* and *relational* components of agency, power, and interests. In regard to the relational dimension, the idea of policy networks has an advantage over the traditional political science approach to the study of "pressure groups". In policy network analysis, state and non-state actors are not assumed to have fixed or structurally "given" interests. Aspects of agency, of power, and of actors' forms of thought and their formulations of their interests are seen as relatively contingent and processual *outcomes* of social relations between, for example, state and non-state actors. Take, for instance, the agricultural policy network. How the Ministry of Agriculture thinks about issues, and what the Ministry will want to do, and what it will be able to do, are matters that are influenced by wider conditions of action (international capital flows, world food prices, and the like) as well as contingent events such as the crisis in 1996 over "Mad Cow Disease", and also, crucially so, by ongoing, institutionalized exchanges and negotiations with other actors within the agricultural policy network (actors such as the National Farmers Union, and the Directorate General VI of the European Commission).

In the last chapter we saw that a problem with conventional theories of the state (theories such as pluralism, elitism, corporatism, and Marxism) is their tendency towards ontological inflexibility. Each of these general theories makes *a priori* assumptions about the nature of the state and of civil society in regard to factors affecting the distribution of power, and in regard to the nature of political and policy dynamics. Such theories, it was suggested in the previous chapter, tend to oversimplify complex relations among individual and social actors in civil society, and relations between those actors and state actors. For example, it could be that the distribution of power in one policy sector or maybe in the handling of a single policy issue is relatively pluralistic, while another policy sector or the handling of another policy issue might be distinctly corporatist, or elitist. Another way of putting this is to say that neither the power of social groups nor of state actors is identical in all policy sectors (agriculture, education, trade policy, consumer policy, etc). Hence the policy network approach, at least in my version of it, makes no *a priori* assumptions about power distributions and policy dynamics in the various policy sectors. In addition, policy network analysis facilitates an ontologically flexible approach to the state/civil society distinction (see the section dealing with this distinction in chapter two). A major theme in contemporary political science and policy analysis is the blurring of the state/ civil society distinction and a growing tendency to reject binary thinking (state/society, plan/market, public/ private). Such blurring, which is a key characteristic of policy networks, is a fairly widespread process that is bound up with social, economic, and political patterns of change. In Britain and elsewhere, specific developments that make it harder to identify the boundaries of state and non-state activities include privatization and closer co-operation between state, private, and voluntary sector actors in the financing, design, and delivery of services; quangos and the "Next Steps" organizations associated with reform of the Civil Service; and the creation of new regulatory bodies (for example, Oftel) that do not sit comfortably with the traditional state/non-state distinction. Moreover, the picture is one of variability: the extent of state/civil society boundary blurring may shift over time, and may also vary from one policy sector (or policy network) to another. This is relevant to the design of empirical studies. That is, we have here yet another example of linkage between theory and methodology; one of the advantages of a processual and anti-reductionist approach to policy network analysis is that it equips the policy researcher with a conception that the state/civil society relation is not structurally predetermined and there is therefore no reason to expect that the relation should be uniform across all policy sectors.

Policy networks may take more than one form. In the first chapter in the section on social networks I drew an analogy between Callon's (1991) sociological distinction between tightly coupled networks and "loose" networks, and Marsh and Rhodes's (1992: 251) political science approach which makes a distinction between two different types of policy network. In *policy communities* (examples widely cited in the political science literature are British health policy, at least until recently, and British agriculture) there tends to be a very small number of actors, with few non-state actors and usually no more than one state actor; a fairly high level of interaction and consensus among the actors; a stable rather than shifting membership; and in terms of mutual resource dependencies, each of the major actors in the network has some power in so far as they have valued resources (technical or professional knowledge, financial resources, legal power, political influence, etc) that they are able to "exchange" with other actors in the network. An *issue network* (examples are American agricultural policy and British industrial policy) is a much less integrated type of policy network. In issue networks there tends to be: a shifting membership; a large number of pressure groups and other actors, including more than one state actor (for example, more than one government department); a politicized policy scenario with little consensus in respect of policy goals and policy instruments; variable quality and generally low quantity of interactions among the actors; and very few mutual resource dependencies. The distinction between policy communities and issue networks is, as I noted in the first chapter, one of degree: we are speaking here of a continuum rather than a sharp dichotomy. And because no structural predetermination is involved, it is necessary to allow for the possibility that policy communities over the course of time may become issue networks, and vice versa.

The coming into being of any particular type of policy network, and its reproduction or change, are relatively contingent matters that involve diachronic and synchronic linkages between agency, structure/conditions, and social chance. In an anti-reductionist sociology of public policy, no substantive general principle of explanation of policy networks is sought. Grand social theories – such as structural-functionalism, rational choice theory, Marxism, feminism, and recent theories of "post-industrial society", "the information society", "post-modern society", "globalization", and so on – tend towards reductionism; each theory in its own way is an attempt to deploy an analytical prime mover that seeks to reduce the complexity of social relations to a single unifying principle of explanation. Of course, it may well be that there are circumstances in which it is legitimate to speak of general social trends (for example, "post-industrialism"): but notice that, firstly, general trends are not necessary effects of the social totality, and secondly, the form and impacts of general trends – because not structurally predetermined – may be variable or uneven. Hence there are no good reasons for supposing that policies and practices in the various policy sectors – health, education, agriculture, trade and industry, foreign policy, urban renewal, and so on – are predetermined in a singular or universal way by, let us say, "post-industrialism" or "globalization", or by any other social phenomenon (Marsh and Rhodes 1992a, 1992b; Wilsford 1994). In other words, government, politics and policy exhibit a great deal more time-space diversity than can adequately be accounted for by reductionist single-order theories. This is noted by, for example, Williams (1994: 56–57) in her apt criticisms of post-Fordist theory of the welfare state.

A similar point is made by M J Smith (1993: 224–5) who observes that it is unhelpful to try to construct a *general* theory of why different types of policy networks exist: instead, it is necessary to account for policy networks – their emergence, mode of operation, and their reproduction or transformation – in terms of empirically and interpretatively "open-ended" investigation of the events and circumstances that influence political and policy development. This does not mean, for reasons that were touched on in theoretical terms in the introductory chapter, that social science cannot legitimately develop any "general" statements at all. For instance, M J Smith (1993), though he offers no explicit and systematic theoretical/methodological framework for addressing macro-mezo linkages, observes that it is possible to develop a few cautious generalizations concerning the emergence of different types of policy networks. He cites empirical evidence which suggests, for example, that policy communities are more likely in a relatively centralized political system (such as the UK) than in a "fragmented" system like the USA (ibid. 138–9, 234), although there are exceptions; for example, US trade policy in the 1950s and 1960s was a highly integrated policy community (ibid. 222) and US agriculture from the 1940s to the 1960s was in most respects a policy community (223). There is also a tendency for policy communities to develop in those policy sectors where the state has a definite policy (224–5) and an interventionist rather than laissez-faire orientation (ibid.), and where the state is reliant on well-resourced non-state actors for policy development and policy implementation (234). Clearly, it is not only large scale macro factors that affect variations in the development of policy networks. For example, issue networks are more likely in highly politicized and "non-technical" policy areas where there is little consensus, or in areas regarded by the government as of secondary importance (for example, policy concerning abortion), or in a new policy area where groups are not yet fully formed and relations between groups are not yet regularized (65–6). Moreover, in the preceding section of the chapter we observed that differing levels of the policy process – micro, mezo and macro – are not embedded in a unified social totality: the levels are relatively autonomous, although there may well be contingently sustained linkages between them. The *relative autonomy* of different levels of social process is a theoretical postulate that facilitates the development of non-reductionist explanations of variations in patterns of governance not only as between policy networks/policy sectors, but also *within* policy sectors. For example, Grant et al (1988) show that although the British industrial policy sector as a whole is a loosely integrated issue network, the sub-sectoral field of industrial policy concerned with the chemicals industry is a highly integrated policy community. Another example of intra-sectoral variation and the relative autonomy of policy levels is provided by M J Smith (1993: 152) who shows that the US coffee production sub-sectoral network is far more tightly integrated than the US trade policy network as a whole.

Earlier, I referred to exchange theory (this was discussed in general theoretical terms in the first chapter) and to the associated notion of mutual resource dependencies. Exchange theory, which tends to be employed extensively by political science writers on policy networks, can explain some instances of social behaviour and interaction among individual actors or among social ("organizational") actors within a policy network. However, I also observed in the first chapter that exchange theory together with rational choice theory has a narrow conception of actors' forms of thought. A similar point is made by Miller (1994) with particular reference to the policy process and policy networks. He refers to individual human actors, but his observations can equally apply to social ("organizational") actors. Miller (ibid. 380) reminds us that exchange theory views actors as rational utility maximizers who exchange resources and rewards (information, status, legitimacy, technical knowhow, etc) and he notes that exchange theory has its uses in so far as it can almost certainly account for *some* interaction. The problem is, however, that exchange theory *per se* is a reductionist attempt to explain *the whole* or most of social interaction in terms of a single principle of explanation, that is, the principle of "rational" utility maximization. Alongside exchange theory what is also required is a phenomenological and social constructivist approach which investigates actors' meanings and intentionalities (ibid.). This requires a research focus on meanings, language, discourses and actors' forms of thought. Miller makes the point that policy actors sometimes subscribe to what might be called altruistic motives and objectives (for example, protection of the ecosystem), and these do not fit easily with a single explanatory principle based on the idea of self-interest maximization. What is needed is a broader, social constructivist approach which does not exclude exchange theory, but which incorporates a much more ontologically "open" frame of reference (ibid.):

Meanings of events (or ideas, individuals, groups or actions) are socially formulated . . . Participants in the policy network interact, and through that process make sense of things, form impressions, and make meaning of their experiences. There is minimal ontological baggage using a phenomenological approach such as social constructivism (Berger and Luckmann 1972). It is not necessary to pre-judge as self-interested participants' intentions, meanings, and values. By moving beyond (but not abandoning) the idea of the self interested individual, a new function of policy networks, the meaning-making function, is evident.

It is not simply that exchange theory and rational choice theory attempt to reduce social interaction to the principle of self-interest maximization in a way that fails to address instances of "altruistic" behaviour. More generally, as I noted in the first chapter with reference to Hindess (1988: 68), rational choice theory and exchange theory fail to appreciate the significance of – and the need to investigate – actors' differential access to discourses, actors' use of a variety of deliberative tools in assessing and acting upon situations, and actors' techniques for turning decisions into actions. It should also be noted that rational choice/exchange theory, as I observed in the first chapter, fails to grasp the significance of the micro-interactional order and, as described earlier in the present chapter, fails to comprehend the part that interpersonal relations play in the social construction of at least some aspects of meanings and practices in local sites.

I suggested earlier that policy network analysis in the form developed within political science chimes with anti-reductionist sociology's approach to the study of public policy, an approach which rejects reductionist single-order theories, including theories of macro-structural predetermination. This is not to say, however, that all political scientists adopt the same approach to policy networks. There is, for example, disagreement over the question of the extent to which policy communities are stable and homogeneous entities. Wright (1996: 49–50) takes the view that all too often in political science the concept policy network refers to an abstraction (a policy sector such as "education"), when the empirical reality is that there is no such thing as "education" policy: instead, he argues, policy formulation and development takes place in *sub-sectors*, for example, higher education policy, further education policy, policy for secondary education, for primary education, and for nursery education. Likewise in regard to "industrial" policy; here, policy is formed in distinct sub-sectors each concerned with a particular industry rather than with "industry" as a whole. The heterogeneity and variability of policy sectors and policy networks is also a theme that concerns Jordan et al (1994) who argue that political science research into agricultural policy-making has tended to assume, wrongly, that there exists a "corporatist" and tightly integrated policy community dominated by the Ministry of Agriculture and the National Farmers Union (NFU). Jordan et al (507) suggest that M J Smith (1993: 103) attributes too much policy dominance to the NFU, and that Smith and others fail to appreciate the sheer empirical variability that characterizes the modern agriculture policy sector. For example, policy on the introduction of land registration forms in 1992 was formulated after discussions with no less than a dozen organizations and groups including, as well as the NFU, the Country Landowners Association, the Tenant Farmers Association, the Royal Institute of Chartered Surveyors, the Institute of Agricultural Secretaries, two groups of consultants, and various other organizations (Jordan et al 1994: 508): this was, in other words, a highly specialized policy community set up for the specific purpose of dealing with a one-off decision-making process (ibid.). Jordan et al argue (509) that there may be several sub-sectoral or even issue-specific policy communities within policy sectors such as health, social services, foreign policy, education, etc. Moreover, partly as a reflection of intra-departmental differences of perspective (512), some sub-sectoral policy communities within a policy sector (for example, agriculture) may be in conflict with each other; and it may be that some actors find themselves members of more than one of these policy communities (510). Jordan et al's (1994) criticisms of M J Smith (1993) are not entirely warranted. Smith (65–66) clearly is aware of sub-sectoral and also issue-based variations of membership of the agricultural policy community; nevertheless, it is true that Smith does not develop this very far and in general he tends to depict the agricultural policy sector in the way that Jordan et al describe. The more general point here, however, is that in employing the concept "policy networks" we should always be aware of the dynamic and variable nature of policy sectors. While there may be occasions when sectoral commonalities and continuities are sufficiently developed to enable us to legitimately speak of the agricultural policy community, the health policy community, and so on, we should also be aware of the possible existence of multiple sub-sectoral policy networks and of issue-specific networks of social relations. This is hardly a startling revelation; in the light of the anti-reductionist theoretical understandings described in chapters one and two, we should not expect to find anything other than that the policy world is a contingently sustained and sometimes empirically messy mixture of spatial and temporal continuities and disconti-nuties.

CHAPTER FIVE

THE NEW SOCIOLOGY OF PUBLIC POLICY

The purposes of this final chapter are to draw together the various theoretical and methodological materials that constitute the new sociology of public policy; to highlight a vital area that will require further development in the future; and to consider possible connections between academic knowledge and the design and implementation of public policy. The chapter is divided into three main sections. The first is a summary of the conceptual content of the new sociology of public policy. The second section of the chapter recognizes that while at the macro level of analysis this book's main emphasis is national governance, and to some extent transnational governance as in the case of the European Union, future work will increasingly need to focus on *post-national* policy dynamics. This is followed by a review of issues centred on the important distinction between a sociology *of* policy, and social science knowledge *for* policy.

Theory and Methodology in the New Sociology of Public Policy: A Summary

In the early chapters I introduced a sociological approach that moves beyond critique of reductionism to formulate a non-reductionist theoretical framework. *Reductionist* theories, it was observed, employ analytical prime movers in an attempt to reduce social life to a single unifying principle of explanation (Lyman and Scott 1970: 16; Hindess 1986a, 1986b, 1988). Examples include theories associated with methodological individualism (such as rational choice theory) and with methodological collectivism (for example, Marxism, and radical feminism), and also theories of "post-Fordism", "post-industrialism", "post-modern society", "globalization", etc. I also noted that *essentialism*, which is closely related to reductionism, presupposes on *a priori* grounds a unity or homogeneity of social phenomena. The phenomena in question might be, for example, the state, the law, culture, social movements, social institutions, or taxonomic collectivities such as "women", "black people", or "the working class".

In order to adequately address these and related conceptual issues it was first of all necessary to look briefly at some metatheoretical considerations. In the introductory chapter I suggested that "grand theories" (which are similar to what post-modernists call "meta-narratives") are inadequate. Structural-functionalism, structuralism, Marxism, feminism, and rational choice theory, are examples of grand theory. I observed that a problem with such theories is that, even though some potentially useful concepts may be extracted from them, they are so general – that is to say, so universal in terms of the range of periods, places, and phenomena that they purport to explain – that they tend to be, as Mouzelis (1995: 34) puts it, either incomplete (holding only in certain conditions not specified by the theory) or trivial. However, *contra* post-modernism, to reject grand theories is not to say that no valid social science generalizations are possible. Substantive generalizations of limited scope are, I suggested, desirable: in any case, a certain amount of generalization – some reliance on assumptions rooted in general categories of knowledge associated with formal and/or informal ("lay") theories – is unavoidable, and it is better that any such generalized assumptions should not be left tacit. The question of generalizations led to a consideration of the distinction between *sensitizing* theory and *substantive* theory: the latter, it was noted, endeavours to explain social happenings, whereas the former – which is the type of theory developed in this book – is a collection of linked concepts (a theoretical framework) that provides us with general ways of thinking about the social world and assists in the formulation of specific substantive theories of a kind that are open to empirical investigation. Sensitizing theories, such as Giddens's structuration theory, may well involve "large" sensitizing generalizations; however this is a legitimate procedure that is, I suggested, entirely different from approaches which lead to the substantive generalizations associated with reductionist grand theories such as Marxism.

The first and second chapters, though primarily theoretical, employed various policy illustrations of the concepts and postulates introduced in those chapters as the conceptual basis for the new sociology of public policy. It was observed that the main underlying concepts of sociology and social science are agency, structure/social conditions, contingency/social chance, and micro-macro: it was shown that the various other concepts associated with anti-reductionist sociology derive from or are in some way relatable to these basic concepts. The first chapter, which touched upon most aspects of the conceptual material that underpins contemporary sociology, began with a critique of the post-modern rejection of social science. It was suggested that while post-modern theory has a few potentially useful ideas (to do with contingency, spatial variation, and anti-essentialism) the post-modern *genre* as a whole is inadequate and self-contradictory. I observed that the post-post-modern thrust of the new sociology of public policy builds upon a relatively eclectic synthesis that employs recent social science concepts, together with reworked versions of concepts drawn from some long-established theoretical traditions.

In order to locate contemporary sociological thought in the context of the recent intellectual history of the discipline, the first chapter looked at structural-functionalism as an influential *macro-to-micro* sociological perspective that has also influenced political science and some other disciplines. The review of the theoretical components of structural-functionalism was used as an opportunity to also introduce some general theoretical themes that have important implications for virtually all of the social sciences, including political science and public policy. These themes are to do with the distinction between *causal analysis* and *functionalist analysis*; *teleology* (the illegitimate attempt to explain the *cause* of a social or cultural item in terms of its effects/consequences); *reification* (an illegitimate form of analysis that attributes agency and causal powers to entities that are not actors); and the need to employ both a figurational or *social integration* approach (the study of agency and of social relations – whether cooperative or conflictual – between actors) and a systemic or *system integration* approach (the study of relations between roles/positions and social institutions). The first chapter also examined a *micro-to-macro* type of theory – rational choice theory – that is based on methodological individualism, and exchange theory. It was noted that although the notions of "rational" utility maximization and utility maximizing social exchange undoubtedly have empirical explanatory value, they cannot account for the whole of social action. (This was also discussed in chapter four with reference to policy networks). Nor can methodological individualism – the notion that "society" is the aggregated outcome of the decisions and actions of countless individuals – account for the emergent structural properties of social systems (the idea that the whole is "more than" the sum of the parts, whether the system in question be a micro, mezo, or macro system). It was also observed that theorists and researchers who employ an individualist perspective cannot adequately grasp the significance of the interactional/micro-situational social order. And of course, by focusing only on individuals, methodological individualism fails to grasp the significance of social ("organizational") actors. To assume that agency can be exercised only by individuals is, as we have seen, profoundly mistaken. Many of the key decisions affecting society are made by social actors, and these are entities whose actions cannot be reduced to the decisions of individuals.

The first chapter also introduced some other concepts and themes. Crucial among these is the anti-reductionist and non-reified definition of the concept *actor* (or agent). An actor is an entity with the means of formulating decisions and, in principle, of acting upon decisions. I have a reason for saying "in principle": whether an actor (an individual or social actor) will be able to implement *all* of the decisions made by that actor is not a constant but is, rather, a variable factor that will to a large extent depend upon the prevailing conditions of action. The concepts of locale and spatial variation, materials and social networks, social systems, and recursion, were introduced and illustrated in policy terms, together with the idea of material diffusion (or transformation) across time-space. The chapter ended with a discussion of the proposition that society is not a unified totality, and with a reaffirmation of the view that society cannot legitimately be reduced to a single general principle of explanation (such as "capitalism", "patriarchy", "the information society", "post-modern society", or whatever).

The second chapter began by demonstrating that while there is room in social science for a wide variety of approaches, a synthetic/integrative approach is legitimate, not least when the approach in question is an ontologically flexible sensitizing framework. This was followed by a review of the case for a broad conception of power that includes both the *systemic* ("power storage") and the *relational* (Foucauldian) faces of power; it was also noted, in regard to power and interests, that most social scientists nowadays reject the notion of "real" (or "objective") interests. In addition, the concept of actor or agent, having been introduced in the first chapter, was re-examined in the light of some complications pertaining to agency; these were illustrated by means of a discussion of agency in relation to the state, policy networks, policy organizations, and transnational policy organizations such as the European Union. The chapter also established the grounds for regarding the following as important analytical tools in the sociology of public policy: actors' forms of thought and a dialectical conception of the relation of discourses to their social contexts; the conditions of action/social conditions; unintended consequences; time-space; network analysis; material diffusion; and Mouzelis's typology of role/positional, dispositional, and situational – interactional dimensions of social action. The chapter ended with a brief account of three social science themes: the state/civil society distinction, postindustrialism, and citizenship.

Chapter three focused primarily on the institutional context of policy. The institutional framework of government and politics – parliamentary democracy, central government, central/local relations, local government, the new public management, and the European Union – was described and analyzed in terms that drew on the theoretical and methodological tools developed in the previous chapters. In particular, the institutional framework was seen as relatively contingent and non-unified, rather than as a necessary effect of, or part of, a unified social totality. As well, the theme "the state and public policy" was examined by means of a discussion of conventional theories of the state and policy (pluralism, elitism, Marxism, and corporatism), and a review of post-Foucauldian conceptions of governance.

The fourth chapter highlighted, with reference to the policy process, the importance of contemporary social sciences' central theoretical and methodological conceptualizations: these are synchronic and diachronic connections between agency, structure/conditions and social chance; and micro, mezo, and macro as relatively autonomous but linked levels of social process. These were amplified and extended with illustrations drawn from politics, government, and various policy sectors. This led to the presentation of a case in favour of an integrated multi-level theoretical and methodological framework for the new sociology of public policy. Finally, it was observed that many of the issues discussed in chapter four and in earlier chapters are encapsulated in policy network analysis, which a number of political scientists regard – with some justification – as a particularly useful analytical tool.

Comparative Analysis and Post-National Analysis

So far I have not discussed comparative public policy (or comparative analysis) which is, as I shall show in the following pages, an important field of study that forms an integral part of the new sociology of public policy. In their text *Comparative Public Policy*, Heidenheimer et al (1990: 3) define their field of study: "Comparative public policy is the study of how, why, and to what effect different governments pursue particular courses of action or inaction". In his account of comparative policy analysis, Harrop's (1992a: 1) opening words are:

> Why has Japan found it easier than the United States to pursue a consistent industrial policy? Why does Britain provide health care collectively whereas France relies on private provision? Why is the United States government unable to ensure the safety of its citizens as they walk the city streets whereas personal safety is not even an issue in Japan?
>
> These are the kinds of questions asked in the study of comparative public policy ... The comparative study of public policy is a relatively new approach in politics.

Harrop regards comparative policy analysis as a recent and highly promising field of political science. Notice, however, that comparative public policy emphasizes the *national* level of government and policy; that is, it compares policy-making and implementation in a number of individual nation-states. The increasing tendency towards transnational policy processes and towards "globalization" (which is discussed later in the chapter) implies that major policy processes operate *across* states, not within states, and that comparing one state with another in the manner of comparative public policy/comparative analysis misses out on the crucial transnational element. Does this mean comparative public policy is redundant? The answer to this must surely be no. As we shall see later, there is no reason to take seriously the more fashionable and exaggerated versions of the globalization thesis. The nation-state "still matters". As Jones (1996: 12) observes: "States ... remain the primary agency for the provision of security against external threats, the major source of protection against domestic disruption and the dominant provider of a range of those welfare functions that require substantial scale for their effective supply". I shall make the point in what follows that comparative analysis can help identify national variations in policy styles and identify the reasons for those variations, and this in turn aids our understanding of the policy process within any particular country. However, as I shall go on to observe later in the chapter, it is clear that transnational and globalization processes are important and they require analysis in ways that cannot rely entirely on the methods and perspectives of comparative public policy. There is therefore much to be said in favour of a broader, synthetic orientation that retains comparative analysis/comparative public policy, but which also employs the methods and perspectives that are currently emerging in the exciting new field of "post-national" policy analysis which abandons crude either/or formulations and instead recognizes that policy dynamics operate at the sub-national, national, and transnational levels of social process (Sibeon 1996). Let us begin, however, with a review of the aims and methodology of comparative public policy.

Comparative public policy

Lane and Ersson (1994b: 45) refer to "the emerging field of comparative public policy". Although interest in comparing systems of government goes back to the time of Aristotle, the systematic comparative study of policy is a fairly recent phenomenon (Heidenheimer et al 1990: 7). Why, however, study comparative public policy? In response to this question, Harrop (1992: 3) writes:

the case is similar to the case for studying any form of politics comparatively: comparison is essential for understanding. "What know they of England", asked Kipling, "who only England know?" By examining policies comparatively, we can discover how countries vary in the policies they adopt, gain insight into why these differences exist, and identify some of the conditions under which policies succeed or fail. Comparative public policy is therefore a source of generalizations about public policy. In turn these are essential for understanding policy in any particular country.

Lane and Ersson (1994a; 1994b: 48) refer to the importance of investigating the extent to which inter-state policy variations reflect differences in systems of government, and/or reflect wider social, cultural, economic, or political differences between societies. The range of relevant variables that have to be taken into account in comparative analysis is very wide indeed and this sometimes leads to methodological problems that require resolution. If, for example, we wish to compare a number of nation states in terms of the percentage of gross domestic product that each spends on social work and the personal social services, it is necessary to recognize that the term "social

work" is itself a variable factor. In the United States and the United
Kingdom, social work has a professional or, at least, a semi-professional
status with university-based training, whereas this is not the case in Spain,
and in the former Soviet Union the notion of social work as understood in,
say, the United Kingdom, simply does not exist (Munday 1989: 8–9). Great
care is required, therefore, to ensure that when engaging in comparative
analysis we are comparing like-with-like.

Feick (1992) refers to differences in political cultures. He describes the
United States in terms of "individualistic and democratic values in the classic
liberal tradition" (ibid. 271), and "a weak-state ideology; politicians and
bureaucrats do not rank high in the esteem of their fellow citizens" (ibid.). On
the other hand (272)

> the Swedish political and administrative culture is characterized by
> attributes almost opposite of America. The democratic credo is commun-
> ity-orientated. The state, its administrations and actors enjoy a rather high
> degree of trust and esteem. We encounter a strong state ideology and a
> certain deference towards political and administrative authorities.

The British case is regarded by Feick as a hybrid that contains elements of
both the American and Swedish political cultures (273). It is often claimed
that the United States is a weak and fragmented state – this being related to
the US constitutional emphasis on a strongly marked separation of powers as
between the executive, legislature, and judiciary, together with the distinction
between federal and state governments – and that this fragmentation of the
political system makes for fragmented policy implementation with a large
number of decision points (Ikenberry et al 1988: 11). This is perhaps true to
some extent, as is the view that the UK has a relatively centralized and
integrated policy process. However, crude generalizations are wide of the
mark. It should not automatically be assumed that there are national policy
styles that override sectoral differences; for instance, in the case of research
concerned with industrial policy it is clear that the sectoral approach as a way
of comparing policy styles has challenged the "strong state versus weak
state" and "national policy styles" approaches that had guided earlier research
(Dunn and Perl 1994: 312). In terms of variations in policy styles, Feick
(1992: 259) argues for an approach to comparative analysis that does "not
exclude the possibility that the characteristics of policy sectors could be more
important as policy-influencing variables than country differences, meaning
that one should find more variation among sectors than among countries. This
is an empirical question". The point that Feick is making is that there may be
more variation of policy style between the different policy sectors (industry,
agriculture, trade, education, etc) within a country than between that country
and other countries. Sectoral variations, as distinct from purely international
variations, are also significant in terms of the extent of states' involvement in
different policy areas. In his review of data relating to comparative analysis

of four countries (France, Japan, the USA, and the UK), Harrop (1992: 273) notes:

> the involvement of the state in the policy process varies more by sector than by country. State involvement is greatest in law and order and immigration control, more recent and indirect in industrial and health policy, and least developed in minorities policy. These contrasts between sectors are clear and consistent. The only major exception is the health sector, where state provision does vary enormously between nations.

In terms of the question of "strong state/weak state" and policy fragmentation, I have already referred to the importance of intra-state sectoral variation. There are numerous illustrations of this. Although Britain is often categorized as a strong state, some British policy sectors are relatively fragmented: examples are drug control, environment, labour market and industrial policy (Feick 1992: 264). This relates to the discussion of policy networks in chapter four, where I referred to the work of M J Smith (1993) who notes that empirical data tend to support the making of cautious general propositions and statements of general tendency, so that, other things being equal, we are more likely to find loose issue networks (as distinct from integrated policy communities) in societies, such as the US, that have a relatively fragmented political system. But as we saw earlier, there are numerous exceptions to this general pattern. For example, US trade policy in the 1950s and 1960s was a highly integrated policy community. It was also noted earlier that another source of variation arises from the fact that issue nets are more likely in highly politicized "non-technical" policy fields, irrespective of the nature of the system of government; and issue nets are also likely in new policy areas, where networked relations among actors may have not had time to become established.

Comparative public policy should, as I have observed, be alert to variations of a kind that are not "national". But of course, and as I also noted earlier, this is *not* to say that nation states, and variations between them, are unimportant (Feick 1992: 259). Some globalization theorists are guilty of underestimating the significance of the nation state. Without for one moment denying that a sense of nation-hood (or indeed, of a "global" order) is a social construction, we should not entertain exaggerated claims that the nation-state is no longer a significant entity. As Anderson (1991: 3) observes: "nation-ness remains the most universally legitimate value in the political life of our time". The nation-state continues to be an important element within the policy process and this is as true of the formulation of foreign policy (Jones 1991: xx) as it is for "domestic" policy. What this suggests is that to say that the issues which enter the policy agenda have an increasingly global dimension is not to say that policy decisions and their implementation are necessarily global: "The policy agenda may be global, but decision-making and delivery remain national" (Parsons 1995: 235). Nor should it be assumed that national governments are insignificant in the formulation of policy agendas (ibid. 242). The more general point to be made here, however, is that despite the existence of international organizations, few such organizations are available at the decision-making and implementation stages of the policy process (242–43):

> Because a problem is considered to be international or global does not mean that international or global institutions and policy-making (and implementation) processes will be established to facilitate a solution ... Issues and problems may well be increasingly constructed in international and global terms, but decision-making and implementation still remain domains which must be analyzed within the context of nation states.

Hence it is necessary to recognize (243) that "internationalization of the policy agenda facing policy makers is not something which necessarily makes for convergence in decision-making". Let me provide a concrete illustration of the point that Parsons is making. Given the existence of nation-states' different cultural and political traditions and unidentical economic circumstances, and given that national actors play a part in shaping welfare policy and its implementation, it is hardly surprising that there should be significant differences between, for example, the Japanese, Swedish and British welfare states. (For an analysis of these differences, see Gould 1993).

Another illustration of the idea that national governance "matters" is to do with conceptions of citizenship. In the second chapter I described Marshall's notion of citizenship, which involves three distinct types of rights: these are *civil* rights, *political* rights, and *social* rights. Roche (1992:77–78) notes that the dominant post-war paradigm of citizenship in the United Kingdom, a paradigm which is congruent with Marshall's thinking, is statist and also emphasizes social rights. In contrast, American conceptions of citizenship emphasize civil society rather than the state, and give more attention to civil rights and political rights than to social rights; Europe in general tends to be more committed than the US to Marshall's idea of social rights and social citizenship. Roche's (1992) observations suggest that these national variations in conceptions of citizenship, and the implications of these variations for the development of public policies, are at least partly related to national differences in political culture and in political traditions: from this it can be argued that comparative analysis, in the present example comparative analysis of differences in conceptions of citizenship and the implications of these differences for public policy, is an important integral part of the sociology of public policy.

In their text on comparative public policy, Heidenheimer et al (1990) suggest that as well as looking, at the national level, at general social, historical, and cultural factors as sources of influence upon public policy, it is essential to look at what the authors refer to as the "more proximate" sources of policy development: these consist of "the interactions of politicians, bureaucrats, interest groups, public opinion, program beneficiaries, and any other elements that bear on policy-making" (ibid. 4). The authors also observe (ibid.) that

> what is needed, what is seriously lacking in the scholarly literature, is a comparative approach that can span levels of government and public/ private sectors, as well as different nations ... Perhaps more than ever before, public policy has become a mosaic pieced together by government authorities at different levels and by private sector actors with public policy responsibilities.

This important statement identifies highly significant developments in contemporary governance, aspects of which were discussed in earlier chapters in regard to the blurring of the state/civil society distinction (see chapter two), the new public management and "governance" which were examined in chapter three, and policy networks which were discussed in chapter four. Also of close relevance to the above statement by Heidenheimer et al is the need to explore the case, outlined below, for a non-reductionist sociology of "*post-national*" governance that spans subnational, national, and transnational levels of the policy process.

Post-national governance

In order to put the idea of post-national governance into context it is necessary to first of all consider the notion of *globalization*. McGrew (1992: 23) defines globalization in these terms:

> Globalization refers to the multiplicity of linkages and interconnections between the states and societies which make up the modern world system. It describes the processes by which events, decisions, and activities in one part of the world can come to have significant consequences for individuals and communities in quite distant parts of the globe.

Analysis of the globalization of economy, polity, and culture has become, according to some, the central defining characteristic of contemporary sociology. Waters (1995: 1) writes: "just as postmodernism was *the* concept of the 1980s globalization may be *the* concept of the 1990s, a key idea by which we understand the transition of human society into the third millennium". This should not be taken to mean that the idea of globalization is new. For example, Erich Marcks in 1903 observed that "the world is ... more than ever before, one great unit in which everything interacts and affects everything else" (see Barraclough 1967: 53). Nevertheless, and despite Etzioni's (1968: 607) plea that modern social science should adopt an explicitly global perspective, it remains true that major social scientific interest in globalization is a fairly recent phenomenon.

Camilleri and Falk (1992: 3) examine globalizing tendencies in five areas: the internationalization of trade, finance and corporate organization; the globalization of the security system; the rapid transformation of technology; the accompanying spread of ecological problems; and the emergence of new social movements with both a local and transnational consciousness. More and more issues that appear on nation-states' policy agendas now have a global dimension to them. Today this applies not only to defence and foreign policy but also to economic and ecological policy, and policy in relation to drugs, AIDS, terrorism, telecommunications and many other issues (McGrew and Lewis 1992). Globalizing tendencies have caused political scientists such as Williams et al (1993: 7) to argue that "the old distinction between domestic and international politics . . . seems increasingly inappropriate". In the course of these debates, the discipline of International Relations has come under fire. Some critics have argued that International Relations theorists have concentrated too much on nation-states and relations between nation-states, and "have not regarded the international arena as a distinct and to some extent autonomous sphere of social life with features and forces of its own" (Scholte 1993: 17). Such criticisms, and the more general criticism that international relations has been a somewhat insular discipline, are not entirely unjustified; however there are signs that the discipline is becoming more theoretically reflective and receptive to wider currents of epistemological and ontological debate in the social sciences (Macmillan and Linklater 1995: 8–9; Halliday 1994: 18).

It was observed earlier that the nation state "matters". Equally, the themes of globalization and the transnational are of considerable importance and therefore comparative public policy, though it has, as I have shown, a valid contribution to make to the sociology of public policy, has to be supplemented by research that does not confine itself to nation states as the focus of analysis. Comparative public policy involves, of course, inter-state comparisons of policy, but the unit of analysis remains the nation-state. This makes it difficult for comparative analysts to grasp the emergent structural properties of transnational social systems and of transnational processes in general. As Andersen and Eliassen (1993: 12) put it: "Most studies of policy-making have retained a national bias and this is true even in the case of comparative studies. The national system has been taken as the unit of analysis". This does not mean, however, that we should think in terms of simply adding a "global" or globalization perspective to a comparative public policy perspective. Not only the nation-state, but also world-regional *blocs* (such as the European Union) should be taken into consideration alongside globalized phenomena (Ling 1993: 259):

The term "international" implies a relationship between independent nation states whilst the term "globalization" implies both that the nation state is no longer the most significant causal unit and that most important developments within each nation state are driven by the global system.

The idea of Europeanization is different again. It might imply that we are seeing a regionalization of the "West" around three major regions: the Pacific rim, the Americas and Europe. According to this argument the characteristics of Western states are conditioned more by regional than global factors.

This raises important questions that I shall return to shortly. To avoid the possibility of terminological confusion, it should also be noted that the term "region", though used by Ling and others to refer to world-regional blocs, can also, of course, refer to regions within a country; regions in this second sense are, as we shall see later, an increasingly important part of contemporary governance.

Globalization suggests that there is a high level of global connectedness of phenomena, a diminution of the significance of territorial boundaries, and a lessening of the significance of the national level of governance. However, a problem with the work of some writers who are keen to promulgate the globalization thesis is their tendency to exaggerate the scale and/or the intensity of globalization. Such writers tend to underplay the highly uneven impact of globalizing tendencies, and to also imply that "objective" and irreversible globalizing forces are at work. This orientation tends towards reductionism, and also towards essentialism insofar as it erroneously assumes the existence of a social process (globalization) that is relatively unified. Bretherton (1996: 12) is right to observe that "Globalization is . . . a set of overlapping processes that are neither inexorable nor irreversible, the impact of which varies in intensity and is highly differentiated in effect. Simply put – globalization is an uncertain process that affects some people more than others". In regard to *political globalization* it is true that transnational organizations have become increasingly important (Groom 1994). In Europe, the European Union is, of course, a key transnational organization. And on a larger geopolitical scale there are various transnational organizations (such as the Organization for Economic Cooperation and Development (OECD), United Nations organizations, the World Bank, and international banks and corporations) that have become an established part of the international scene. However, the overall significance of transnational organizations, relative to other types of organizations, is by no means clear. Likewise, the notion of a *global civil society* (Falk 1995: 3) is rather vague. Nor is *cultural globalization* a clear-cut phenomenon. Globalized electronic communications and other media undoubtedly contribute to an increasingly globalized diffusion of cultural materials. But this need not mean that locality and nation are no longer significant social and cultural foci; indeed, a seemingly increasing emphasis on ethnicity, religion, and other forms of differentiation and fragmentation is just as much a feature of the (post)modern world as globalized forms of thought. *Economic globalization* is sometimes said to be one of the driving forces of the globalization process. Here also it is important to avoid exaggerated claims. There are, it is true, some important indicators of economic globalization. One is the high level of intra-firm trade across national boundaries as components and semi-finished goods are moved from one country to another between the subsidiaries of large firms (Jones 1996: 10). It is wrong, however, to suppose that nowadays the level of external trade, as a percentage of gross domestic product, is exceptionally high. It is not; for most of the leading industrial nations (the exceptions are Germany and the USA) it has not risen above pre-World War 1 levels (ibid. 9–10). And in the case of transnational corporations it is all too easy to exaggerate the extent of globalization: for example, share ownership of transnational corporations as well as their senior managements tend to be drawn from the home country (10). It is also the case that not all of the regions of the world are involved to the same extent in global production, and some regions – such as Sub-Saharan Africa – are barely involved at all (Bretherton 1996: 7). Moreover, the extent of globalization varies by policy sector (Harrop 1992: 4): there is, for example, some evidence that industrial policy is more highly globalized than policy towards ethnic minorities (ibid.). And we have already seen that national governments "matter"; even in the case of problems which in some respects are transnational, policy efforts to resolve those problems in large part continue to be developed and implemented at the national level of governance.

In looking at globalization and its implications for governance, it is important to recognize that as well as *transnational* and *national* policy processes of the kind that I have referred to, it is also necessary to consider *subnational* governance. The idea of locale and spatial variation, as well as being part of post-modernists' predilection for "local narratives" (Krokidas 1993: 534), has in recent years figured fairly strongly in historical sociology and theories of social change (Boudon 1986; Mann 1986; Sztompka 1993). An aspect of the renewed emphasis on locale and on subnational governance, is the growing recognition of the significance of regions in the policy process. For example, Storper (1995) refers to increased academic interest – among economists, planners, geographers, and political scientists – in the resurgence of regional economies: Amin and Thrift (1995) outline a socioeconomic focus on mezo-level governance and policy networks within the regions of Europe; and Jenson (1995: 103–4) in her interesting study of Canada shows that regional governance may be embraced enthusiastically as a way of asserting regional or ethnic autonomy (as in Quebec), or exercised reluctantly (as in New Democratic-led Ontario) where subnational governments perceive a tendency for central governments to abdicate responsibility for maintaining national standards of economic and social welfare.

The growing emphasis on regional governance is evident in Europe. Bew and Meehan (1994) argue that the increasing economic and political power of regions is linked to European Union regional policy, which rests on three principles. These are *"additionality"*, which means that the EU's regional development funds must be spent in the regions and not used to top up national coffers; the principle of *"partnership"*, which specifies that projects funded from EU regional-policy monies must be the subject of consultation with local/regional "social partners" (local authorities, trades unions, employers associations, voluntary organizations, etc); and *"subsidiarity"*, which refers to the desirability of decentralization in policy implementation so that, as with the principle of "partnership", emphasis is placed on the involvement of local and regional organizations.

However, regionalism *per se* is only one aspect of sub-national European governance and to grasp other aspects we have to look at transnational European policy networks. The increased emphasis on regionalism is often taken as an indication that sub-national actors are gaining increased autonomy from national governments. This matter can usefully be approached from the standpoint of transnational policy networks. In part, the question of whether subnational policy actors are becoming more autonomous viz-a-viz national governments, is a question that hinges on the distinction made in chapter four between two main types of policy network (that is, policy communities and issue networks). Subnational actors from the member states might for whatever reasons become participants in a transnational EU policy network. This, as M J Smith (1993: 93–94) observes, might to some extent increase the network participants' autonomy from domestic politics and from national government controls. But, on the other hand, transnational networks tend to have a large number of members (national government actors, at least one interest group from each country, the respective directorate-general from the European Commission, perhaps committees of the European Parliament, etc) and this tends to make less likely the establishment of consensus and a "closed" policy community (ibid.). Thus, to the extent that sub-national actors' power has a *relational* component that derives from membership of and interaction with other members of a "closed" and tightly integrated policy community, it is an empirically open question whether membership of a transnational EU policy network will enhance the autonomy of subnational actors in terms of their relation to national actors. Moreover, if national government actors become less powerful in particular policy spheres, it should not be automatically assumed that this is because power has flowed "downwards" to sub-national or regional actors: in agriculture, for example, control of food prices has to some extent shifted "upwards" from national governments to the European Union (M J Smith 1993: 104–5).

Bennington and Harvey (1994: 22) note that the European policy process is simultaneously being subjected, via the European Union, to both centralizing and decentralizing tendencies: an expression of the latter is transnational and inter-regional local authority policy networks composed of governmental and non-governmental actors. Involvement in these new transnational policy networks is attractive to local authorities, for a number of reasons. Participation helps local authorities to monitor local, regional, and national impacts of European restructuring and new regulations; and assists local authorities in their lobbying and pressure-group activities directed towards the securing of Eurofunds and the promotion of local/regional economic development. Participation also symbolizes a sense of European identity and status (some local authorities regard a high profile "European" identity as a way of enhancing their prestige and power). For Bennington and Harvey (1994), the growing number and scale of transnational policy networks indicates that a transformation is occurring in political representation and participation; they perceive a shift away from vertical "tiers" of government towards a style of governance involving overlapping and interlocking "spheres" (22, 28). Bennington and Taylor (1993: 128–29) argue that in some policy sectors there is a movement not only towards institutional (for example, local authority) transnational networks, but also towards issue-based rather than institution-based transnational networks that include participants from public, private, and voluntary sectors. The authors speak of a "paradigm shift" (129) in the European policy process, and they comment: "New kinds of coalition are emerging where a common interest is forged on a specific policy issue between actors and organizations which, traditionally, have negotiated separately or even in opposition to each other" (128). As already mentioned, it is also argued that in Europe the idea of separate hierarchical "tiers" (or levels) of government (local, regional, national, European) is being "complemented and challenged" (129) by a new model of governance consisting of transnational policy networks that involve overlapping and interlocking "spheres" of governance, as distinct from separate "tiers" of government (ibid.).

Interest in transnational governance has resulted in a steadily expanding literature on patterns of European governance. The development of the European Union has been a special factor in this. But of course, it is also necessary to look outside Europe. Here it will be helpful to first of all acknowledge a distinction between corporative and regulative methods of policy co-ordination. Genschel and Werle (1993: 207) in their account of international governance relating to telecommunications, adopt Common's (1961: 342) distinction between corporative and regulative modes of policy co-ordination. The corporative mode is where nation states set up a transnational organization and transfer certain national sovereign rights to it, so that states agree to be legally bound by decisions of the transnational actor. The transnational actor, in other words, is empowered to act on behalf of the member states. While the corporative model leads to what might be called a transnational "hierarchy', the regulative mode, though it might involve the creation of a new transnational organization for administrative, legal, or advice-giving purposes, does not rest on a transfer of sovereign rights to a new supranational organization. Rather, a set of formally binding rules is agreed among states, rather like an international law or treaty (Stein 1982: 301). The regulative mode of international co-ordination within a particular policy domain or issue area is very often referred to as an international *regime*.

Undoubtedly, the notion of "regime" has some analytical value (Thrift

1994: 25). However, for reasons set out earlier, a focus on transnational policy networks affords a particularly fruitful method for investigating post-national governance. At the transnational level, some policy spheres (for example, international financial systems) are more highly globalized than others. This is illustrated in Thrift's (1994) interesting account of international financial systems. To fully engage with his wide-ranging paper would require a lengthy digression. Here, I shall mention but one of his empirical interpretations, which concerns not only globalized networks but also two theoretical foci – micro-macro and time-space – that I have referred to at various points throughout the book. Thrift (1994: 4, 16, 25–26, 43, 47) convincingly demonstrates that – despite some globalization theorists' claims that "objective" and impersonal globalizing "forces" dominate world affairs – international systems based largely on electronic communication and the rapid global diffusion of large amounts of data, do not necessarily result in a drastic lessening of the importance of actors nor of localized social relations which include face-to-face relations in micro settings. On the one hand, it is true that the international financial system – within which global electronic networks have become increasingly important – has to some extent become "disembedded from place" (25–27). But on the other hand, transnational financial networks generate a vast amount of data and also generate a range of meanings surrounding the possible interpretation of those data, so that, paradoxically, inter-personal exchanges in meetings to negotiate, discuss, interpret, and act upon the data, assume special importance (ibid.). This refers not only to ongoing operations; in special circumstances, face-to-face contact is necessary so as to enable the relevant actors to respond quickly to events (43). These locales and meeting places – which may be thought of, in Law's (1994: 104) terminology, as "ordering centres" that process information – are sometimes "cosmopolitan" (Thrift 1994: 26) with participants from many different countries. Notice that there is here a version of a micro-macro dialectic in which the cognitive and decisional outcomes of these meetings feed back into the "disembedded" electronic space that is associated with the international financial communication system (ibid.). The idea that there is a dialectical relation between policy materials and their social contexts, also relates to the question (discussed in chapters one and two) of the relative spatial mobility and temporal durabilities of the various materials that circulate across locales and across networks. Although I cannot pursue this here, it is worth noting that insufficient attention has been given to the development of conceptual and methodological tools for the purpose of investigating material diffusion processes (Fararo 1992) that operate across transnational contexts (Braithwaite 1994).

As we have seen, there are problems both with traditional state-centric orientations and with crude globalization approaches that emphasize only the transnational. There is a definite place for comparative public policy in so far as nation states "matter", though the comparative analysis approach – because its unit of analysis remains the nation state – needs to be complemented by a transnational orientation and also, as I have shown, by an awareness of subnational policy processes. In the last few pages I have tried to convey something of the complex nature of governance. I have shown that contemporary governance, at least in part, is about different forms of spatiality and linkages between them; and I have also shown that there is no reason for thinking that localism and particularity cannot co-exist with globalism and universality. Hence a sociological approach to the study of "post-national" governance recognizes the importance of *subnational, national*, and *transnational* policy processes. It should also be observed that the theoretical contents of the earlier chapters support the view that these levels of policy process are not embedded in a unified social totality. That is to say, there are no structurally "necessary" connections between these levels and none of them wholly determines the others; rather, they are relatively autonomous levels of social process, although there may well be important contingently produced and contingently sustained linkages between them.

It seems likely that debates to do with globalization will in the future become an increasingly important part of the new sociology of public policy. This is as it should be, providing the rather crude and exaggerated globalization approaches mentioned earlier are rejected in favour of a "post-national" perspective and methodology. For reasons to which I have already referred, it is important to keep in focus the subnational, national, and transnational levels of governance, rather than give causal primacy to any one of these levels on *a priori* grounds. The question of which of these levels is the more important and whether and in what form there are linkages between them, are empirical questions to be determined in each instance, not matters for theoretical predetermination in advance of empirical enquiry. In some situations, sub-national (for example, regional) conditions of action will come to the fore, in others it may be national or transnational conditions that are the more significant.

In the disciplines of sociology and social theory, concept formation has without doubt been affected by the idea of globalization, not least in terms of theorizing about time-space. In this connection, as in some others, Giddens's work is of particular importance. Giddens (1990) refers to a globalized re-ordering of time-space. His conceptions (1991: 21) of small-scale locale and of globalization, are not antithetical; rather, globalization is the "largest" expression of time-space distanciation. A more general point arising from Giddens's and others' work concerns the importance of avoiding either/or dichotomies that emphasize localism and particularity *or* globalism and homogenizing tendencies; instead, sociology should be concerned with the study of time-space in a way that keeps both material continuities and discontinuities in focus.

Some political scientists are beginning to show interest in employing sociological constructs pertaining to, for example, agency/structure and social chance, as a basis for formulating methodologies appropriate to the study of globalizing tendencies. For instance, Axford (1995: 2–3, and ch 3), though he wrongly supposes that agency is restricted to individual human actors, nevertheless moves into an exciting new area of theoretically informed policy research; his aim is (ibid. 3)

> to integrate aspect of [Giddens's] structurationist account of the active constitution of social systems by agents with some of the insights from institutionalist analyses applied to the study of global systems, of the extent to which individual identities and actions are "anchored" in social and cultural "scripts" of greater generality and longevity.

Axford speaks, too, of the possibility of employing the concept *system* in a way that avoids teleology (ibid. 6). Jones (1996: 7) is another recent writer who raises the question of agency/structure in relation to globalization. He shows that, even in the case of highly globalized phenomena such as international financial systems, it is mistaken to suppose that these systems are the product of wholly "objective" forces: various actors played a part in their creation and – as Thrift (1994) also notes – actors are involved in their reproduction.

It is noticeable that today an increasing number of political scientists reject mechanical, unitary, and reductionist conceptions of globalization. Bretherton (1996: 12) observes that globalization is an uncertain, uneven set of overlapping processes. Axford (1995: 2) rejects reductionist theories of globalization that are based on "ineluctable single logics" such as economic forces, market exchanges, power relations, or globalized cultural communications. His anti-reductionism leads him to reject the view that "the global system is being integrated by a single causal logic" (ibid. 33). Axford's understanding is, then, that the global system is not a unified totality (25) but is, rather, a highly fluid and contingent set of processes (8). The themes of contingency and anti-reductionism are also developed by another political scientist, O'Neill (1996). Although O'Neill's particular interest is European integration and the EU, his remarks can nevertheless be applied more generally to globalization. O'Neill observes that in analyzing the politics of European integration it is futile to look for an analytical prime mover (ibid. 81). The synthetic approach favoured by O'Neill is described by him in these terms (81–82):

> Instead of the certainties of both process and outcome that tend to characterize the classical paradigms, it ... chooses to see the EU as a hybrid composed of international and domestic variables; a process driven by mixed motives, in several directions and at variable speeds. European integration is ... a contingent process which depends on the issue agendas, leadership skills and the configurations of both the supranational and domestic agencies involved in its policy making.

As I have just indicated, O'Neill's approach is not restricted to the study of

European politics and policy. In more general terms he notes (ibid. 82) that recent approaches to the study of social and political life employ "the fluid metaphors of variable geometry or multi-speed change", to replace "the old certitudes of the established paradigms". There are, then, indications that at the present time some exciting new conceptual developments emanating both from sociology and from political science are becoming established as materials for the future development of a new and non-reductionist interdisciplinary approach to the study of post-national governance (Sibeon 1996). However, to refer to the study of post-national governance leaves open the question of the *purpose* of such study in terms of academic and/or practical policy-oriented goals. This question of purpose raises the important distinction between analysis "of" and "for" policy; it is this distinction, and more especially analysis "for" policy, that forms the basis for the discussion in the remaining pages of the chapter.

Analysis "For" Policy

In the introductory chapter I indicated that a sociology *of* public policy is not oriented to the production of knowledge for practical application by policy actors; it is, rather, an exercise in intellectual understanding, an attempt to construct a body of sociological knowledge pertaining to public policy, its institutional context, and the policy process. This book has concentrated on conceptual and methodological materials that form the basis for the development of a contemporary sociology *of* public policy. I noted in the introductory chapter that a sociology *for* public policy is orientated towards the formulation of theoretical and methodological insights and empirical data of a kind intended for practical application. I noted, too, that while the distinction sometimes becomes blurred, it is appropriate to retain a conceptual distinction between analysis "of" and "for" policy. This relates closely to questions of purpose. A sociology of public policy rests upon academic values (the pursuit of knowledge for its own sake) and it is important that these values should be preserved. The notion that the only kind of knowledge that is worth pursuing is that which has practical application, is a notion that should play no part in academic social science nor in the wider academic community. Cochrane (1994: 118) refers to Dunleavy's (1980: 7) observation that writing on local government in the 1960s and 1970s reflected close relationships between academics and local government administrators and professionals, and that this may have removed some of the critical edge from academic writing on local government. Cochrane (ibid. 118) argues that this close relationship continues to pose a problem today: some academics in this field rely on training and consultancy contracts with local government and this tends to inhibit the development of hard-hitting academic critique. Whether a problem of this kind actually exists to the extent implied by Cochrane is open to debate, though he undoubtedly has put his finger on a potential problem. In a moment, however, I will suggest that there *is* a legitimate place for academic knowledge of a kind that is capable of informing public policy; but I shall also observe that the relation between academic knowledge and public policy is variable and complex, and very often tenuous.

Another important consideration that was flagged for attention in the introductory chapter is the idea that the sociology of public policy, though located as a purely academic activity within the discipline of sociology and therefore a sociological sub-field in its own right, can *also* be viewed as a contribution to the development of a multidisciplinary field of study that might appropriately be termed *Policy Analysis* (Ham and Hill 1993: 4–21). It is this cross-disciplinary mode that I propose to concentrate on here, having in the previous chapters drawn not only on social theory and sociology but also political science and public policy. Rather than refer to sociology of/for policy, in what follows I will wherever necessary refer to analysis of policy and to analysis for policy: neither of these expressions is tied to a single discipline, for they refer to all of the social science disciplines that are capable of contributing to policy analysis (disciplines such as sociology, social theory, political science, public policy, economics, planning, and human geography). It should also be noted that like Ham and Hill (1993: 4, 18) my broadly-based use of the term policy analysis refers to an academic activity that, as well as being interdisciplinary, can be divided into analysis *of* policy and analysis *for* policy.

Smith and Stanyer's (1976/1980) observations on analysis "for" policy, are worthy of note. Smith and Stanyer, who discuss in historical perspective the relation of academic knowledge to the management of public sector organizations and to public administration generally, divide the literature on public administration into two broad types (ibid. 22–29). Firstly, the older tradition of the inter-war years whereby practising or former administrators wrote articles based on their personal experiences; these kinds of articles were published in journals such as *Public Administration* (12). In this older tradition in which the public administration literature was dominated by practitioners, the underlying cognitive processes involved in the production of written knowledge entailed the formulation of generalizations from particular ("idiographic") instances and extrapolation from personal experience (26–7). The second and more recent development described by Smith and Stanyer is a shift towards a body of public administration literature that is dominated by academics (27). Here the underlying cognitive processes entail particularizing from general ("nomothetic") categories of knowledge, that is, the application of general social scientific theory and of generalized bodies of data to particular cases or problems. In the view of Smith and Stanyer this more recent academic orientation has not, however, had much influence upon public policy organization, management, and practice (27–28):

Unfortunately it has to be admitted that the management movement has not made a great deal of progress in British public administration . . .

Recent thinking is obviously an advance on the generalized personal experiences of civil servants and local government officers, but the difficulty is that outside the sphere of specialized administration techniques there is little that can easily be transferred.

Smith and Stanyer adduce two reasons for this. The first is that in order to be practically useful, academic social science knowledge about organization and management "must be something which stands in the same relation to management behaviour as do physics and chemistry to engineering, and as engineering does to the building of a particular bridge" (28). In regard to this the authors observe that academic social science is uncertain, multi-paradigmatic, and with no clear, ready-made guidelines on how it might be applied. Secondly, Smith and Stanyer make the point that moving from the general to the particular is fraught with difficulty: applying generalized (nomothetic) knowledge to individual cases is never a straightforward, mechanical, or routine matter (29).

Notice that Smith and Stanyer discuss the relation of social science to organization and management practice. Others emphasize the use of social science techniques for policy monitoring and policy evaluation purposes. And a crucial consideration is whether social science affects the formulation of policy goals. It is not easy to determine how far social science influences policy objectives, and many academics working in applied fields feel that their work has little or no impact upon the policy community. It would be wrong, however, to suppose that social science knowledge has no impact at all upon the direction of policy. Bulmer (1986: 16–25) provides some examples. One is the influence on policy of the data produced as part of the "rediscovery of poverty" in the 1960s, data which resulted in some changes in the social security field. Another is the use that Royal Commissions make of research data. Bulmer (ibid. 20) also notes that in Britain the Robbins Committee on Higher Education in the 1960s employed a considerable amount of statistical data and the Robbins Report of 1963 stimulated a climate of changed opinion concerning the expansion of higher education and in this way contributed to the later expansion of higher education in universities and polytechnics. Banting (1986: 46) points out that social scientists and professionals are regularly appointed to advisory bodies. He goes as far as claiming that: "In effect, social scientists and professionals have been partially integrated into Britain's policy elites" (ibid.). He goes on to observe (ibid.) that in his case-studies of housing, rent regulation, educational priority, and family poverty, "the most striking finding is the pervasive influence of intellectuals and professionals. The conceptual changes that are the preconditions of policy innovation regularly start with them". He further notes (47) that the involvement of social science in vocational and professional training and the expansion of university training programmes for public sector professionals (teachers, social workers, health visitors, psychologists, housing officials, etc) and for managers and administrators, is another factor that strengthens the relationship between academic social science knowledge and public policy.

In chapter three I referred to the principle of parliamentary democracy and to the politics/administration distinction as important elements of the institutional framework of government and public policy. Some writers, such as Benveniste (1973), have focused on a tension between, on the one hand, the principle of political democracy, and on the other, the idea that policy might be shaped by the academic opinion of unelected "experts". This, it should be noted, relates not only to the politics/administration distinction but also to the question of whether social science can or should be an entirely "objective" or "value-free" activity. Wilson (1993), whose particular interest is the policy relevance of sociology, suggests that social science can be relevant to policy in so far as there is a distinction between instrumental value judgments and categorical value judgments (ibid. 5–6):

> For example, if research has firmly established that the least prejudiced individuals are those who have grown up in a permissive rather than a restrictive environment, then an instrumental value judgement would state that if our society wants to embark on a long-term programme to reduce prejudice, then it is better to raise children in a permissive than in a restrictive way. Such a statement clearly represents an empirical assertion amenable to scientific test ... although it would be inappropriate for sociologists, in their role as social scientists, to make categorical value judgements, they can certainly make instrumental judgement of value, judgements that would be consistent with the assumptions of the logic of scientific enquiry.
>
> However, this is not to say that sociologists or social scientists cannot or should not address the issues of categorical value judgements in their studies of basic values and belief systems in society. Often a social scientist can point out the contradictions or inconsistencies in what are taken to be categorical judgements of values.

Wilson's observations give a particular slant to the question of whether social science can or should be "value-free", and to the relation of this question to the possible relevance of social science to public policy. Here we enter a minefield of controversy. Post-modernists, among others, object to claims that social science is ethically and politically "neutral" or value-free, and object to the idea that social science may legitimately contribute to the formulation or implementation of public policies. As noted in the first chapter, post-modern theorists go as far as saying that the world is entirely a product of language and discourse: there is nothing more to reality than discourse, and therefore social science discourse, like any other, is merely "constructing" in an arbitrary manner a social world which has no prior (pre-discursive) ontological reality. I suggested in the first chapter that this aspect of post-modern theory is open to challenge, and that a more adequate conception, based on a non-reified understanding of agency/structure, is that the relation of discourses to their context is loosely dialectical: discourse is partly shaped by the social context and the context is partly shaped by discourse, but neither fully determines the other – each has a degree of autonomy.

Weiss (1986, 1993), a leading writer on the topic of the relation of social science to public policy, and herself an advocate of closer connections between social science knowledge and policy (1993: 36), is one of a number of writers whose work suggests that post-modern theorists are tilting at a pretentious social scientific self-image which is not typical of the majority of social scientists, most of whom are only too aware of the epistemological and ontological uncertainties that attend their work. She observes (ibid. 32–33) that currents of social concern and ways of thinking in the wider society affect, though do not wholly or consistently determine, how social scientists think about issues and which topics they select for investigation. Weiss is a policy-oriented sociologist, not a social theorist. An analogous theme to Weiss's, however, is also to be found among theorists. For instance, Friedrich (1972: 298–99) notes that sociology does not stand in grand isolation from "lay" discourses. Nowadays, not many social scientists would want to cling to outmoded claims that their discipline is entirely value-free or entirely devoid of forms of thought that circulate within the wider society. My use of the word "entirely", is deliberate: we should avoid an either/or approach to this matter, and instead think in terms of the relative but not total autonomy of social science discourse from its social contexts. As I have already intimated, it can be argued that the relation of academic discourse to lay discourse and to social conditions, is in a loose sense dialectical. Lay concepts filter into social scientific discourse, and social science discourse in a variety of ways – through the mass media, the incorporation of social scientific concepts in public policies, the inclusion of social science in university and college based programmes of vocational and professional training, etc – enters into the world of lay and policy-related cognitions (Bryant 1991: 192–200). On the question of the relation of social scientific discourse to society, Giddens (1987: 32) suggests the concepts and theories generated by social science "spiral in and out" of social life, although there is no "necessary match" between changes in lay and social science discourses (Giddens 1993: 13–14). This does not mean that social science discourse is indistinguishable from "lay" discourse, only that each contains elements of the other. Another way of putting this is to say that while social science knowledge can never be entirely "value-free" or entirely uninfluenced by its social context, academic knowledge may, nevertheless, be *relatively* detached and have relative autonomy from the social context in which it is produced.

Moreover, it can be argued that the relation of academic knowledge to public policy is based not on some academic purist notion of the direct practical application of academic knowledge but, rather, on a combination of what Weiss (1993) calls the "enlightenment" model, which I shall discuss in a moment, and the "interactive" model in which actors located in policy networks engage in the negotiation of policy materials of which research data and academic knowledge are but one element. In the interactive model it is assumed that academic knowledge is itself negotiable in so far as whether such knowledge is employed by policy actors, and if so in what form, are decisional outcomes that emerge through processes of exchange and interaction in policy networks. The "enlightenment" model as conceived by Weiss is quite unlike the positivist version of claims to enlightenment that, as some post-modern critics have been quick to note, was a feature of some early social science theories such as Marxism. Weiss's (1993: 28) point is that social science knowledge, whether conceptual, methodological, or empirical, or some combination of these, does not necessarily have to lead to an immediate, specific policy measure in order for us to conclude that the knowledge in question has had some effect upon the policy community. Research carried out by Weiss over a period of some years suggests that very often there is what she calls an "enlightenment" effect. This occurs when social science knowledge percolates into the world of public policy in a fairly general, diffuse way that, however, does contribute, either in the short term or over a longer period, to the ways in which policy actors think about problems. Weiss refers to an "amorphous percolation of sociological ideas into the policy arena" (ibid. 28), and she goes on to say of the enlightenment model (29–30) that

> there is still a long way to go . . . The creep of sociological ideas into policy arenas remains an erratic phenomenon. Some ideas are distorted or misunderstood; others are ignored. Those findings and theories that support existing positions are better heard than those that do not. Still, there are significant areas in which social science has influenced the way that public problems are conceptualized and the solutions that are considered.

I have already referred to Weiss's "interactive" model of the relation of social science to public policy. This model has an affinity with Giddens's dialogical model of interactions between researchers, policy makers, and others involved in the policy process (Bryant 1991: 194). Policy outcomes may to some extent be affected by social science knowledge, but even when this happens, outcomes involve a great deal more than the straightforward application of social science knowledge. The operation of values, judgments, resource limits, organizational and professional interests, changes in the conditions of action, shifting configurations of power in actor networks, etc, are all factors that combine in complex and sometimes unpredictable ways to influence policy decisions and outcomes. This is illustrated in Nies's (1992) study of policy planning in respect of the needs of elderly people requiring long-term care (ibid. 2, emphasis added):

The assessment of need, either based on scientifically obtained data or on "grass-roots" knowledge constitutes only one element of policy-making. Ideological convictions, political considerations, practical problems, pressure from interest groups and other contextual factors also have a substantial impact on decision-makers and decision-making . . . planning is strongly influenced by inter – and intraorganizational interests . . . it is an *interactive* process . . . This implies that rational models of planning are too idealistic and even unrealistic, since intergroup relationships and interactions (eg. interest group struggles) are not accounted for.

The interactive model of the relation of social science to public policy, though it may disappoint some academics who expect that academic knowledge will be applied to policy and practice in a straightforward, linear or "undiluted" fashion, is a fairly realistic model upon which to base analysis *for* policy. Weiss, one of the leading researchers on the utilization of social scientific knowledge by policy practitioners, is not, as I observed earlier, a theoretician. Bryant's (1991) interests in this topic overlap with Weiss's, although Bryant is more theoretically oriented in his approach. Bryant (1991: 197–98) in his criticism of Bulmer's (1990: 121–22) rejection of Giddens's dialogical model – which in some respects is similar to Weiss's interactive model – argues that a dialogical/interactive conception of the relation of social science to public policy does *not* mean that social science is restricted to an instrumental concern with means; social science in this conception can also legitimately be concerned with policy goals. Giddens's model, though it rejects positivist conceptions of social science, involves dialogue and interaction between social scientists, policy actors and other interested parties in such a way that social scientists may legitimately be regarded as having something to contribute, through dialogue and interaction with others, to the formulation of policies (Bryant 1991: 194–98). Actually, dialogical models of the relation of social science to policy and practice are not of recent origin: see, for example, Lees's (1975) account of "action-research" strategies in social work (ibid. 4–5), these being research strategies that also guided the EPA (Education Priority Area) and CDP (Community Development Project) programmes in the 1960s (ibid. 8). Lees notes that "the aim of action research is not simply to provide a detached assessment . . . but rather to set up a dynamic interaction between the social scientist and the practitioner" (4). The argument developed by Lees is that although the CDPs were perhaps not a successful example of the action-research principle, this does not mean the principle itself is unsound: mistakes have been made in the past, as in the case of the planning and organization of the CDPs, but it is possible to learn from these mistakes (ibid. 69–76). All in all, there seems to be a fairly strong argument in favour of the view that the dialogical/interactive model of the relation of social science to public policy, rather than the pretensions of a "pure science" or "social engineering" model, is the most likely way forward when it comes to the deployment of social scientific analyses *for* policy.

Many of the discussions of analysis "for" policy refer, in the main, to approaches that neglect comparative analysis. Comparative public policy is a field of enquiry that may lead to improvement in the quality of policy design. For example, a comparative approach helps us to understand which policy successes or policy failures are due to general cross-national conditions, and which are due to factors that relate only to particular countries. An instance cited by Heidenheimer et al (1990: 2) is the economic shock – which was experienced across all of the industrially developed nations – of the oil-price increases of the 1970s. Some countries responded to this economic shock more effectively than others. Why? As Heidenheimer et al (ibid.) note, comparing different ways of coping with similar problems, and observing the relative success or otherwise of different policy responses, may provide valuable data that can in the future be incorporated into the design of public policies. Harrop (1992: 3) comments:

The study of comparative public policy provides particular opportunities for cross-national learning. If neighbourhood watch schemes reduce crime in the United States, why not give them a try in France? If the United States could reduce deaths from coronary heart disease by a quarter in the 1970s, why not try to repeat the success among the Scots in the 1990s (whose hearts are the most unhealthy in the world)? What can the French and Japanese experience with national health insurance contribute to the American debate about whether public insurance should be introduced there? The practical benefits from studying policy comparatively are one of the distinctive strengths of the approach.

Harrop (ibid. 4) is clearly aware that we cannot assume that what works in one society (for example, Japan) will necessarily work in another (such as the USA), for the reason that there may be large differences of culture, political values and institutions, economics, etc, between one country and another. From a practical policy-design point of view what is important in comparative analysis is the use of data to help decide when and how some policies that are successful in one country can effectively be transposed to another. This, incidentally, does not exclude the investigation of national responses to contingent events (a terrorist incident, say, or an oil-spill) and cross-national learning from the study of national governments' responses to such events.

Lastly, in considering possibilities for the development of analyses *for* policy, I agree with Wilson (1993: 9–10) who makes the point that it is not only empirical data that is capable of informing policy. Theoretical ideas and methodological insights that contribute to an understanding of how the world works, and how the policy process itself works, can, providing they are communicated in a form that is meaningful to practitioners, have an analytically sensitizing effect upon policy actors. Examples include the idea of contingency; the methodological significance, discussed in chapters one and two, of employing both a *social integration* and *system integration* perspective whenever one is investigating social phenomena such as social problems; the distinction, discussed in the first chapter, between functionalist analysis and causal analysis; the need to avoid reductionist, single-order accounts (such as "post-Fordism', "post-industrialism", or "globalization") of the genesis, reproduction or change of social phenomena; the conceptual and methodological sensitization of the policy researcher to the dynamics of micro, mezo, and macro levels of social process; and the notion of synchronic and diachronic linkages between agency, structure/social conditions, and social chance. These are all potential sources of direct or indirect academic influence upon the design of policy research and upon policy actors' understanding of problems and of the policy environment in which the problems to be addressed are located, and also their understanding of the policy process itself. As Weiss (1993) puts it (ibid. 37, emphasis added):

> Although good data are useful and build credibility, equally important is the *sociological perspective* on entities, processes and events. Participants in the policy process can profit from an understanding of the forces and currents that shape events, and from the structures of meaning that sociologists derive from their theories and research.

The relationship between social science and public policy is, as I have tried to show, complex and variable. I would argue that social science does indeed have a legitimate and credible applied role. It is, admittedly, difficult to find very many instances where social science knowledge has had a direct and immediate impact upon policy. However, this does not mean that analysis *for* policy is a hopeless enterprise. To the contrary, research by Weiss and others on the "enlightenment" model and the dialogical/interactive model would seem to suggest that the ideas associated with the new sociology of public policy will in the course of time influence the design of policy research and will, as these ideas percolate the world of public policy, have a certain amount of influence on policy actors' forms of thought and hence upon the formulation of public policy.

Concluding Observations

I hope that in this book I have convincingly demonstrated that in the sociology of public policy, and in the social sciences in general, theory is of central importance. Theory of one kind or another also figures in everyday life, in the workplace, at home, or in the street. Another way of putting this is to say that everyone is a version of the social theorist. Theories, whether informal and homespun ("commonsensical" theory) or the formal academic variety, or the kinds of theoretical assumptions that circulate across political, professional or policy communities, are unavoidable. Certainly in our everyday lives we use theories all the time: theories about people and situations; theories about what constitutes appropriate behaviour; theories pertaining to relationships between causes and effects; and so on. Likewise it is impossible to conceive of a theoryless social science, whether the theories in question be of the substantive or sensitizing kind. Moreover, in the early chapters as well as in the present chapter, I referred to the idea that the relation of social science theory to society (or more precisely, to those social contexts that relate to the theory in question) is dialectical. Over a period of time theory partly shapes and is partly shaped by social contexts. My use of the term "partly" is, as I noted earlier, intended to indicate that social science theory has relative, though not total autonomy from social contexts. In any event, theory of some kind unavoidably influences (a) decisions pertaining to the selection of particular topics for empirical investigation; (b) research design; and (c) analysis and interpretation of the resultant data. That is to say, in the design and implementation of any piece of social scientific research, it is inevitable that the researcher will have to make certain theoretical assumptions about, in particular, micro-macro, and agency/structure and social chance. Far better that the theoretical assumptions be made explicit, rather than allow them to influence the course of social investigation in tacit, surreptitious ways. It is, of course, only by making our theoretical assumptions explicit that we can subject them to our own and others' critical evaluation; and it is also through this process that theoretical concepts and postulates are formulated, codified in written form and made available to other theorists and to empirical researchers.

Finally, this book's disciplinary and interdisciplinary contexts should not be lost sight of. Recent political science in some instances uses theoretical and methodological postulates of a kind that are not dissimilar to those employed in sociological approaches which recognize the contingent, processual features of the social world. Occasionally, political scientists draw explicitly upon sociological ideas: an example referred to earlier is Axford's (1996) political science approach to the study of globalization. This is quite rare. For example, Judge et al (1994) in their informative study of the European Parliament and the policy process display an empirically-based awareness of contingency in the European policy process, although the authors, each of whom is a political scientist, make hardly any reference to sociology. Much the same can be said of O'Neill's (1996) work on European integration, which was mentioned earlier in the chapter. These and other political science studies that blend descriptive political analysis with an attempt to rigorously theorize the ontological character of the social world, are invaluable sources of social science material that, unfortunately, tend not to be read by sociologists. This is sociology's loss. On the other hand, sociological theory and methodology can validly contribute to political science. Take, for example, the pieces of work to which I have just referred (those by Judge et al and O'Neill). These political scientists exhibit analytical skill, and they also display a fine-grained knowledge of political institutions and political processes that, I suspect, very few sociologists would be able to match. Nevertheless, their work would, I suggest, have greater explanatory power had the authors drawn upon sociology in regard to, for instance, the systemic and relational faces of power, the system integration/social integration distinction, time-space and material diffusion processes, and Mouzelis's typology of positional, dispositional, and situational-interactional dimensions of social action.

The case for greater emphasis on an interdisciplinary orientation as a way of furthering the development of policy analysis as a multidisciplinary field does not, however, only involve the need for more collaborative work between sociologists and political scientists. As I indicated in my Preface, the literature on *public policy* – as distinct from political science – is generally far removed from contemporary sociology. A further schism, although perhaps not as marked as in the cases to which I have just referred, is the relation of political science to public policy as a field of enquiry. In America, where the term "public administration" continues to be used to describe a disciplinary or interdisciplinary academic activity that in Europe is nowadays far more likely to be called public policy, policy studies, policy science, or policy analysis (Lane 1993), there is considerable tension between political science and public administration: interesting accounts of this tension are provided by Denhardt (1990), Whicker et al (1993), and Waldo (1990). The intensity of this debate is perhaps not surprising, in so far as a fairly large proportion of American public administration academics tend to adopt a "technical" emphasis on skills and practical techniques in a way that is rather divorced from the larger corpus of social science knowledge (see Chandler 1991: 42). In Britain there is among public administration/public policy academics a somewhat more appreciative stance towards the broader and more explicitly theorized approaches of social science. Moreover, the relationship of public policy to political science is, as I observed in the introductory chapter, sometimes very close. Even in Britain, however, the managerialist approaches of the 1980s – which to some extent were associated with Thatcherism – contributed to a certain amount of conflict that reflected the fear of some academics that a broad social science approach to the teaching of public administration was being swept aside as certificate, diploma and degree curricula in public administration became more narrowly technical and vocational (ibid. 44). There are some indications that this is changing, and certainly policy analysis is showing signs of becoming a rigorous social scientific activity (Lane 1993). That said, there is clearly a long way to go before it can be claimed that policy analysis is a well-founded field of multidisciplinary enquiry. It is against this background that I have tried to show that the new sociology of public policy, as well as standing in its own right as a developing sociological sub-field, is also potentially a major contributor to the future development of policy analysis as an expanding area of contemporary social scientific discourse that spans analysis *of* and *for* public policy.

REFERENCES

Abell, P. (1977) "The many faces of power and liberty: revealed preference, autonomy, and teleological explanation" *Sociology*, 11, 1: 3–24

Aberle, D.F. (1967) "The functional prerequisites of a society" in N.D. Demerath and R. Peterson (eds) *System, Change and Conflict*, New York, Free Press

Abrahamson, M. (1978) *Functionalism*, Englewood Cliffs, N.J., Prentice-Hall

Abrams, P. (1982) *Historical Sociology*, Ithaca, Cornell University Press

Adams, I. (1993) *Political Ideology Today*, Manchester, Manchester University Press

Alexander, J. (ed) (1985) *Neofunctionalism*, London, Sage

Alexander, J. (1992) "General theory in the postpositivistic mode: the 'epistemological dilemma' and the search for present reason" in S. Seidman and D.G. Wagner (eds) *Postmodernism and Social Theory*, Cambridge (Mass.) and Oxford, Blackwell

Alexander, J. and Colomy, P. (1992) "Traditions and competition: preface to a postpositivist approach to knowledge cumulation" in G. Ritzer (ed) *Metatheorizing*, London and Newbury Park, Calif., Sage

Amin, A. and Thrift, N. (1995) "Institutional issues for the European regions: from markets and plans to socioeconomics and powers of association" *Economy and Society*, 24, 1: 41–66

Anderson, B. (1991) *Imagined Communities: Reflections on the Origins and Spread of Nationalism*, London, Verso

Andersen, S.S. and Eliassen, K.A. (1993) "The EC as a new political system" in S.S. Andersen and K.A. Eliassen (eds) *Making Policy in Europe: The Europeification of National Policy-Making*, London, Sage

Antonio, R. J. and Kellner, D. (1992) "The limits of postmodern thought" in D. Dickens and A. Fontana (eds) *Postmodernism and Social Inquiry*, Chicago, University of Chicago Press

Archer, M. (1988) *Culture and Agency: The Place of Culture in Social Theory*, Cambridge, Cambridge University Press

Aron, R. (1967) *Eighteen Lectures on Industrial Society*, London, Weidenfeld and Nicolson

Axford, B. (1995) *The Global System: Economics, Politics and Culture* Cambridge, Polity

Bagguley, P. (1994) "Prisoners of the Beveridge dream? The political mobilization of the poor against contemporary welfare regimes" in R.

Burrows and B. Loader (eds) *Towards a Post-Fordist Welfare State*? London, Routledge

Banting, K. (1986) "The social policy process" in M. Bulmer, K. Banting, S.S. Blume, M. Carley, and C.H. Weiss *Social Science and Social Policy*, London, Allen and Unwin

Barbalet, J. (1985) "Power and resistance" *British Journal of Sociology* xxxvi, 4: 531–48

Barbalet, J.M. (1988) *Citizenship*, Milton Keynes, Open University Press

Barberis, P. (1996) "Whitehall since the Fulton Report" in P. Barberis (ed) *The Whitehall Reader*, Buckingham, Open University Press

Barker, R. and Roberts, H. (1993) "The uses of the concept of power" in D. Morgan and L. Stanley (eds) *Debates in Sociology*, Manchester, University of Manchester Press

Barraclough, G. (1967) *An Introduction to Contemporary History*, Harmondsworth, Penguin

Baudrillard, J. (1983) *In the Shadow of the Silent Majorities . . . or the End of the Social and Other Essays*, New York, Semiotext(e)

Baudrillard, J. (1994) *The Illusion of the End*, Cambridge, Polity

Bauman, Z. (1987) *Legislators and Interpreters*, Oxford, Polity

Bauman, Z. (1989a) "Hermeneutics and modern social theory" in D. Held and J.B. Thompson (eds) *Social Theory of Modern Societies: Anthony Giddens and his Critics*, Cambridge, Cambridge University Press

Bauman, Z. (1989b) "Sociological responses to postmodernity" *Thesis Eleven*, 23: 35–63

Bauman, Z. (1992a) "Foreward" In F. Crispi *Social Action and Power*, Oxford, Blackwell

Bauman, Z. (1992b) *Intimations of Postmodernity*, London, Routledge

Bell, D. (1973) *The Coming of Post-Industrial Society*, London, Heinemann

Bennington, J. and Harvey, J. (1994) "Spheres or tiers? The significance of transnational local authority networks" *Local Government Policy Making*, 20, 5: 21–30

Bennington, J. and Taylor, M. (1993) "Changes and challenges facing the UK welfare state in the European Union of the 1990s" *Policy and Politics*, 21, 2: 121–34

Benveniste, G. (1973) *The Politics of Expertise*, Berkeley, Calif., Glendessary Press

Berger, P. and Luckmann, T. (1972) *The Social Construction of Reality*, Penguin, Harmondsworth.

Bernardes, J. (1985) "Family ideology: identification and exploration" *The Sociological Review*, 33, 2: 275–97

Bertens, H. (1995) *The Idea of the Postmodern*, London and New York, Routledge

Best, S. and Kellner, D. (1991) *Postmodern Theory: Critical Interrogations*, London, Macmillan

Betts, K. (1986) "The conditions of action, power, and the problem of interests" *Sociological Review*, 34, 1: 39–64.

Bew, P. and Meehan, E. (1994) "Regions and borders: controversies in Northern Ireland about the European Union" *Journal of European Public Policy*, 1, 1: 95–113

Blau, P. (1964) *Exchange and Power in Social Life*, New York, Wiley

Blumer, H. (1954) "What is wrong with social theory?" *American Sociological Review*, 19: 3–10

Blumer, H. (1969) *Symbolic Interactionism: Perspectives and Methods*, Englewood Cliffs, N.J., Prentice-Hall

Bolderson, H. (1994) Review *Journal of Social Policy*, 23, 2: 271–73

Bonnett, A. (1993) "The formation of public professional radical consciousness: the example of anti-racism" *Sociology*, 27, 2: 281–97

Bouchier, D. (1977) "Radical ideologies and the sociology of knowledge; a model for comparative analysis" *Sociology*, 11, 1: 25–46

Boudon, R. (1982) "Educational institutions and perverse effects: short-cycle higher education" in R. Boudon *The Unintended Consequences of Social Action*, London, Macmillan

Boudon, R. (1986) *Theories of Social Change*, Cambridge, Polity Press

Bourdieu, P. (1977) *Outline of a Theory of Practice*, Cambridge University Press, Cambridge

Bourdieu, P. (1990) *In Other Words: Essays Towards a Reflexive Sociology* Cambridge, Polity

Bourricaud, F. (1981) *The Sociology of Talcott Parsons*, Chicago, University of Chicago Press

Braithwaite, J. (1994) "A sociology of modelling and the politics of empowerment" *British Journal of Sociology*, 45, 3: 444–79

Braverman, H. (1974) "Labour and monopoly capitalism: the degradation of work in the twentieth century" *Monthly Review Press*, New York: 85–123

Bretherton, C. (1996) "Introduction: global politics in the 1990s" in C. Bretherton and G. Ponton (eds) *Global Politics: An Introduction*, Oxford, Blackwell

Breton, A. (1974) *The Economic Theory of Representative Government*, London, Macmillan

Bryant, C. (1976) *Sociology in Action: A Critique of Selected Conceptions of the Social Role of the Sociologist*, London, Allen and Unwin

Bryant, C. (1991) "The dialogical model of applied sociology" in C. Bryant and D. Jary (eds) *Giddens's Theory of Structuration: A Critical Approach*, London, Routledge

Bryant, C. (1995) *Practical Sociology: Post-Empiricism and the Reconstruction of Theory and Application*, Cambridge, Polity

Bryant, C. and Jary, D. (1991) (eds) *Giddens's Theory of Structuration: A Critical Approach*, London, Routledge

Bryant, C. and Mokrzycki, E. (1994) "Introduction: theorizing the changes in East-Central Europe" in C. Bryant, and E. Mokrzycki, (eds) *The New Great*

Transformation? Change and Continuity in East-Central Europe, London and New York, Routledge

Buchanon, J.M. (1975) *The Limits of Liberty: Between Anarchy and Leviathan*, Chicago, University of Chicago Press

Buchanon, J.M. (1977) *Freedom in Constitutional Contract*, College Station, Texas A and M University Press

Bulmer, M. (1982) *The Uses of Social Research: Social Investigation in Public Policy-Making*, London, Allen and Unwin

Bulmer, M. (1986) ''The policy process and the place in it of social research'' in M. Blumer, K. Banting, S. Blume, M. Carley, and C.H. Weiss *Social Science and Social Policy*, London, Allen and Unwin

Bulmer, M. (1990) ''Successful applications of sociology'' in C. Bryant and H. Becker (eds) *What Has Sociology Achieved?* London, Macmillan

Bulmer, S. (1993) ''The governance of the EU: a new institutionalist approach'' *Journal of Public Policy*, 13, 4: 351–80

Bulmer, M., Banting, K., Blume, S., Carley, M., and Weiss, C.H. (1986) *Social Science and Social Policy*, London, Allen and Unwin

Burns, T. (1986) ''Actors, transactions, and social structure'' in U. Himmelstrand (ed) *The Social Reproduction of Organization and Culture*, London, Sage

Burrows, R. and Loader, B. (eds) (1994) *Towards a Post-Fordist Welfare State?* London, Routledge

Bury, M. (1986) ''Social constructionism and the development of medical sociology'' *Sociology of Health and Illness*, 8, 2: 137–169

Butcher, T. (1995) ''A new civil service? The next steps agencies'' in R. Pyper and L. Robins (eds) *Governing the UK in the 1990s*, London, Macmillan

Calhoun, C. (ed) (1994) *Social Theory and the Politics of Identity*, Oxford UK and Cambridge USA, Blackwell

Callon, M. (1986) ''Some elements of a sociology of translation: domestication of the scallops and the fishermen of St. Brieuc Bay'' in J. Law (ed) *Power, Action and Belief: A New Sociology of Knowledge?* London, Routledge

Callon, M. (1991) ''Techno-economic networks and irreversibility'' in J. Law (ed)
A Sociology of Monsters: Essays on Power, Technology and Domination, London, Routledge

Callon, M., Courtial, J. P., Turner, W. A., and Bauin, S. (1983) ''From translation to problematic networks; an introduction to co-word analysis'' *Social Science Information*, 22: 199–235

Callon, M. and Latour, B. (1981) ''Unscrewing the big Leviathan: how actors macro-structure reality and how sociologists help them to do so'' in K. Knorr-Cetina and A. V. Cicourel (eds) *Advances in Social Theory and Methodology: Towards an Integration of Micro- And Macro- Sociologies*, London, Routledge

Callon, M. and Law, J. (1982) ''On interests and their transformation: enrolment and counter-enrolment'' *Social Studies of Science*, 12: 615–25

Callon, M., Law, J. and Rip. A. (eds) (1986) *Mapping Out the Dynamics of Science and Technology: Sociology of Science in the Real World*, London, Macmillan,

Camilleri, J.A. and Falk, J. (1992) *The End of Sovereignty? The Politics of a Shrinking and Fragmenting World*, Aldershot, Edward Elgar

Carlen, P. (1977) "Magistrates courts; a game theoretic analysis", in M. Fitzgerald, P. Halmos, J. Muncie, and D. Zeldin (eds) *Welfare in Action*, London, Routledge

Cerny, P. (1990) *The Changing Architecture of the State*, London, Sage, 27, quoted in M.J. Smith (1993) *Pressure, Power and Policy: State Autonomy and Policy Networks in Britain and the United States*, Hemel Hempstead, Harvester Wheatsheaf, 72

Challis, L., Fuller, S., Henwood, M., Klein, R., Plowden, W., Webb, A., Whittington, P. and Wistow, G. (1994) "Investigating policy coordination: issues and hypotheses" in D. McKevitt and A. Lawton (eds) *Public Sector Management: Theory, Critique and Practice*, London, Sage

Chandler, J.A. (1991) "Public administration: a discipline in decline" *Teaching Public Administration*, xi, 2: 39–45

Charon, J. M. (1995) *Symbolic Interactionism*, Englewood Cliffs New Jersey, Prentice Hall

Child, A. (1941) "The problem of imputation in the sociology of knowledge" *Ethics*, 51, 2: 200–19

Cicourel, A. V. (1980) "Language and social interaction: philosophical and empirical issues" *Sociological Inquiry*, 50: 1–30

Cicourel, A. V. (1981) "Notes on the integration of micro- and macro-levels of analysis" in K. Knorr-Cetina and A. V. Cicourel (eds) *Advances in Social Theory and Methodology: Towards an Integration of Micro-and Macro-Sociologies*, London, Routledge

Clapham, D. (1986) "Management of the local state: the example of corporate planning" *Critical Social Policy*, 14: 27–42

Clegg, S. (1989) *Frameworks of Power*, London, Sage

Cochrane, A. (1994) "Restructuring the welfare state" in R. Burrows and B. Loader (eds) *Towards a Post-Fordist Welfare State?*, London, Routledge

Cockburn, C. (1977) *The Local State: Management of Cities and People*, London, Pluto

Cohen, I. (1989) *Structuration Theory: Anthony Giddens and the Constitution of Social Life*, London, Macmillan

Cohen, I. (1993) "Structuration theory and social praxis" in A. Giddens and J. Turner (eds) *Social Theory Today*, Cambridge, Polity Press

Cohen, P. (1968) *Modern Social Theory*, London, Heinemann

Cole, I. and Goodchild, B. (1995) "Local housing strategies in England: an assessment of their changing role and content" *Policy and Politics*, 23, 1: 49–60

Coleman, J. (1990) *Foundations of Social Theory*, Cambridge USA, Harvard University Press

Collins, R. (1992) "The romanticism of agency/structure versus the analysis of micro/macro" *Current Sociology*, 40, 1: 77–97

Collins, R. (1994) *Four Sociological Traditions*, New York and Oxford, Oxford University Press

Commons, J.R. (1961) *Institutional Economics: Its Place in Political Economy*, Madison, University of Wisconsin Press

Cook, K.S., O'Brien, J. and Kollock. P. (1990) "Exchange theory: a blueprint for structure and process" in G. Ritzer (ed) *Frontiers of Social Theory: The New Synthesis*, New York, Columbia University Press

Cooke, P. (ed) (1989) *Localities: The Changing Face of Britain*, London, Unwin Hyman

Couch, C. (1990) *Urban Renewal: Theory and Practice*, London, Macmillan

Coxall, B. and Robins, L. (1994) *Contemporary British Politics*, 2/e, London, Macmillan

Craib, I. (1992) *Anthony Giddens*, London, Routledge

Crespi, F. (1992) *Social Action and Power*, Oxford, Blackwell

Dahl, R. (1958) "A critique of the ruling elite model" *American Political Science Review*, 52: 463–69

Dahl, R. (1961) *Who Governs? Democracy and Power in an American City*, New Haven, Yale University Press

Dahrendorf, R. (1959) *Classes and Class Conflict in an Industrial Society*, London, Routledge

Davies, K. and Moore, W. (1945) "Some principles of stratification" *American Sociological Review*, 10: 242–49

Defronzo, J. (1991) *Revolutions and Revolutionary Movements*, Oxford and San Francisco, Westview Press

Degeling, P. (1995) "The significance of 'sectors' in calls for urban health intersectoralism: an Australian perspective" *Policy and Politics*, 23, 4: 289–301

Demertzis, N. (1993) Review *The Sociological Review*, 41, 2: 385–90

Denhardt, R.B. (1990) "Public administration theory: the state of the discipline" in N. Lynn and A. Wildavsky (eds) *Public Administration: The State of The Discipline*, Chatham N.J., Chatham House

Dickens, P. (1990) *Urban Sociology: Society, Locality and Human Nature*, London, Harvester Wheatsheaf

Dominelli, L. and McLeod, E. (1989) *Feminist Social Work*, London and Basingstoke, Macmillan

Dowding, K. (1993) "Civil service" in R. Maidment and G. Thompson (eds) *Managing the United Kingdom: An Introduction to Its Political Economy and Public Policy*, London, Sage

Dowding, K. (1995) *The Civil Service*, London, Routledge

Duncan, S. (1989) "What is locality?" in R. Peet, and N. Thrift, (eds) *New Models in Geography*, London, Edward Arnold

Duncan, S. and Goodwin, M. (1988) *The Local State and Uneven Development*, Cambridge, Polity

Dunleavy, P. (1980) *Urban Political Analysis*, London, Macmillan
Dunleavy, P. (1986) ''Explaining the privatization boom: public choice versus radical approaches'' *Public Administration*, 64: 13–34
Dunleavy, P. and O'Leary, B. (1987) *Theories of the State: The Politics of Liberal Democracy*, London, Macmillan
Dunn, J. (1989) *Modern Revolutions*, Cambridge, Cambridge University Press
Dunn, J.A. and Perl, A. (1994) ''Policy networks and industrial revitalization: high speed rail initiatives in France and Germany'' *Journal of Public Policy* 14, 3: 311–43
Duster, T. (1981) ''Intermediate steps between micro- and macro-integration: the case of screening for inherited disorders'' in K. Knorr-Cetina and A. V. Cicourel (eds) *Advances in Social Theory and Methodology: Towards an Integration of Micro- and Macro-Sociologies*, London, Routledge
Eccleshall, R., Geoghegan, V., Jay, R., Kenny, M., Mackenzie, I. and Wilsford, R. (1994) *Political Ideologies*, 2/e, London, Routledge
Ehrenreich, B. and Ehrenreich, J. (1979) ''The professional-managerial class'' in P. Walker (ed) *Between Labour and Capital*, Sussex, Harvester Press
Elias, N. (1978) *What is Sociology?* London, Hutchinson
Elliot, P. and Mandell, N. (1995) ''Feminist theories'' in N. Mandell (ed) *Feminist Issues: Race, Class and Sexuality*, Ontario, Prentice Hall
Elster, J. (1989) *Nuts and Bolts for the Social Sciences*, Cambridge, Cambridge University Press
Emerson, R.M. (1981) ''Social exchange theory'' in M. Rosenberg and R.H. Turner (eds) *Social Psychology: Sociological Perspectives*, New York, Basic Books
Esping-Anderson, G. (1990) *The Three Worlds of Welfare Capitalism*, Cambridge, Polity
Etzioni, A. (1968) *The Active Society: A Theory of Societal and Political Processes*, New York, Free Press
Eyerman, R. and Jamison, A. (1991) *Social Movements; A Cognitive Approach*, Oxford, Polity
Falk, R. (1995) *On Humane Governance: Towards a New Global Politics*, Cambridge, Polity
Fararo, T. J. (1992) *The Meaning of General Theoretical Sociology: Tradition and Formalization*, Cambridge, Cambridge University Press
Farganis, S. (1994) *Situating Feminism: From Thought to Action*, Thousand Oaks Calif., and London, Sage
Farnham, D. and Horton, S. (eds) (1993) *Managing The New Public Services*, London, Macmillan
Feick, J. (1992) ''Comparing comparative policy studies – a path towards integration?'' *Journal of Public Policy*, 12, 3: 257–85
Fimister, G. and Hill, M. (1993) ''Delegating implementation problems: social security, housing and community care in Britain'' in M. Hill, (ed) *New Agendas in the Study of the Policy Process*, London, Harvester Wheatsheaf
Flynn, N. (1993) *Public Sector Management*, London, Harvester

Foucault, M. (1972) *The Archaeology of Knowledge*, New York, Random House

Foucault, M. (1980a) *Power/Knowledge*, New York, Pantheon

Foucault, M. (1980b) *The History of Sexuality*, New York, Vintage Books

Foucault, M. (1982) ''The subject and power'' in H.L. Dreyfus and P. Rabinow *Michel Foucault: Beyond Structuralism and Hermeneutics, with an Afterword by Michel Foucault*, Brighton, Harvester Wheatsheaf

Fox, N.J. (1991) ''Postmodernism, rationality and the evaluation of health care'' *Sociological Review*, 39, 4: 709–44

Freeman, J.L. (1965) *The Political Process: Executive Bureau-Legislative Committee Relations*, New York, Random House

Friedman, D. and Hechter, M. (1988) ''The contribution of rational choice theory to macrosociological research'' *Sociological Theory*, 6: 201–218

Friedman, D. and Hechter, M. (1990) ''The comparative advantages of rational choice theory'' in G. Ritzer (ed) *Frontiers of Social Theory: The New Syntheses*, New York, Columbia University Press

Frohlich, N., Oppenheimer, J.A. and Young, O.R. (1978) *Modern Political Economy*, Englewood Cliffs, N.Y., Princeton University Press

Friedrichs, R. W. (1972) *A Sociology of Sociology*, New York, Free Press

Fuller, R. and Myers, R. (1941) ''The natural history of a social problem'' *American Sociological Review*, 6 (June): 320–28

Gane, M. and Johnson, T. (1993) ''Introduction: the project of Michel Foucault'' in M. Gane and T. Johnson (eds) *Foucault's New Domains*, London, Routledge

Garfinkel, H. (1967) *Studies in Ethnomethodology*, Englewood Cliffs, N.J., Prentice-Hall

Garside, P. (1993) ''Housing needs, family values and single homeless people'' *Policy and Politics*, 21, 4: 319–28

Gellner, E. (1993) *Postmodernism, Reason and Religion*, London and New York Routledge

Genschel, P. and Werle, R. (1993) ''From national hierarchies to international standardization: model changes in the governance of telecommunications'' *Journal of Public Policy*, 13, 3: 203–225

Giddens, A. (1976) *New Rules in Sociological Method*, Hutchinson, London.

Giddens, A. (1979) *Central Problems in Social Theory: Action, Structure and Contradiction in Social Analysis*, London, Macmillan; Berkeley, University of California Press

Giddens, A. (1981) ''Agency, institution, and time-space analysis'' in K. Knorr-Cetina and A.V. Cicourel (eds) *Advances in Social Theory and Methodology; Towards an Integration of Micro– and Macro–Sociologies*, London, Routledge

Giddens, A. (1982) *Profiles and Critiques in Social Theory*, London, Macmillan

Giddens, A. (1984) *The Constitution of Society*, Polity, Cambridge.

Giddens, A. (1987) *Social Theory and Modern Sociology*, Cambridge, Polity

Giddens, A. (1989a) *Sociology*, Cambridge, Polity

Giddens, A. (1989b) "A reply to my critics" in D. Held and J. Thompson (eds) *Social Theory and Modern Societies: Anthony Giddens and his Critics*, Cambridge University Press.

Giddens, A. (1990) *The Consequences of Modernity*, Cambridge, Polity

Giddens, A. (1991) "Structuration theory: past, present and future" in C. Bryant and D. Jary (eds) *Giddens's Theory of Structuration: A Critical Appreciation*, London, Routledge

Giddens, A. (1993) *New Rules of Sociological Method*, 2/e, Cambridge, Polity

Gillatt, S. (1991) "Putting the public in policy: notes towards the revival of a discipline" *Towards Public Administration*, xi, 2: 22–30

Ginsberg, N. (1992) *Divisions of Welfare: A Critical Introduction to Comparative Social Policy*, London, Sage

Glennerster, H., Power, A. and Travers, T. (1992) "A new era for social policy: a new enlightenment or a new Leviathan?" *Journal of Social Policy*, 20, 3: 389–414

Goldthorpe, J.H. and Marshall, G. (1992) "The promising future of class analysis" *Sociology*, 26: 381–400

Gould, A. (1993) *Capitalist Welfare Systems: A Comparison of Japan, Britain and Sweden*, London and New York, Longman

Gouldner, A. (1971) *The Coming Crisis of Western Sociology*, London, Heinemann

Grant, W.P., Peterson, W. and Whitson, C. (1988) *Government and the Chemical Industry*, Oxford, Clarendon

Gray, A. and Jenkins, W.I. (1985) *Administrative Politics in British Government*, Brighton, Harvester

Gregory, D. (1989) "Presences and absences: time-space relations and structuration theory" in D. Held and J. B. Thompson (eds) *Social Theory of Modern Societies; Anthony Giddens and his Critics*, Cambridge, Cambridge University Press

Greenwood, J. and Wilson, D. (1989) *Public Administration in Britain Today*, London, Unwin Hyman

Groom, A.J.R. (1994) "The setting in world society" in A.J.R. Groom and P. Taylor (eds) *Frameworks For International Co-operation*, London, Pinter

Gurnah, A. and Scott, A. (1992) *The Uncertain Science: Criticism of Sociological Formalism*, London, Routledge

Gwartney, J.D. and Wagner, R.E. (eds) (1988) *Public Choice and Constitutional Economics*, Greenwich, CT, Jai Press

Gyford, J. (1991) *Citizens. Consumers and Councils: Local Government and the Public*, London, Macmillan

Habermas, J. (1986) *The Theory of Communicative Action, Vol. 1: Reason and the Rationalization of Society*, Cambridge, Polity

Habermas, J. (1987) *The Theory of Communicative Action, Vol. 2: The Critique of Functionalist Reason*, Cambridge, Polity

Haimes, E. (1993) "Theory and method in the analysis of the policy process: a case study of the Warnock Committee on Human Fertilisation and Embryology'' in Hill, M. (ed) *New Agendas in the Study of the Policy Process*, London, Harvester Wheatsheaf

Hall, S. and Held, D. (1989) "Left and Rights" *Marxism Today* June: 16–23

Halliday, F. (1994) *Rethinking International Relations*, London, Macmillan

Ham, C. and Hill, M. (1993) *The Policy Process in the Modern Capitalist State*, London, Harvester Wheatsheaf

Hambleton, R. and Hoggett, P. (1990) *Beyond Excellence: Quality Local Government in the 1990s*, Working Paper 25, University of Bristol, School for Advanced Urban Studies

Hamilton, P. (1974) *Knowledge and Social Structure*, Routledge, London.

Harloe, M., Pickvance, C. and Urry, J. (eds) (1990) *Place. Policy and Politics: Do Localities Matter?*, London, Unwin Hyman

Harre, R. (1981) "Philosophical aspects of the macro-micro problem" in K. C. Knorr-Cetina and A. V. Cicourel (eds) *Advances in Social Theory and Methodology: Towards an Integration of Micro-And Macro-Sociologies*, London, Routledge

Harrop, M. (1992a) Introduction in M. Harrop (ed) *Power and Policy in Liberal Democracies*, Cambridge, Cambridge University Press

Harrop, M. (ed) (1992b) *Power and Policy in Liberal Democracies*, Cambridge, Cambridge University Press

Heap, S.P.H. and Varoufakis, Y. (1995) *Game Theory: A Critical Introduction*, London, Routledge

Heater, D. (1990) *Citizenship*, London, Longman

Hechter, M. (1988) "Rational choice theory and the study of race and ethnic relations" in J. Rex and D. Mason (eds) *Theories of Race and Ethnic Relations*, Cambridge, Cambridge University Press

Heidenheimer, A.J., Heclo, M., and Adams, C.T. (1990) *Comparative Public Policy: The Politics of Social Choice in America, Europe and Japan*, 3/e, New York, St. Martin's Press

Held, D. (1995) *Democracy and the Global Order: From the Modern State to Cosmopolitan Governance*, Cambridge, Polity

Heller, A. (1986) "The sociology of everyday life" in U. Himmelstrand (ed) *The Social Reproduction of Organization and Culture*, London, Sage

Heller, A. and Feher, F. (1988) *The Postmodern Political Condition*, Cambridge, Polity

Hencke, D. (1996) "Right-wingers who pull the strings" *Education Guardian*, 19 March: 2

Hill, M. (1972) *The Sociology of Public Administration*, London, Weidenfeld and Nicolson

Hill, M. (1993a) *Understanding Social Policy*, 4/e, Oxford, Blackwell

Hill, M. (ed) (1993b) *New Agendas in the Study of the Policy Process*, London, Harvester Wheatsheaf

Hills, H. (1993) Review *The Sociological Review*, 41, 2: 377–81

Hindess, B. (1982) "Power, interests, and the outcomes of struggles" *Sociology* 16, 4: 488–511.

Hindess, B. (1986a) "Actors and social relations" in M. L. Wardell and S. P. Turner (eds) *Sociological Theory in Transition*, London, Allen and Unwin

Hindess, B. (1986b) "Interests in political analysis" in J. Law (ed) *Power. Action and Belief: A New Sociology of Knowledge?* London, Routledge

Hindess, B. (1988) *Choice. Rationality and Social Theory*, London, Unwin Hyman

Hindess, B. (1990) "Liberty and equality" in B. Hindess (ed) *Reactions of the Right*, London, Routledge

Hindess, B. (1996) *Discourses of Power: From Hobbes to Foucault*, Oxford, Blackwell

HMSO (Cabinet Office) (1994) *Civil Service Yearbook*, London, HMSO

Hoggett, P. (1991) "A new management in the public sector?" *Policy and Politics* 19, 4: 243–56.

Hollinger, R. (1994) *Postmodernism and the Social Sciences: A Thematic Approach*, London, Sage

Holzner, B. (1968) *Reality Construction in Society*, New York, Schenkman

Holzner, B. (1978) "The construction of social actors: an essay on social identities" in T. Luckmann (ed) *Phenomenology and Sociology*, Harmondsworth, Penguin

Homans, G. (1958) "Social behaviour as exchange" *American Journal of Sociology*, 63: 597–606

Homans, G. (1961) *Social Behaviour: Its Elementary Forms*, New York, Harcourt, Brace and World

Homans, G. (1974) *Social Behaviour: Its Elementary Forms*, Rev. ed., New York, Harcourt, Brace and Jovanovich

Hoppe, R. (1993) "Political judgement and the policy cycle: the case of ethnicity policy arguments in the Netherlands" in F. Fischer and J. Forester (eds) *The Argumentative Turn in Policy Analysis and Planning*, Duke University Press/London, UCL Press

Horowitz, J.L. (1967) "Consensus, conflict and co-operation" in N. Demerath and R. Peterson (eds) *System, Change, and Conflict*, New York, Free Press

Hudson, B. (1993) "Collaboration in social welfare: a framework for analysis" in M. Hill (ed) *The Policy Process: A Reader*, London, Harvester Wheatsheaf

Hughes, O. (1994) *Public Management and Administration: An Introduction*, London, Macmillan

Hunter, F. (1953) *Community Power Structure*, Chapel Hill, University of North Carolina Press

Hutton, R. (1995) "Whitehall amateur drama" *Guardian Society*, 10 May: 9

Ikenberry, G.J., Lake, D.A. and Mastanduno, M. (1988) "Introduction: Approaches to explaining American foreign economic policy" in G.J. Ikenberry, D.A. Lake, and M. Mastanduno (eds) *The State and American Foreign Economic Policy*, Ithaca and London, Cornell University Press

Isaac-Henry, K., Painter, C. and Barnes, C. (1993) *Management in the Public Sector: Challenge and Change*, London, Chapman and Hall

Jackson, N. and Carter, P. (1991) "In defence of paradigm incommensurability" *Organization Studies*, 12, 1: 109–27

Jenson, J. (1995) "Mapping, naming and remembering: globalization at the end of the twentieth century" *Review of International Political Economy*, 2, 1: 96–116

Jewson, N. and Mason, D. (1992) "The theory and practice of equal opportunities policies: liberal and radical approaches" in P. Braham, A. Rattansi, and R. Skellington, (eds) *Racism and Anti-Racism: Inequalities. Opportunities and Policies*, London, Sage

Joas, H. (1993) "Symbolic interactionism" in A. Giddens, and J. Turner, (eds) *Social Theory Today*, Cambridge, Polity

Johnson, N. (1991) "The break-up of consensus: competitive politics in a declining economy" in M. Loney, R. Bocock, J. Clark, A. Cochrane, P. Graham, and M. Wilson (eds) *The State or the Market; Politics and Welfare in Contemporary Britain*, London, Sage

Jones, B. and Kavanagh, D. (1994) *British Politics Today*, 5/e, Manchester, Manchester University Press

Jones, R.J.B. (1996) "Globalization, regionalization and 'national' action" *Paper presented to the Annual Conference of the British Sociological Association*, (April), Reading, University of Reading

Jones, W.S. (1991) *The Logic of International Relations*, 7/e, New York, Harper Collins

Jordan, G. (1994) *The British Administrative System: Principles Versus Practice*, London, Routledge

Jordon, G., Maloney, W., and McLaughlin, A.M. (1994) "Characterizing agricultural policy-making" *Public Administration*, 72, 4: 505–26

Judd, D. and Parkinson, M. (eds) (1990) *Leadership and Urban Regeneration*, London, Sage

Judge, D. (1993) *The Parliamentary State*, London, Sage

Judge, D., Earnshaw, D. and Cowan, N. (1994) "Ripples or waves: the European Parliament in the European Community policy process" *Journal of European Public Policy* 1, 1: 27–52

Kalberg, S. (1994) "Max Weber's analysis of the rise of monotheism: a reconstruction" *British Journal of Sociology*, 45, 4: 563–83.

Kasarda, J. (1989) "Urban industrial transition and the underclass" *The Annals of the American Academy of Political and Social Science*, 501: 26–47

Keane, J. (1988) *Democracy and Civil Society*, London, Verso

Kellner, D. (1990) "The postmodern turn: positions, problems and prospects" in G. Ritzer (ed) *Frontiers of Social Theory: The New Syntheses*, New York, Columbia University Press

Kickert, W. (1993) "Complexity, governance and dynamics: conceptual explorations of public network management" in J. Kooiman (ed) *Modern Governance: New Government – Society Interactions*, London, Sage

Kirkpatrick, I. and Lucio, M.M. (eds) (1995) *The Politics of Quality in the Public Sector*, London, Routledge

Knoke, D. and Kuklinski, J.H. (1991) "Network analysis: basic concepts" in G. Thompson, J. Frances, R. Levacic, and J. Mitchell (eds) *Markets, Hierarchies and Networks: The Coordination of Social Life*, London, Sage

Knorr-Cetina, K. D. (1981) "Introduction: the micro-sociological challenge of macro-sociology: towards a reconstruction of social theory and methodology" in K. D. Knorr-Cetina and A. V. Cicourel (eds) *Advances in Social Theory and Methodology: Towards an Integration of Micro– And Macro– Sociologies*, London, Routledge

Knorr-Cetina, K. D. and Cicourel, A. V. (1981) (eds) *Advances in Social Theory and Methodology: Towards an Integration of Micro– And Macro– Sociologies*, London, Routledge

Kooiman, J. (1993a) "Social-political governance: introduction" in J. Kooiman, (ed) *Modern Governance: New Government-Society Interactions*, London, Sage

Kooiman, J. (ed) (1993b) *Modern Governance: New Government-Society Interactions*, London, Sage

Krokidas, A. (1993) Review *Sociology*, 27, 3: 534–36.

Kumar, K. (1978) *Prophecy and Progress: The Sociology of Industrial and Post-Industrial Society*, London, Penguin

Kumar, K. (1995) *From Post-Industrial to Post-Modern Society: New Theories of the Contemporary World*, Oxford, Blackwell

Lane, Jan-Erik (1993) *The Public Sector: Concepts, Models and Approaches*, London, Sage

Lane, Jan-Erik and Ersson, S. (1994a) *Comparative Politics: An Introduction and New Approach*, Cambridge, Polity

Lane, Jan-Erik and Ersson, S. (1994b) *Politics and Society in Western Europe*, 3/e, London, Sage

Larrain, J. (1979) *The Concept of Ideology*, London, Routledge

Larrain, J. (1994) "The postmodern critique of ideology" *The Sociological Review*, 42, 2: 289–314

Latour, B. (1986) "The powers of association" in J. Law (ed) *Power. Action and Belief: A New Sociology of Knowledge?*, London, Routledge

Latour, B. (1987) *Science in Action: How to Follow Engineers and Scientists Through Society*, Milton Keynes, Open University Press

Latour, B. (1991) "Technology is society made durable" in J. Law (ed) *A Sociology of Monsters; Essays on Power. Technology and Domination*, London, Routledge

Lave, J. (1986) "The values of quantification" in J. Law (ed) *Power, Action and Belief: A New Sociology of Knowledge?*, London, Routledge

Law, J. (1986a) "On power and its tactics: a view from the sociology of science" *Sociological Review* 34 1: 1–38

Law, J. (ed) (1986b) *Power. Action and Belief: A New Sociology of Knowledge?*, London, Routledge

Law, J. (1986c) "Power/knowledge and the dissolution of the sociology of knowledge" in J. Law (ed) *Power. Action and Belief: A New Sociology of Knowledge*, London, Routledge

Law, J. (1986d) "On the methods of long-distance control: vessels, navigation and the Portuguese route to India" in J. Law (ed) *Power. Action and Belief: A New Sociology of Knowlege?*, London, Routledge

Law, J. (ed) (1991a) *A Sociology of Monsters: Essays on Power. Technology and Domination*, London, Routledge

Law, J. (1991b) "Power, discretion and strategy" in J. Law (ed) *A Sociology of Monsters; Essays on Power. Technology and Domination*, London, Routledge

Law, J. (1994) *Organizing Modernity*, Oxford, Blackwell

Lawton, A. and Rose, A. (1991) *Organization and Management in the Public Sector*, London, Pitman

Layder, D. (1993) *New Strategies in Social Research: An Introduction and Guide*, Oxford, Polity

Layder, D. (1994) *Understanding Social Theory*, London, Sage

Lees, R. (1975) *Research Strategies for Social Welfare*, London, Routledge

Lemert, C. (1993) "After modernity" in C. Lemert (ed) *Social Theory: The Multicultural and Classic Readings*, San Francisco, Westview Press

Levitas, R. (1976) "The social location of ideas" *The Sociological Review*, 24, 3: 545–57

Lewis, N. (1992) *Inner City Regeneration: The Demise of Regional and Local Government*, Buckingham, Open University Press

Lidz, V. (1981) "Transformational theory and the internal environment of action systems" in K. D. Knorr-Cetina and A. V. Cicourel (eds) *Advances in Social Theory and Methodology: Towards an Integration of Micro– and Macro- Sociologies*, London, Routledge

Ling, T. (1993) "Overview" in R. Maidment and G. Thompson (eds) *Managing The United Kingdom: An Introduction to Its Political Economy and Public Policy*, London, Sage

Lister, R. (1990) *The Exclusive Society: Citizenship and the Poor*, London, Child Poverty Action Group

Lister, R. (1995) "Dilemmas in engendering citizenship" *Economy and Society*, 24, 1: 1–40

Lockwood, D. (1956) "Some remarks on the social system" *British Journal of Sociology*, 7: 134–46

Luhmann, N. (1982) *The Differentiation of Society*, New York, Columbia University Press

Luhmann, N. (1988) "Tautology and paradox in the self-descriptions of modern society" *Sociological Theory*, 6: 26–37

Luhmann, N. (1989) *Ecological Communication*, Cambridge, Polity

Lukes, S. (1974) *Power: A Radical View*, London, Macmillan

Lyman, S. and Scott, M. (1970) *A Sociology of the Absurd*, New York, Appleton Century Crofts

Lyon, D. (1987) *The Information Society: Issues and Illusions*, Cambridge, Polity

Lyon, D. (1993) "An electronic panopticon? A sociological critique of surveillance theory" *The Sociological Review*, 41, 4: 653–78

Lyon, D. (1994) *Postmodernity*, Buckingham, Open University Press

Lyotard, J. F. (1986) *The Postmodern Condition: A Report on Knowledge* tr. G. Bennington and B. Massumi, Manchester, Manchester University Press

Macmillan, J. and Linklater, A. (1995) Introduction in J. Macmillan and A. Linklater (eds) *Boundaries in Question: New Directions in International Relations*, London, Pinter

Maidment, R. and Thompson, G. (eds) (1993) *Managing the United Kingdom: An Introduction to its Political Economy and Public Policy*, London, Sage

Mann, M. (1984) "The autonomous power of the state: its origins, mechanisms and results" *Archives Europeennes de Sociologie*, 25: 185–213

Mann, M. (1986) *The Sources of Social Power: Volume 1*, Cambridge, Cambridge University Press

March, J.G. and Simon, H. (1958) *Organizations*, New York, Wiley

Marglin, G. (1980) "The origins and functions of hierarchy in capitalist production" in T. Nichols (ed) *Capital and Labour*, London, Fontana

Marsh, D. and Rhodes, R.A.W. (eds) (1992a) *Policy Networks in British Government*, Oxford, Oxford University Press

Marsh, D. and Rhodes, R.A.W. (1992b) "Policy communities and issue networks: beyond typology" in D. Marsh and R.A.W. Rhodes (eds) *Policy Networks in British Government*, Oxford, Oxford University Press

Marshall, T.H. (1950/1963) "Citizenship and social class" in T.H. Marshall (1963) *Sociology at The Crossroads*, London, Heinemann

Mason, D. (1988) Introduction in J. Rex and D. Mason (eds) *Theories of Race and Ethnic Relations*, Cambridge, Cambridge University Press

May, C. (1993) Review in *Sociology*, 27, 3: 558

Mayer, T. (1994) *Analytical Marxism*, London, Sage

Mayntz, R. (1993) "Governing failures and the problem of governability: some comments on a theoretical paradigm" in J. Kooiman (ed) *Modern Governance: New Government – Society Interactions*, London, Sage

McLennan, G. (1995) "After postmodernism: back to sociological theory?" *Sociology*, 29, 1: 117–32

McGrew, A.G. (1992) "Conceptualizing global politics" in A.G. McGrew and P.G. Lewis (eds) *Global Politics: Globalization and the Nation-State*, Cambridge, Polity

McGrew, A.G. and Lewis, P.G. (eds) (1992) *Global Politics: Globalization and the Nation-State*, Cambridge, Polity

McKevitt, D. and Lawton, A. (eds) (1994) *Public Sector Management: Theory, Critique and Practice*, London, Sage

McNay, L. (1992) *Foucault and Feminism: Power, Gender and the Self*, Cambridge, Polity Press

McNay, L. (1994) *Foucault: A Critical Introduction*, Cambridge, Polity

Mead, G. H. (1967) *Mind, Self and Society*, Chicago, University of Chicago Press

Melucci, A. (1984) *Altrici, Aree di movimento nella metropoli*, Bologna, Il Mulino

Merton, R. (1968) *Social Theory and Social Structure* (Enlarged edition), New York, Free Press

Metcalfe, L. and Richards, S. (1990) *Improving Public Management*, London, Sage

Miller, H.T. (1994) "Post-progressive public administration: lessons from policy networks" *Public Administration Review*, 54, 4: 378–85

Miller, P. and Rose, N. (1988) "The Tavistock programme: the government of subjectivity and social life" *Sociology*, 22, 2: 171–92

Miller, P. and Rose, N. (1993) "Governing economic life" in M. Gane and T. Johnson (eds) *Foucault's New Domains*, London, Routledge

Miller, W. W. (1993) "Durkheim's Montesquieu" *British Journal of Sociology*, 44, 4: 693–712

Mills, C. Wright (1956) *The Power Elite*, Oxford, Oxford University Press

Mills, C. Wright (1970) *The Sociological Imagination*, Harmondsworth, Penguin

Mishra, R. (1990) *The Welfare State in Capitalist Society: Policies of Retrenchment and Maintenance in Europe, North America, and Australia*, London, Harvester Wheatsheaf

Moran, M. (1990) "Financial markets" in J. Simmie and R. King (eds) *The State in Action: Public Policy and Politics*, London and New York, Pinter

Morgan, D. and Stanley, L. (1993) "Debates in sociology: contextual and procedural dynamics in the production of a discipline" in D. Morgan and L. Stanley (eds) *Debates in Sociology*, Manchester, Manchester University Press

Mouzelis, N. (1989) "Restructuring structuration theory" *The Sociological Review*, 37, 4: 613–35

Mouzelis, N. (1991) *Back to Sociological Theory; The Construction of Social Order*, London, Macmillan

Mouzelis, N. (1993a) "The poverty of sociological theory" *Sociology*, 27 4: 675–95

Mouzelis, N. (1993b) "Comparing the Durkheimian and Marxist traditions" *The Sociological Review*, 41, 3: 572–82

Mouzelis, N. (1995) *Sociological Theory: What Went Wrong? Diagnosis and Remedies*, London, Routledge

Mouzelis, N. (1996) "After postmodernism: a reply to Gregor McLennan" *Sociology*, 30, 1: 131–35

Moynihan, D.P. (1989) "Towards a post-industrial social policy" *The Public Interest*, 96: 16–27

Mueller, D. (1989) *Public Choice II*, Cambridge, Cambridge University Press

Mullard, M. (ed) (1995) *Policy Making in Britain*, London, Routledge

Munch, R. (1987) "Parsonian theory today: in search of a new synthesis" in A. Giddens and J. Turner (eds) *Social Theory Today*, Cambridge, Polity

Munch, R. and Smelser, N. (1987) "Relating the micro and macro" in J. Alexander, B. Giesen, R. Munch, and N. Smelser (eds) *The Micro-Macro Link*, Berkeley, University of California Press

Munck, G. (1995) "Actor formation, social co-ordination, and political strategy: some conceptual problems in the study of social movements" *Sociology*, 29, 4: 667–85

Munday, B. (1989) "Introduction" in B. Munday (ed) *The Crisis in Welfare: An International Perspective on Social Services and Social Work*, London, Harvester Wheatsheaf

Nicholson, L. and Seidman, S. (1995) Introduction in L. Nicholson and S. Seidman (eds) *Social Postmodernism: Beyond Identity Politics*, Cambridge and New York, Cambridge University Press

Nies, H. (1992) "Research and the local planning of services for elderly people: an interactive approach" *Politics and Policy*, 20, 1: 1–13

Niskanen, W.A. (1973) *Bureaucracy and Representative Government*, New York, Aldine-Atherton

Nixon, J. (1993) "Implementation in the hands of senior managers: community care in Britain" in M. Hill (ed) *New Agendas in the Study of the Policy Process*, Hemel Hempstead, Harvester Wheatsheaf

Norton, P. (1982) *The Constitution in Flux*, Oxford, Martin Robinson

Nugent, N. (1994a) *The Government and Politics of the European Union* 3/e, London, Macmillan

Nugent, N. (1994b) "Britain in the European Community" in B. Jones (ed) *Political Issues in Britain Today*, Manchester, Manchester University Press

Oliver, D. and Heater, D. (1994) *The Foundations of Citizenship*, London, Harvester Wheatsheaf

Olson, M. (1965) *The Logic of Collective Action*, Cambridge, Mass., Harvard University Press

O'Neill, M. (1996) *The Politics of European Integration*, London, Routledge

O'Toole, B. (1994) "The British civil service in the 1990s: are business practices really best?" *Teaching Public Administration*, xiv, 1: 24–35

Parker, M. (1992) "Post-modern organizations or postmodern organization theory?" *Organization Studies*, 13, 1: 1–17

Parsons, T. (1947) Introduction in *The Theory of Social and Economic Organization (Max Weber)*, edited by T. Parsons and A.M. Henderson, New York, Free Press

Parsons, T. (1951) *The Social System*, New York, Free Press

Parsons, T. (1954) "The present position and prospects of systematic theory in sociology" in T. Parsons *Essays in Sociological Theory*, Rev. edition, New York, Free Press

Parsons, T. (1966) *Societies: Evolutionary and Comparative Perspectives*, Englewood Cliffs, New Jersey, Prentice-Hall

Parsons, T. (1967) *Sociological Theory and Modern Society*, New York, Free Press

Parsons, T. (1971) *The System of Modern Societies*, Englewood Cliffs, New Jersey, Prentice-Hall

Parsons, W. (1995) *Public Policy: An Introduction to the Theory and Practice of Policy Analysis*, Aldershot, Edward Elgar

Peele, G. (1995) *Governing the United Kingdom* 3/e, Oxford, Blackwell

Peters, G. (1994) "Agenda-setting in the European Community" *Journal of European Public Policy*, 1, 1: 9–26

Peters, T.J. and Waterman, R.H. (1982) *In Search of Excellence*, New York, Harper and Row

Pickvance, C.G. (1990) "The institutional context of local economic development: central controls, spatial policies and local economic policies" in M. Harloe, C. Pickvance, and J. Urry (eds) *Place, Policy and Politics: Do Localities Matter?* London, Unwin Hyman

Pilkington, C. (1995) *Britain in the European Union Today*, Manchester, Manchester University Press

Pollack, M. A. (1994) "Creeping competence: the expanding agenda of the European Community" *Journal of Public Policy*, 14, 2: 95–145

Ponting, C. (1986) *Whitehall: Tragedy and Farce*, London, Hamish Hamilton

Poulantzas, N. (1975) *Classes in Contemporary Capitalism*, London, New Left Books

Pyper, R. and Robins, L. (eds) (1995a) *Governing the UK in the 1990s*, London, Macmillan

Pyper, R. and Robins, L. (1995b) "The nature and challenge of governing in the 1990s" in R. Pyper and L. Robins (eds) *Governing the UK in the 1990s*, London, Macmillan

Ranson, S. and Stewart, J. (1994) *Management for the Public Domain: Enabling the Learning Society*, London, Macmillan

Reed, M. (1985) *Redirections in Organizational Analysis*, London and New York, Tavistock

Reed, M. (1992) *The Sociology of Organizations: Themes, Perspectives and Prospects*, Hemel Hempstead, Harvester

Rex, J. (1961) *Key Problems in Sociological Theory*, London, Routledge

Rhodes, R.A.W. (1988) *Beyond Westminster and Whitehall*, London, Unwin Hyman

Rhodes, R.A.W. (1990) "Policy networks: a British perspective" *Journal of Theoretical Politics*, 2: 293–317

Richards, P.G. (1988) *Mackintosh's The Government and Politics of Britain*, London, Hutchinson

Richardson, J. and Jordan, A.G. (1985) *Governing Under Pressure*, 2/e, Oxford, Martin Robinson

Richardson, J. and Lindley, R. (1994) "Editorial" *Journal of European Public Policy*, 1, 1: 1–7

Ritzer, G. (1990) "Micro-macro linkages in sociology; applying a metatheoretical tool" in G. Ritzer (ed) *Frontiers of Social Theory; The New Syntheses*, New York, Columbia University Press

Ritzer, G. (1992a) "Metatheorising in sociology: explaining the coming of age" in G. Ritzer (ed) *Metatheorizing*, Newbury Park California and London, Sage

Ritzer, G. (1992b) *Sociological Theory*, 3/e, New York, McGraw Hill

Robertson, R. and Turner, B.S. (1991) "An introduction to Talcott Parsons: Theory, Politics and Humanity" in R. Robertson and B.S. Turner (eds) *Talcott Parsons: Theorist of Modernity*, London, Sage

Roche, M. (1992) *Re-thinking Citizenship: Welfare, Ideology and Change in Modern Society*, Cambridge, Polity

Roemer, J. (1981) *Analytical Foundations of Marxian Economic Theory*, Cambridge, Cambridge University Press

Roemer, J. (1982a) "Methodological individualism and deductive Marxism" *Theory and Society*, 11, 4: 253–87

Roemer, J. (1982b) "New directions in the Marxian theory of exploitation and class" *Politics and Society*, 11, 3: 375–94

Rootes, C. A. (1981) "The dominant ideology thesis and its critics" *Sociology*, 15, 3: 436–44

Rose, G. (1988) "The postmodern complicity" *Theory, Culture and Society*, 5, 2/3: 357–71, quoted in A. Gurnah and A. Scott (1992) *The Uncertain Science: Criticism of Sociological Formalism*, London, Routledge, 151

Rose, N. and Miller, P. (1992) "Political power beyond the state: problematics of government" *British Journal of Sociology*, 43, 2: 173–205

Rubinstein, D. (1988) "The concept of structure in sociology", in M. Wardell and S. Turner (eds) *Sociological Theory in Transition*, London, Allen and Unwin

Runciman, W.G. (1972) *Relative Deprivation and Social Justice*, Harmondsworth, Penguin

Rustin, M. (1993) "Ethnomethodology" in D. Morgan and L. Stanley (eds) *Debates in Sociology*, Manchester and N.Y., Manchester University Press

Salmon, T. (1995) "The European Union dimension" in R. Pyper and L. Robins (eds) *Governing The UK in the 1990s*, London, Macmillan

Sapir, E. (1966) *Culture. Language and Personality*, Berkeley and Los Angeles, University of California Press

Saunders, P. (1990) *A Nation of Home Owners*, London, Unwin Hyman

Scholte, J. (1993) *International Relations of Social Change*, Buckingham and Philadelphia, Open University Press

Schumpter, J.A. (1965) *Capitalism, Socialism and Democracy*, London, Unwin University Books

Schutz, A. (1962) "Symbol, reality and society" in M. Natanson (ed) *Collected Papers vol. 1: The Problem of Social Reality*, The Hague, Martinus Nijhoff

Schwarzmantel, J. (1994) *The State in Contemporary Society*, Hemel Hempstead, Harvester Wheatsheaf

Scott, A. (1990) *Ideology and the New Social Movements*, London, Unwin Hyman

Scott, J. (1988) "Trend report: social network analysis" *Sociology*, 22, 1: 109 27

Scott, J. (1995) *Sociological Theory: Contemporary Debates*, Aldershot, Edward Elgar

Seidman, S. (1994) *Contested Knowledge: Social Theory in the Postmodern Era*, Oxford UK and Cambridge USA, Blackwell

Sharp, R. (1980) *Knowledge. Ideology and Politics of Schooling: Towards a Marxist Analysis of Education*, London, Routledge

Sibeon, R. (1996) "A sociology of post-national governance" *Paper presented to the Annual Conference of the British Sociological Association* (April) Reading, University of Reading

Simon, H. (1957) *Models of Man*, New York, Wiley

Skocpol, T. (1980) "Political responses to capitalist crisis: neo-Marxist theories and the case of the New Deal" *Politics and Society*, 10: 155–201

Smart, B. (1991) "Modernity, postmodernity and the present" in B.S. Turner (ed) *Theories of Modernity and Postmodernity*, London, Sage

Smelser, N. (1962) *Social Change in the Industrial Revolution: An Application of Theory to the Lancashire Cotton Industry 1770–1840*, London, Routledge

Smith, B.C. and Stanyer, J. (1976) *Administering Britain*, London, Fontana/Collins (re-issued Oxford, Martin Robinson 1980)

Smith, M.J. (1990) *The Politics of Agricultural Support in Britain: The Development of the Agricultural Policy Community*, Aldershot, Dartmouth

Smith, M. J. (1993) *Pressure, Power and Policy: State Autonomy and Policy Networks in Britain and the United States*, London, Harvester Wheatsheaf

Smith, M. (1993) "Changing sociological perspectives on chance" *Sociology*, 27, 3: 513–31

Standing, G. (1986) *Unemployment and Labour Market Flexibility: The UK*, Geneva, International Labour Office

Stein, A. (1982) "Co-operation and collaboration: regimes in an anarchic world" *International Organization*, 35: 299–323

Stewart, M. (1994) "Between Whitehall and town hall: the realignment of urban regeneration policy in England" *Policy and Politics*, 22, 2; 133–45

Stoker, G. (1991) *The Politics of Local Government*, 2/e, London, Macmillan

Storper, M. (1995) "The resurgence of regional economies" *European Urban and Regional Studies*, 2, 3: 191–221

Sudnow, D. (1965) "Normal crimes: sociological features of the penal code in a public defender's office" *Social Problems*, 12: 255–76

Sztompka, P. (1993) *The Sociology of Social Change*, Oxford U.K. and Cambridge U.S.A., Blackwell

Taylor-Gooby, P. (1991) *Social Change, Social Welfare and Social Science*, Hemel Hempstead, Harvester Wheatsheaf

Taylor-Gooby, P. (1994) "Postmodernism and social policy: a great leap backwards?" *Journal of Social Policy*, 23: 3: 385–404

Thompson, G. (1982) ''The firm as a dispersed social agency'' *Economy and Society*, 2, 1: 233–50

Thompson, G., Frances, J., Levacic, R., and Mitchell, J. (eds) (1991a) *Markets, Hierarchies, and Networks: The Co-ordination of Social Life*, London, Sage

Thompson, G., Frances, J., Levacic, R., and Mitchell, J. (1991b) ''Introduction'' in G. Thompson, J. Frances, R. Lavacic, and J. Mitchell (eds) *Markets, Hierarchies, and Networks: The Co-ordination of Social Life*, London, Sage

Thompson, S. and Hoggett P. (1996) ''Universalism, selectivism, and particularism: towards a postmodern social policy'' *Critical Social Policy*, 16, 1: 21–43

Thrift, N. (1994) ''A phantom state? International money, electronic networks, and global cities'' *Paper presented to the Centre for Social Theory and Comparative History* (June), UCLA

Thurber, J.A. (1991) ''Dynamics of policy subsystems in American politics'' in A.J. Cigler and A. Loomis (eds) *Interest Group Politics*, 3/e, Washington DC, Congressional Quarterly

Tiryakian, E.A. (1992) ''Pathways to metatheory: rethinking the presuppositions of macrosociology'' in G. Ritzer (ed) *Metatheorizing*, Newbury Park USA and London, Sage

Touraine, A. (1974) *The Post-Industrial Society*, London, Wildwood

Touraine, A. (1981) *The Voice and the Eye: An Analysis of Social Movements*, Cambridge, Cambridge University Press

Tullock, G. (1965) *The Politics of Bureaucracy*, Washington DC, Public Affairs Press

Tullock, G. (1975) *The Vote Motive*, London, Institute for Economic Affairs

Turner, B.C. (1990) ''Outline of a theory of citizenship'' *Sociology*, 24, 2: 189–217

Turner, B. S. (1990) ''Conclusion: peroration on ideology'' in N. Abercrombie, S. Hill and B. S. Turner (eds) *Dominant Ideologies*, London, Unwin Hyman

Turner, J. (1988) *A Theory of Social Interaction*, Cambridge, Polity

Turner, J. and Maryanski, A.Z. (1979) *Functionalism*, Menlo Park, Calif., Benjamin/Cummings

Uehara, E. (1990) ''Dual exchange theory, social networks, and informal social support'' *American Journal of Sociology*, 96: 521–57

Vincent, A. (1992) *Modern Political Ideologies*, Oxford, Blackwell

Walby, S. (1994) ''Is Citizenship gendered?'' *Sociology*, 28, 2: 379–95

Waldo, D. (1990) ''A theory of public administration means in our time a theory of politics also'' in N. Lynn and A. Wildavsky (eds) *Public Administration: The State of the Discipline*, Chatham NJ, Chatham House

Wallace, R. and Wolf, A. (1995) *Contemporary Sociological Theory: Continuing The Classical Tradition*, Englewood Cliffs NJ., Prentice-Hall

Wallace, W. (1992) ''Metatheory, conceptual standardization, and the future of sociology'' in G. Ritzer (ed) *Metatheorising*, London, Sage

Waltzer, M. (1992) ''The civil society argument'' in C. Mouffe (ed) *Dimensions of Radical Democracy*, London, Verso

Waters, M. (1994) *Modern Sociological Theory*, London, Sage

Waters, M. (1995) *Globalization*, London, Sage

Webb, A. (1991) "Co-ordination: a problem in public sector management" *Policy and Politics*, 19, 4: 229–41

Weber, M. (1921/1978) *Economy and Society*, Berkeley, University of California Press

Webster, F. (1995) *Theories of the Information Society*, London, Routledge

Weir, M. and Skocpol, T. (1985) "State structures and the possibility of 'Keynesian' responses to the Great Depression in Sweden, Britain and the United States" in P.B. Evans, D. Rieschemeyer and T. Skocpol (eds) *Bringing The State Back In*, Cambridge, Cambridge University Press

Weiss, C. H. (1986) "The many meanings of research utilization', in M. Bulmer, K. G. Banting, S. S. Blume, M. Carley, and C. H. Weiss, *Social Science and Social Policy*, London, Allen and Unwin

Weiss, C.H. (1993) "The interaction of the sociological agenda and public policy" in W.J. Wilson (ed) *Sociology and the Public Agenda*, London, Sage

Whicker, M.L., Strickland, R.A., and Olshfski, D. (1993) "The troublesome cleft: public administration and political science" *Public Administration Review*, 53, 6: 531–41

White, Harrison C. (1992) *Identity and Control: A Structural Theory of Social Action*, New Jersey, Princeton, Princeton University Press

Whorf, B. L. (1956) *Language. Thought and Reality*, New York, MIT Press and John Wiley

Wilding, P. (1982) *Professional Power and Social Welfare*, London, Routledge

Williams, F. (1994) "Social relations, welfare and the post-Fordist debate" in R. Burrows and B. Loader (eds) *Towards a Post-Fordist Welfare State?* London, Routledge

Williams, H., Wright, M., and Evans, T. (1993) Introduction in H. Williams, M. Wright, and T. Evans (eds) *A Reader in International Relations and Political Theory*, Buckingham, Open University Press

Williams, R. (1985) *Towards 2000*, Harmondsworth, Penguin

Wilsford, D. (1994) "Path dependency, or why history makes it difficult but not impossible to reform health care systems in a big way" *Journal of Public Policy*, 14, 3: 251–83

Wilson, D. (1995) "Elected local government and central-local relations" in R. Pyper and L. Robins (eds) *Governing the UK in the 1990s*, London, Macmillan

Wilson, W.J. (1993) "Can sociology play a greater role in shaping the national agenda?" in W.J. Wilson (ed) *Sociology and The Public Agenda*, Newbury Park, Calif., and London, Sage

Wootton, A. (1975) *Dilemmas of Discourse: Controversies about the Sociological Interpretation of Language*, London, Allen and Unwin

Wright, M. (1996) "Policy community and policy network" in P. Barberis (ed) *The Whitehall Reader*, Buckingham, Open University Press

Wrong, D. (1967) "The oversocialized concept of man in modern sociology" in L. Coser and B. Rosenberg (eds) *Sociological Theory: A Book of Readings*, London, Collier-Macmillan

INDEX